BEST WEEKEND GETAWAYS

Best
WEEKEND

JACK CHRISTIE

• • •

GETAWAYS

from Vancouver

GREYSTONE BOOKS

Douglas & McIntyre Publishing Group
Vancouver/Toronto/Berkeley

For Louise

Greystone Books
A division of Douglas & McIntyre Ltd.
2323 Quebec Street, Suite 201
Vancouver, British Columbia
Canada V5T 4S7
www.greystonebooks.com

Library and Archives Canada Cataloguing in Publication
Christie, Jack, 1946–
Best weekend getaways from Vancouver : favourite trips and overnight destinations / Jack Christie.

ISBN 978-1-55365-256-4

1. British Columbia—Tours. 2. Outdoor recreation—
British Columbia—Guidebooks. I. Title.
FC3807.C468 2008   917.1104′5   C2008-900378-0

Editing by Iva Cheung
Cover design by Jessica Sullivan
Cover photograph © Brandon Cole/Getty Images
Interior design by Peter Cocking and Jessica Sullivan
Photos by Louise Christie
Printed and bound in Canada by Friesens
Printed on acid-free paper that is forest friendly (100% post-consumer recycled paper) and has been processed chlorine free.
Distributed in the U.S. by Publishers Group West

We gratefully acknowledge the financial support of the Canada Council for the Arts, the British Columbia Arts Council, the Province of British Columbia through the Book Publishing Tax Credit, and the Government of Canada through the Book Publishing Industry Development Program (BPIDP) for our publishing activities.

Contents

. . . . .

Preface *vii*
Overview map *x*

LOWER MAINLAND

1 Harrison Hot Springs 2
2 Hope 10
3 Bowen Island 18
4 Squamish 25
5 Whistler 35
6 Pemberton 45
7 Lillooet 53

SUNSHINE COAST

8 Gibsons and Roberts Creek 62
9 Sechelt and Halfmoon Bay 70
10 Pender Harbour and Egmont 78
11 Powell River and Lund 86

GULF ISLANDS

12 Galiano Island 96
13 Mayne Island 106
14 North and South Pender Islands 114
15 Salt Spring Island 122
16 Saturna Island 130

VANCOUVER ISLAND

17 Victoria *140*
18 Sooke *151*
19 Cowichan Valley *161*
20 Nanaimo *170*
21 Gabriola Island *178*
22 Comox Valley *186*

THOMPSON OKANAGAN

23 Kamloops *196*
24 Sun Peaks Resort *205*
25 Vernon *212*
26 Kelowna *220*
27 Penticton *231*
28 Osoyoos and Oliver *240*

Destination index *249*
Activities index *257*

Preface

. . . . .

S
o you want to get away. And you want to make the trip last more than a day, although probably not for as long as you'd like. But a weekend—be it two or three days—is better than no break at all, especially when contentment lies just a short journey from home. Your reward is a comfy bed, tasty food, and as little or as much adventure as you'd prefer. That's exactly what the destinations in *Best Weekend Getaways from Vancouver* are designed to offer.

After years of combing B.C. in search of the best outdoors attractions and activities, I've amassed a filing cabinet or two of notes to draw on when narrowing the focus of this book to those special destinations perfectly suited to a quick break, where, no matter what the weather, you can relax in comfort without busting your budget or returning home more stressed than when you started.

My intention with this guide is to suggest places where you can enjoy as soft or as challenging an experience as you wish. Want to ski or ride a bike? It's all here. Want to relax in a spa or picnic by a river? I'm with you on that, too. And although I can't help recommending special places where you might want to camp overnight under the stars, my emphasis is predominantly on setting you up with a roof over your head that's a little more waterproof than a tent, and with room service to boot. Where the only inflatable air mattresses are the ones by the heated pool. Where the margaritas are always made with freshly squeezed juice. And where the menus feature the best in local flavours. Wherever suitable, wheelchair access is also noted with a wheelchair icon (ঙ) at the beginning of each attraction.

Each of the destinations in this guide are within a maximum five-hour drive of Vancouver, including ferry travel where necessary. Most are much closer than that, but it hardly seems fair to exclude regions such as the Okanagan, which, with a little advance planning, some astute schedule juggling, and a jump on rush-hour traffic, you can reach within the stated time frame.

Bottom line: enjoy yourself. Life's better than you think, and nowhere more so than close to home. Slow travel, anyone?

ACKNOWLEDGMENTS

Rob Sanders, publisher of Greystone Books, is chiefly responsible for this new endeavour. He gathered the team to make it happen, principally editor Iva Cheung, managing editor Susan Rana, and art director Peter Cocking. Louise Christie took and organized the photographs.

Encouragement came from many quarters, including Charlie Smith, John Burns, Martin Dunphy, Dan McLeod, and Yolanda Stepien at the *Georgia Straight*; Janice Greenwood, Mika Ryan, Carla Montt, and Cindy Burr at Tourism British Columbia; Lana Kingston at Tourism Vancouver Island; Darlene Small at Tourism Whistler; and Michelle Leroux and Tabetha Boot at Whistler Blackcomb. As well, thanks go to Chelsea Barr and Hanah King, Sarah Cotton, Meaghan Cursons, Mike Duggan, Catherine Frechette, Kristine George, Denise Imbeau, Michelle Jefferson, Eric Kalnins, Holly Lenk, Jayne Lloyd-Jones, Jeff McDonald, Heather McGillivray, Christopher Nicholson, Naomi Pauls, Jennifer Rhyne, Kelly Reid, Edith Rozsa, Laura Serena, Steve Threndyle, and Norah Weber.

Family and friends who adventure with us and inspire us deserve special thanks. Jacqueline Christie, Athal and Arrlann Christie, Gord White and Jane McRae, Larry Emrick, Ruth Tubbesing, Charles Campbell and Lainé Slater, Brigit and Bill Sirota, Juergen and Jacquie Rauh, Peter and Toni Kelley, Judith and Ian Kennedy, Rob Kowalchuk, Kevin Ibbestson, Gwilym and Sharon Masui Smith, Lisa, Keith, and Jade Wilcox-Whitaker, Britta Wagner, the Loadmans, the Collinses, and the Browns are always there to cheer us on.

Thank you to all those readers, listeners, and viewers who have offered constant encouragement and suggestions for new destinations. If you'd care to comment on anything that catches your eye while using this book, write to me care of Greystone Books, 2323 Quebec Street, Suite 201, Vancouver, B.C., v5T 4S7, or visit our website, www.jackchristie.com.

BEST WEEKEND GETAWAYS

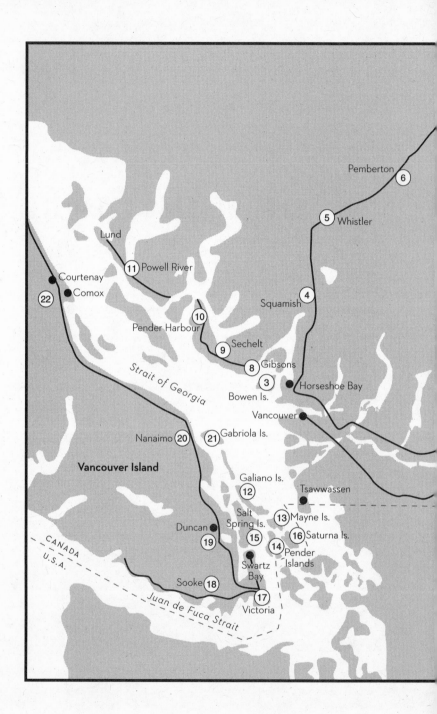

Pemberton **6**

5 Whistler

Lund

11 Powell River

Courtenay

22 ●Comox

Squamish **4**

10

Pender Harbour

9 Sechelt

8 Gibsons

3

Bowen Is.

Horseshoe Bay

Strait of Georgia

Vancouver ●

Nanaimo **20** **21** Gabriola Is.

Vancouver Island

Galiano Is.

12

Tsawwassen

Salt **13** Mayne Is.
Spring Is.

Duncan ●

16 Saturna Is.

19

15 **14** Pender
Islands

CANADA

U.S.A.

Swartz
Bay

Sooke **18**

17

Victoria

Juan de Fuca Strait

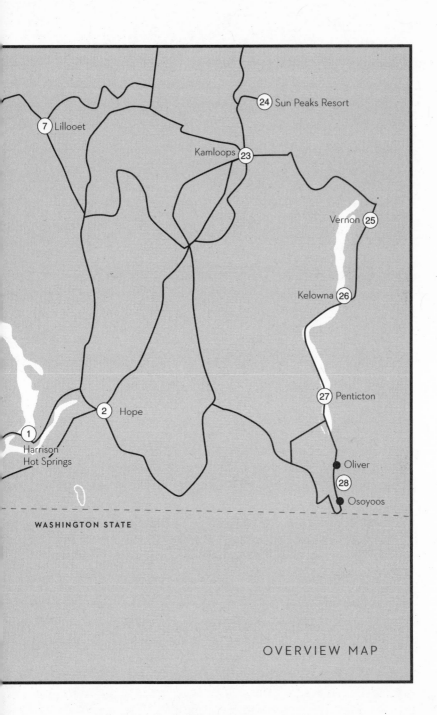

(7) Lillooet

(24) Sun Peaks Resort

Kamloops (23)

Vernon (25)

Kelowna (26)

(27) Penticton

(2) Hope

(1)
Harrison
Hot Springs

● Oliver

(28)

● Osoyoos

OVERVIEW MAP

LOWER MAINLAND

HARRISON HOT SPRINGS

HOPE

BOWEN ISLAND

SQUAMISH

WHISTLER

PEMBERTON

LILLOOET

HARRISON HOT SPRINGS

· · · · ·

> ACCESS: The quickest approach to Harrison Hot Springs is via Highway 1 to the east side of Chilliwack. From Exit 135, follow Highway 9 north as it crosses the Fraser River then twists and turns through Agassiz and on to Harrison Hot Springs, a distance of about 130 km from Vancouver. A slightly longer approach is via Highway 7, which intersects with Highway 9 east of Mission.

> WHY GO: Nothing can match the sensation of watching the bowl of stars twinkle on the surface of Harrison Lake or waking to the impossible stillness of early mornings in this mountain town.

> KEEP IN MIND: This Fraser Valley hamlet is scary full in the summer months, particularly during the annual Dragon Boat Festival in July. If you don't make reservations the overnight getaway you were hoping for might just have to be scaled back to a day trip instead.

TUCKED IN the folds of the Coast Mountains' Lillooet Range, Harrison Hot Springs boasts a beach that would be the pride of any seaside town, let along a lakefront one. September marks the beginning of what typically is the best time to scout out the farmfield-lined backroads northeast of Chilliwack towards Harrison Hot Springs. Camping sites and motel bungalows suddenly free up as kids stream back to school with all the concentrated energy of the salmon migrating in nearby rivers, including the Fraser, Chehalis, Chilliwack, and Harrison. Local fields yield the tastiest corn imaginable.

To get detailed information on Harrison Hot Springs, including a comprehensive guide to the surrounding region, call 604-796-5581 or visit www.harrisonhotsprings.org.

> HARRISON LAKE AND RIVER

ACTIVITIES: *Paddling, swimming, walking*

All of 15 km long, the Harrison River is one of the shortest in the province as it empties from Harrison Lake—a deep fiord—into the Fraser River. And it's one of the easiest to explore, beginning from the sandy expanse of the town's beach. The best part is that you don't even need a boat, although floating along in one is guaranteed to provide you with a view to the south of Cheam Peak and the surrounding ridge—a setting that looks all the world as if it were in the Alps—or heighten your chances of drifting upon unsuspecting wildlife, such as a cougar perched on a boulder in the act of stalking a flock of Canada geese. Sasquatch Tours (www.sasquatchtours.com) offers Aboriginal cultural cruises on Harrison Lake and River. They also offer interpretive nature walks, traditional ceremonies and dances, and drum-making and cedar basket–weaving workshops.

> HOT SPRINGS ♿

ACTIVITIES: *Picnicking, swimming, walking*

If you're curious about the source of the hot springs' scalding water, which is piped into a public swimming pool as well as the pool at the Harrison Hot Springs Resort, head west of the hotel along a well-maintained pathway suitable for those in wheelchairs. Within minutes you'll arrive at what first appears to be a curved-roof mausoleum built of cinder bricks.

Closer inspection reveals that this structure houses the hot springs, which percolate from a rocky outcropping at a sizzling 62°C degrees. A cement foundation isolates the springs from the lake, and the water is then pumped through a pipeline into town. By the time you get to soak in either the hotel or the town pool, the temperature has been moderated to a more welcoming 40°C. Although the main source of the springs is off limits, a companion seep flows from a pipe into a pond immediately beside the brick building. This one is even hotter: 68°C. Try keeping your hand in it for longer than a second.

Watch for a rougher trail that leads west from the source. Although it climbs steeply for a short distance through the cool interior of a dense forest, this route leads to a smaller expanse of beach at Sandy Cove. The crescent-shaped expanse slopes out into the lake

3

in a much shallower approach than the town's main lido. As a result, water here is warmer for swimming than elsewhere on the glacier-fed fiord. Pick up the trail again at the west end of the beach as it loops around Whippoorwill Point for views south along the Harrison River.

> FRASER VALLEY BALD EAGLE FESTIVAL

In evolutionary terms the question of which species came first, eagles or salmon, may be a moot point. But one thing is certain: each fall 800 to 1,200 bald eagles return to overwinter in the Fraser Valley, the third-largest such colony in North America. Hot on the birds' tail feathers are schools of spawning salmon on whose spent carcasses the majestic birds feast. On the third weekend in November, the Fraser Valley Bald Eagle Festival celebrates this annual cycle of life and death at a series of outdoor and indoor venues in the Mission–Harrison Hot Springs region. Renowned artist, author, and naturalist Robert Bateman is a regular festival participant. So too are members of the Stó:lō nation whose ancestors lived for millennia beside such local rivers as the Fraser, Harrison, and Chehalis. Depending on the weather, eagles may be easier to spot at some viewing sites than others. Watch for their distinctive hunched shapes adorning tall cottonwoods where the Lougheed Highway (Highway 7) rounds the shoreline of Harrison Bay. Begin exploring from the shores of Kilby Park near the bay's confluence with the Fraser River or on the banks of the nearby Chehalis River.

One of the festival's prime locations is Tapadera Estates on Morris Valley Road, where volunteers from the Astronomical Society and the Chilliwack and Central Valley naturalists set up spotting scopes and telescopes to spy eagles in action on Chehalis Flats from the shelter of viewing tents. If you're lucky, some trumpeter swans (which boast the largest wingspan of any birds on Canada's west coast) may also put in an appearance. A roofed gazebo here, complete with roaring fireplace, provides a cozy place to warm up. For a close-up view of spawning salmon, stop at the nearby Chehalis River Hatchery for a self-guided tour. When it's raining, eagles prefer to hunker down and wait for a break in the weather to catch their meal. If this is the case during your visit, head indoors to the quaint Harrison Mills

Riding the wind, Harrison Lake

Community Hall off Highway 7 where guest lecturers on eagle-related topics, as well as local arts and crafts, are featured.

Harrison Mills is also the site of the Kilby Heritage Museum and provincial park, located a further 1.5 km south of the hall along School and Kilby roads. In 1904, Thomas Kilby opened a general store and hotel for business here, which is now preserved as testimony to the Fraser River's glory days. The store stands on stilts: before a dike was built, the surrounding waters had a habit of flooding at this junction of the Harrison and Fraser rivers. Boardwalks link the store with outbuildings. During the festival, an adjacent store's café and Christmas craft shop operate in much the same fashion as they did at the height of the riverside crossroad's prominence in the 1920s, when it was the hub of the community of Harrison Mills.

Across the road from the restaurant, massive relics from the days of logging loom in the forest. A slippery trail leads along the banks of the nearby Harrison River, one of the Fraser's shortest tributaries. Come November, dead salmon begin to litter the shoreline, as rigid as sculptures on the sand. Adjacent to the store is Kilby Provincial Park, a pleasant spot to picnic while enjoying the view across Harrison Bay. Trumpeter swans and bald eagles agree, and this is where they like to gather.

Kilby Historic Store (604-796-9576), adjacent to Kilby Park, is open May to October and at Christmas, and has a wonderful pioneer history. The restored boarding house, post office, and general store give a feel for life on the Fraser River at the beginning of the twentieth century, when sternwheelers linked small towns with the docks downstream at Mission and New Westminster.

> SASQUATCH PROVINCIAL PARK

ACTIVITIES: *Camping, cycling, paddling, picnicking, running, swimming, walking*

Green Point picnic area lies at the entrance to Sasquatch Park on the eastern shore of Harrison Lake, 6 km north of the town centre. Wooden tables, many with barbecues, sit beside an open play area. The beach is bathed in afternoon sun, an important consideration as the waters of Harrison Lake are cold year-round. Sasquatch Park is a favourite with families in summer months. At most other times it's the almost-exclusive preserve of those who come to savour the park's wondrous quiet. Whatever you favour—a walk in the woods, a swim on a sandy beach, or an extended bike ride along level trails—pleasure is there for the taking. Broadleaf maple, white birch, and poplar present an alluring sight in autumn when the leaves change colour. From spring through early fall birdsong fills the air and mingles with a chorus of frogs until late evening. Breathe the rich oxygenated air in deeply as you make your way around Deer and Hicks lakes. Paddle either in an hour without rushing. (Canoe and kayak rentals are available on both lakes during summer months.) From the beaches, walk lakeside trails out to sandy points where fishing or swimming may suit your mood. More isolated sandy stretches sit at the far end of either lake. Watch for mountain goats in the early-morning light on the slopes of Slollicum Bluffs, which rise above Deer Lake's north side. Hicks Lake is twice the size of and not as open as Deer Lake. The peaks of the Skagit Range near Chilliwack Lake stand out on the southern horizon. Good fishing spots abound here on points of land in front of campsites 2 to 17. Rainbow trout, cutthroat trout, and brook char thrive in these waters, as the sight of ospreys—fish hawks—attests. Beaver Pond Trail offers a short but interesting walk around a marshy area near the day-use parking lot.

Boardwalks and bridges lead past a small creek flowing west from Hicks Lake, part of which has been diverted by a beaver dam into a small pond. Put your boat in at the Hicks Lake launch site or walk or cycle the trail ringing the lake to Sandy Beach at the south end. Aim for it as your picnic destination if you're travelling light. You'll reach the beach in 1 hour after a stroll in the shade along an old logging road. Partway around is the group campsite, in front of which is another good beach.

> **OTHER ATTRACTIONS**

The Agassiz Fall Fair and Corn Festival: This festival takes place mid-September. For information check out agassizfallfair.ca.

Fraser Country Circle Farm Tours: One of the most rewarding aspects of trekking to Harrison Hot Springs is checking out the numerous farms and craft cottages along the way, including the artisan cow and goat cheeses made at The Farm House Natural Cheeses and the drive-through Sparkes Corn Barn, both in Agassiz. You're guaranteed to go home with a heavier load than you arrived, even if you are slightly lighter in the pocket. Brochures on each of the six Fraser Country Circle Farm Tours are available at Visitor Info Centres throughout the Lower Mainland. For details, visit www.circle farmtour.ca.

Galleries: Native Whispers Gallery and Gifts features a collection of authentic native artwork from local Stó:lō and West Coast First Nations artists. As you travel along Highway 7 via Agassiz, visit the Ruby Creek Art Gallery (www.rubycreekartgallery.com), which features an extraordinary collection of Pacific Northwest native art, including jewellery, masks, pottery, sculptures, glass, and fibre arts.

World Championships of Sand Sculpture: Come September, the town takes full advantage of its sandy strand when it hosts the World Championships of Sand Sculpture, which runs from the day after Labour Day until the following Sunday. Everyone is invited to vote on the "People's Choice" award in three different classes: solo, doubles, and team efforts. Once the prize money has been awarded, the sculptures remain in place until Thanksgiving.

X̱á:ytem Longhouse Interpretive Centre (35087 Lougheed Highway; 604-820-9725; www.xaytem.ca; 5 km east of Mission).

Knowledgeable Stó:lō guides help explain traditional Aboriginal fishing technology as well as the significance of an enormous rock, renowned as one of the Fraser Valley's "stone people." With help, profiles of three chiefs can be discerned on the rockface, which is X̱á:ytem's (*hay-toom*) centrepiece. Older than Stonehenge and the pyramids of Giza, the recently excavated site has yielded artifacts carbon dated to about 9,000 years ago. Peek inside the centre's two cozy pithouses to capture a sense of the ambience of those long-ago times. The centre's cedar longhouse also features a fascinating collection of traditional baskets as well as hands-on displays of weaving and carving. Freshly baked bannock is always a treat, worth a stop here in itself during the Fraser Valley Bald Eagle Festival (see above).

> **DINING**

Kitami Japanese Restaurant (318 Hot Springs Road; 604-796-2728) and *Black Forest Restaurant* (180 Esplanade Avenue; 604 796-9343): Kitami and the Swiss-themed Black Forest Restaurant vie for top foreign honours in Harrison Hot Springs.

Silvano's Restaurant (7056 Cheam Avenue, Agassiz; 604-796-9565): Nearby in Agassiz, Silvano's hosts a Greek-themed menu for those of us who can never get enough calamari.

Harrison Hot Springs Resort's Copper Room (100 Esplanade Avenue; 1-800-663-2266; www.harrisonresort.com): This elegant dining room offers up an old-school dine and dance with Michael Bublé fans in mind.

> **ACCOMMODATION**

Without a reservation, you'll find drop-in space at a premium from May through September. I've almost been skunked here before—almost. Harrison makes a whimsical getaway in the off-season where you can plant yourself at any of these three retreats:

Sasquatch Provincial Park: Three provincial campgrounds nestle beside two of the four lakes within Sasquatch Provincial Park. There's ample room for overnighters at the 177 campsites ($14 per night). Campsites 2 to 17, along with sites 36 to 41, are the most desirable locations at Hicks Lake. Reserve campsites in advance by calling 604-689-9025 or visiting discovercamping.ca. For more information, visit the BC Parks website: www.bcparks.ca.

Fenn Lodge Bed and Breakfast (15500 Morris Valley Road, Harrison Mills; 604-796-9798 or 1-888-990-3399; www.fennlodge. com): This retreat lies 4 km northeast of Highway 7 on Morris Valley Road and is an exotically furnished 1903 Victorian classic, landscaped with a heated spring-fed swimming pool and a meditation maze. Kayak the nearby Chehalis River, which runs red with spawning salmon in autumn and thick with bald eagles, too. Savour yummy breakfasts around Gary and Diane's kitchen table, and try the nearby River's Edge Grill at the Sandpiper Golf Course for lunch or dinner if you simply want to hang out around the property rather than head to Harrison Hot Springs or Agassiz, a 15-minute drive east.

Harrison Hot Springs Resort (100 Esplanade Avenue, Harrison Hot Springs; 1-800-663-2266; www.harrisonresort.com): Move over, Banff. This hotel boasts a drop-dead beautiful lakeside location with its own private hot springs to boot. Request space in the newest of the hotel's three wings where each room has a view of the lake and is within steps of a maze of outdoor hotspring pools. Pamper yourself with the full spa and indoor pools, two restaurants, lovingly landscaped grounds with tennis courts, an exercise circuit, and a handful of motel-style cabins tucked in the woods for privacy.

HOPE

. . . . .

> ACCESS: Hope lies 138 km east of Vancouver via the Trans-Canada Highway (Highway 1) or Highway 7.

> WHY GO: Take in fresher than fresh air in the canyons and a taste of Shakespeare, too.

> KEEP IN MIND: Gas prices in Hope are typically far cheaper than around Metro Vancouver; although there are several service stations downtown, even better prices are usually found along the Old Hope–Princeton Highway that leads along Hope's east side.

CHAINSAW SCULPTURE capital of the world? That's Hope's big ambition. Despite wind and weather—a winter storm took out three sculptures one year—the creations just keep on appearing. They are just one of several good reasons to spend a day or two around Hope, whether exploring the Kettle Valley Railway tunnels or hot-tubbing in the woods at an eco-retreat where you can even arrange to stay in a former KVR cabin. You'll never rush through Hope again. The Hope Visitor Info Centre (919 Water Avenue; 1-866-467-3842; www.hopebc.ca) publishes a visitor guide, *Daytrippers Paradise*, complete with detailed maps of trails, including the Dewdney Mule and Kettle Valley Railway trails.

For fishing, cycling, and camping needs visit Cheyenne Sports (267 Wallace Street; 604-869-5962; www.cheyennesportinggoods. com). *Note:* The store is closed Sundays.

> **NAHATLATCH PROVINCIAL PARK**
ACTIVITIES: *Fishing, paddling, picnicking, rafting*
Tucked between Harrison Lake and the Fraser Canyon, the Nahatlatch's lake-and-river system is a gem of a destination, suited to day

trippers and campers alike. Six campgrounds, each with two or three sites, are easily accessible on the banks of Frances, Hannah, and Nahatlatch lakes. The Nahatlatch flows into the Fraser Canyon 18 km upstream from Boston Bar, a lumber town that lies 66 km north of Hope on Highway 1 and is located on the east side of the canyon, where a bridge links with North Bend on the west. From there the Nahatlatch Forest Service Road, paved for the initial 5 km from North Bend towards the Nahatlatch River Bridge then becoming a well-maintained gravel road, leads north past several farms to an imposing log bridge that spans the Nahatlatch. It's an easy 30-minute drive. After flowing from a series of lakes upstream, the forest-green river meets its match beyond the bridge, where it merges with the chocolate-brown Fraser.

If you're just there for the day, begin by exploring east of the bridge along the Nahatlatch's south shore. As the river flows down towards the Fraser you'll find open spots for fishing and backwater pools for swimming. An old trail begins a short distance south of the bridge and leads down off the road, through the forest, and past the remains of several derelict cabins. Soft moss carpets the ground. Sweet vegetable smells and birdsongs pour down off the hillside. As you make your way, you'll momentarily lose sight of the river before spotting it again under an imposing CNR trestle. This blackened iron structure towers overhead as the Nahatlatch makes a final sprint before exhausting itself in the Fraser.

By mid-July, water levels in the Fraser have receded to the point where you can walk out on the sandbars and smooth boulders. Across the way, traffic on the Trans-Canada can be seen wending through the canyon. Convoys of railway cars roll frequently along tracks on both sides of the Fraser. The friction between steel wheels and rails sets up a musical sound similar to a crazed carillon. These notes carry on the wind and ring through the canyon as the trains pass.

> **OTHELLO-QUINTETTE TUNNELS (COQUIHALLA CANYON PROVINCIAL PARK)** &

ACTIVITIES: *Cycling, hiking, picnicking, viewpoints, walking*
From Hope, follow signs to the Coquihalla Highway (Highway 5). About 15 km east of Hope on Highway 5, take Exit 183. Drive west

across the highway overpass to the Coquihalla Canyon Provincial Park and nearby Kawkawa Lake Park. Alternatively, from Hope follow Kawkawa Lake Road, then Othello Road—a distance of 7 km. Kawkawa Lake is 2.4 km north of Hope. The tunnels are 4.4 km farther north.

Welcome to Bard in the Canyon, or Bard on the Kettle Valley Railway if you will. Romeo and Juliet, Lear and Portia, Iago and Othello: these are whistle stops along the line's Coquihalla subdivision named by chief engineer Andrew McCulloch after some of William Shakespeare's best-known characters. McCulloch's major opus, the four Quintette Tunnels at Othello, are still considered the costliest mile of railway track in the world. After the trains stopped running in 1965, Hope residents smoothed out the rail bed into a broad recreation trail, now part of the Trans Canada Trail system that opened in 2000. Exploring the Coquihalla Canyon is no more strenuous than strolling the Stanley Park seawall. Tack on a stint of hiking on the Dewdney Mule Trail and get the added bonus of climbing through a shady, old-growth forest with viewpoints above the canyon that stretch out towards imposing Mount Hope in the distance. The Dewdney Mule Trail loops above both sides of the Othello tunnel complex and makes for a fascinating one-hour loop hike.

Along the route, you'll develop a new appreciation for the term *tunnel vision*, particularly in the middle of the longest of the four passageways, where light barely seeps in through each end. Step from the heat of the day into the coolness of the shafts as currents of soothing air waft over you, propelled along by the rushing motion of the river. Short spans of bridges link one tunnel to the next, allowing tantalizing glimpses of the Coquihalla Canyon below, the clear river muscling its way through granite walls with all the emotional rage of Othello himself. The Bard would surely have approved. (*Note:* The park is officially closed November to March.)

Decades before the railway blasted through the canyon, surveyor Edgar Dewdney and a group of Royal Engineers cut a single-track trail on the slopes that eventually led from Hope to Fort Steele.

Coquihalla Canyon Park near Hope

> **SKAGIT VALLEY PROVINCIAL PARK**

ACTIVITIES: *Cycling, fishing, hiking, picnicking, walking*

The road into the Skagit Valley begins off Highway 19 (Exit 168) on the western outskirts of Hope. Follow the Hope Business Road exit for a short distance to the well-marked Silver/Skagit Road. The entrance to the park lies 37 km south. From there the road runs an additional 23 km to its end at the Canada–U.S. border. There are no services along this wide and well-maintained road, so make sure to fill your tank at one of the local service stations.

One of North America's finest fishing rivers lies south of Hope in the Skagit Valley. The hour-long drive over a dirt road will be more than justified upon arrival. Even if you aren't interested in dipping a line, make a point of an outing on foot or by bike in this magical

13

valley. You may find the enchantment a hard spell to break. Pack along your camping gear for a night under the stars at one of three campgrounds. Visit www.bcparks.ca for details.

Two of my favourite ways to explore the Skagit Valley are on foot and by bike. To get a feel for the river, try a section of the 15-km Skagit River Trail that runs northeast from 26 Mile Bridge to Sumallo Grove in Manning Park. The first 3 km make for an easy bicycle ride before the trail begins a short, steep climb along the edge of an extensive ancient scree slope. (If you wish to explore farther, leave your bike here.) Treats along the way include views of nearby Silvertip Mountain and its retreating glacier, a copse of rare wild rhododendrons that bloom red in June, sandbars exposed on the Skagit, and a provincial ecological reserve at 9 km protecting a stand of tall cedar and fir. Just before the trail reaches the reserve, it crosses 28 Mile Creek. At times of high water, crossing here is tricky. Tread cautiously.

Farther south in the valley lies the Chittenden Meadow Trail. The Skagit is special because of its U-shaped profile, a rare configuration in southwestern B.C., where most valleys are steep-sided Vs dominated by high mountains. The trails through Chittenden Meadow, 16 km south of 26 Mile Bridge, show off the valley's grandeur. Cycling the trails imparts an enhanced sense for the flatness of the valley bottom that you won't otherwise experience as you pass beneath stands of tall cottonwoods. Come fall, their leaves turn a vivid gold. At that time of year there's such a stillness in the air that the leaves make a racket as they tumble down.

To reach the meadow, park beside the Skagit River and cross the suspension bridge. Trail maps are usually available from the BC Parks kiosk located at the beginning of the meadow trail on the west side of the suspension bridge. The level, hard-packed Chittenden Meadow trail branches off in several directions and leads towards Ross Lake. (A trail leads north from the west side of the bridge to several good fishing spots. Depending on your technique, you can either cast from the riverbank or don waterproof gear and wade in. You'll find a cozy campsite here beneath the sheltering limbs of five magnificent red cedars, from which there is a view of Silvertip and Shawatum mountains to the north and east.)

One of the best ways to tour the meadow is with bicycles along the old logging roads that double as pathways through the meadow. For example, from marker "4" follow a faint trail west that soon becomes much more distinct as it leads to a sign that points towards International Creek. Follow this trail as it leads through the overhanging forest, eventually emerging at the northwest corner of the lake. From here, ride through the field of stumps and tall grass back towards the meadow. A branch of the trail leads to the nearby Ross Lake campground. Allow an hour to do the trail by bike.

> ## OTHER ATTRACTIONS

Arts and carving walk: As you make your way around town, you'll notice large wooden carvings of animals mounted everywhere. Local carvers Pete Ryan and Robert Forde have elevated this form of mechanized carving to a new level. Two dozen (and counting) larger-than-life depictions of animal and humans—including the endangered species–listed gas attendant—anchor the streets and pathways of Memorial Park where the original eagle-and-salmon creation took shape. In summer, displays of artwork are also featured at a variety of businesses around the downtown core. Allow an easy hour for a self-guided tour with a map in hand courtesy of the Hope Arts Gallery (349 Fort Street; 604-869-2408).

Brigade Days: A particularly colourful time to see Hope is the second full weekend in September, when the town hosts Brigade

> # CASTING CALL

· · · · · · · · ·

AS SILVER/SKAGIT ROAD heads south of Silver Lake, it parallels one of North America's finest river systems for fishing. At Silverhope Creek, the Klesilkwa River, and the Skagit River, fly-fishers pull off at designated parking spots to try for rainbow trout. Open season is summer and fall, when there are several strong runs. Watch for postings along the way. The area around the Silvertip campground is especially popular. Fishing is strictly catch-and-release here on the Skagit, with only barbless hooks permitted.

Days, a celebration of its pioneer past. The town lets off steam with fireworks on Friday night, parades and rocks out at the Briggie Ball on Saturday, and whips out the chainsaws for some logger sport and sculpting action on Sunday. The festival is capped by a demolition derby. A roaring, smashing, smoking good time is sure to be had by almost all.

Hope Gliding Centre: Take wings over the Fraser Valley for a soundless flight in a glider. Hope is renowned for its favourable winds. The Vancouver Soaring Association flies out of the Hope Airport on weekends from April through October. For information call 604-869-7211 or visit www.vsa.ca.

Hope Museum: The Hope Museum sits both inside the Visitor Info Centre at the south end of Hope's main street, Water Street, and outside across from the Fraser River. Watch for the waterwheel, part of the restored Home Gold Mine, mounted next to the centre. Admission is free.

Kawkawa Lake Park: The word *kawkawa* is a poetic term in the Halkomelem language that means "much calling of loons." Kawkawa Lake Park is a quiet, roadside municipal park with grassy picnic grounds fronted by a beach and boat launch. In summer, you'll appreciate the lake's warm water. Forest shades the background and shelters the road between here and Coquihalla Canyon Provincial Park.

Spawning Salmon: If you are in the area during salmon spawning season in September, follow Kawkawa Lake Road east of Hope as it passes over the Coquihalla River. Thacker Regional Park sits on the west bank of the river. On the other side, Union Bar Road leads off to the left past Kawkawa Creek, which flows into the Coquihalla at this point. A fish ladder awaits returning salmon here, and a boardwalk beside the creek gives a close-up view of the action.

Yale: Yale is located 24 km north of Hope on Highway 1 at the southern end of the Fraser Canyon. Hunt for antique firewater bottles on the beach at Yale. In its boozy heyday, when the pursuit of intoxication was absolute, seventeen saloons lined the boardwalk where paddlewheelers docked. Empties piled up like a shell midden. Staff at the nearby Hope Museum will point out some likely places to begin digging. Bring your gold pan, too, or rent one from the museum. Each spring the Fraser River washes down a few more grains and nuggets onto these shores. The Yale Museum (604-863-2324), housed in an 1868 heritage home, is located on Douglas Street just off Highway 1. On hot summer days its air-conditioned interior is especially welcoming.

> ## DINING

A quick tour of downtown is all it takes to scope out menu boards in front of the *Blue Moose Café* (322 Wallace Street; www.bluemoose cafe.com) and *KimChi Japanese and Korean Restaurant* (821A–6th Avenue; 604-869-0070).

My favourite lies just west of the Visitor Info Centre, *Georgia's Deli and Bistro* (875 Water Avenue; 604-869-0520) the best bet for soup and sandwiches, gelato, and robust coffee. And if you're looking for some baked goodies for your picnic or while cycling around town taking in the public art, find your way to *Dutchy's Bakery* (825–6th Avenue; 604-869-9886), open Tuesday through Saturday.

> ## ACCOMMODATION

Kw'o:kw'e:hala Eco Retreat (1-877-326-7387; www.eco-retreat.com): Sue VandeVelde-Savola's family has owned this riverside property since the early days of the Kettle Valley Railway just east of the tunnels in Othello and upstream from the Coquihalla Canyon. She and her husband, Henry, host a maximum of six guests in three separate cabins, complete with woodfired outdoor hot tub. Enjoy one of the many creative packages on offer, such as "Eco Spa in the Raw," or simply spend a night in the Othello Cottage and walk off the over-the-top breakfast along the crystal-clear river where the Xe:Xe:ls spirits play.

REO Rafting Resort (604-461-7238 or 1-800-736-7238; www.reorafting.com): An hour's drive upstream from Hope in the always-awesome Fraser Canyon, REO offers a variety of accommodations and rafting adventures on the banks of the Nahatlatch River. With a quarter-century of experience under his life jacket, owner Bryan Fogelman knows how to have a good time and makes sure his guests share in the laughter.

> 3

BOWEN ISLAND

. . . . .

> ACCESS: Head 20 km west of Vancouver on Highway 1/99 via Horseshoe Bay in West Vancouver and from there take a 20-minute ride aboard BC Ferries (1-800-223-3779; www.bcferries.com) or Cormorant Marine Water Taxi (604-250-2630 or 604-947-2243).

> WHY GO: Stay in Snug Cove and explore Crippen Regional Park.

> KEEP IN MIND: At the foot-passenger terminal in Horseshoe Bay, allow plenty of time in advance of sailings to purchase tickets and make your way to the loading ramp.

FOR MANY travellers, the 20-minute ferry ride across Howe Sound between Horseshoe Bay and Snug Cove is a thrill in itself. As soon as you get out on the water the skyline opens up with the familiar sight of the Lions (the Sisters) oddly skewed when compared with their familiar arrangement when seen from Burrard Inlet. The ski trails on Mount Strachan in Cypress Provincial Park are clearly visible, as are the recently blasted sections along the Sea to Sky Highway's smoothed-out route. As you approach Bowen, the island's centrepiece, Mount Gardner, rises like a dumpling with homes clinging to its forested slopes and granite shoreline.

True to its name, Snug Cove presents one of the only inviting places for ships to land on Bowen. The wharf at Snug Cove is also where you'll find Bowen Island Sea Kayaking (604-947-9266; www.bowenislandkayaking.com) for kayak rentals and tours. Aside from several small farms sprinkled around the island, this is one of the few open areas. Almost as soon as you walk off the ferry the street begins to rise towards Mount Gardner. Shops and food stores line one side of Bowen Trunk Road, Snug Cove's main street, while the restored Union Steamship Company store—which now houses the

Tunstall Bay Beach, Bowen Island

town library and Metro Vancouver Parks Info Centre—and leafy entrance to Crippen Regional Park stand opposite. A large map of the island posted on the store's lawn helps to orient the visitor.

Bowen is one of the hilliest islands in southern B.C., and that's saying something. Roads tend to be narrow and winding. Count on a challenging bike ride if you want to explore further afield than Snug Cove. Island roads are not entirely well marked nor well lit at night. To avoid frustration, especially when making your way beyond Snug Cove after dark in search of a bed and breakfast, ask your host for specific directions when you book your B&B stay. One immediately noticeable quirk is that local inns are far less likely to announce their presence with signs than is common on the Gulf Islands and elsewhere; this feature is the reason I'd suggest travelling car-free and staying in Snug Cove. There's more than enough to capture your

interest on foot or by kayak from there. If curiosity gets the better of
you, hop on one of the Bowen Island Community Shuttle buses that
run at peak times and are equipped with bike racks.

For general information check out the Bowen Island Municipal
Office website (www.bimbc.ca) or contact the Bowen Island Chamber of Commerce (604-947-9024; www.bowenisland.org) and
request the *Bowen Island Guide*.

> **CRIPPEN REGIONAL PARK &**

ACTIVITIES: *Cycling, paddling, picnicking, running, swimming,*
viewpoints, walking

Year-round, Crippen Park is a quiet haven and a major part of Bow-
en's charm. All of the trails around Snug Cove, including those leading to and around Killarney Lake, are part of the 240-ha park. Walk
the trails while leaves float gently down and crunch underfoot in
autumn. Enjoy the winter wonderland feeling after a snowfall. Catch
the first hint of spring in a forest where views are not yet obstructed
by the foliage of a new season.

Just steps away from the ferry dock on the west side of Snug Cove
lie Bowen's largest beach and the open fields of the picnic grounds,
site of gala summer gatherings for decades. A steep trail leads up the
hill on the far side of the picnic area to Dorman Point. Look down
from here for a vivid illustration of why this inlet is called Snug Cove.

> **WIND WARNING**
. . . .

ANYONE WHO paddles along B.C.'s coast quickly learns how unpredictable the weather can be. Predictably unpredictable. If you've
ever crossed an exposed inlet or a bay, you likely know how
quickly the ocean's surface can change from mirror calm to white-
capped swells, particularly as temperatures rise on a warm day. Paddling around Bowen is like pacing off four sides of a room. Kayakers
know that on at least one of those sides, they're likely going to have the
wind in their faces. At which point there's not much you can do except
paddle harder.

Uphill on the right past the Union Steamship store, a wide trail leads off past Terminal Creek, which tumbles down a steep embankment and into a lagoon beside Deep Bay, and north along Killarney Creek Trail to the largest freshwater lake on the island. Fish ladders climb the rocky canyon beside the creek. Once fall rains raise water levels in October and November, coho salmon and cutthroat trout may be seen leaping the ladders. Allow 45 minutes to walk to the lake, half that to travel by bike. Once there, allow an hour to circle the lake on foot.

The first third of the trail crosses level ground, then begins to rise gently through second-growth forest. Halfway to Killarney Lake, Meadow Trail leads off to the left and across a small bridge over Terminal Creek. Take this path and you'll discover that a short way along, meadows open up. In one is an exercise paddock for horses. Just beyond the paddock, the trail links up with Mount Gardner Road, which leads back left to the ferry or right to the lake. Island residents often gather around the paddock. A picnic table stands under spreading trees nearby beside the Terminal Creek fish hatchery.

Killarney Creek Trail continues from the halfway point towards the lake, linking with Magee Road just before it reaches the shoreline. Bear left at this junction. Follow Magee as it drops down to the lake and watch for the sign indicating the start of the Killarney Loop Trail. Almost immediately you will see the concrete dam that controls the water level of the lake. There is a small swimming area here and, a short distance beyond, picnic tables in the cool shelter of a fir tree grove. There is parking beside the picnic area.

The going is easy around the north side of the lake, where the ground is level. A short walk or ride leads to a gravel beach where a small creek flows into the lake. In summer the waters of Killarney Lake are warm enough for swimming. This is also a good place to launch a canoe or kayak. From here, trail access is restricted to those on foot. Although bikes are not permitted on this portion of the trail, you might want to check out the skills park on the opposite side of Mount Gardner Road from here.

Past the beach the trail begins to climb slightly, then joins a boardwalk that crosses the marsh at the far end of the lake. The steepest and roughest parts of the trail are here where the hillside rises, providing several good viewpoints of the lake and Mount Gardner, Bowen's highest point (760 m). Rustic benches, hewn from some of the old stumps at trailside, line the way until the trail links up once more with Magee Road.

> ## HOWE SOUND SEA KAYAKING
ACTIVITIES: *Paddling*
Each June, Horseshoe Bay awakens to the sound of hundreds of little wheels as kayakers from around the Lower Mainland and even further afield roll onto the Bowen Island ferry. The occasion is the annual Round Bowen Race, a 38-km paddlefest at the mouth of Howe Sound, the world's southernmost fiord. Even if you're not here to race, or come at times other than early June, the joys of sea kayaking off Bowen are many. For starters, the watertight craft are amazingly stable, even in rough water. For another, paddlers get a good upper-body workout without putting stress on knees or backs. And sea kayaks provide an intimate way to connect with the primal forces of nature as water, wind—and, with luck, a little sunshine— combine to form a potent recipe for adventure. And there's plenty of that in the islands that ring Bowen, including Pasley, Keats, and Gambier. The best way to safely explore them, at least for first timers, is to join a guided tour offered by Bowen Island Sea Kayaking (see above).

> ## OTHER ATTRACTIONS
Cape Roger Curtis: If you do take a vehicle, one of Bowen's most charming and controversial spots to visit is Cape Roger Curtis. Head across island on Grafton and Adams roads, and then Tunstall Boulevard. Turn left on Reef Road, then follow Whitesails Road to a cul-de-sac from where trails begin. To stage a paddle journey around Cape Roger Curtis, hand-launch a boat at Tunstall Bay Beach from the foot of Tunstall Boulevard. In 2002, development slated for this sensitive micro-climate on the southwestern corner of the island triggered the formation of the Cape Roger Curtis Trust Society (caperogercurtis.org). After a contentious five years during which the 255-ha cape was posted as off-limits to the public, the owners reopened its old logging roads and trails to visitors. Pending

the outcome of current negotiations, the point's most ecologically sensitive portion may be set aside as a park.

Twiggleberries Spa (711 Cates Hill Road; 604-947-2876; www.twiggleberries.com): You can find Twiggleberries 2 km west of Snug Cove. Visits are by appointment, so plan ahead. Four guest rooms are also available in this stylish craftsman country home.

> ## DINING

Both fine dining restaurants in Snug Cove are closed on Mondays and Tuesdays. If you've come with a car, the *Galley Bistro and Lounge* (539 Artisan Lane; 604-947-0061; www.thegalleybistro.com) in Artisan Square is your best bet. Just as easy an option is the *Bowen Island Neighbourhood Pub* (604-947-2782) in Snug Cove where the pool balls click in time with finger-picking guitar stylings on live music evenings.

Village Baker Café (992 Dorman Road; Village Square in Snug Cove; 604-947-2869): There's often a line-up here, always a sure sign of a winner (or the only game in town). On warm, sunny days the cafe's patio is a fine place to do brunch and people watching at the same time.

Tuscany (451 Bowen Trunk Road; 604-947-0550; www.tuscanyrestaurant.ca): The Vancouver restaurant–seasoned team of Christophe Langlois and Julie Cree know exactly what visitors from the Big Smoke expect, including weekend brunches. The toasted aroma

> ## ALL ABOARD
· · · · · · ·

THE QUEEN OF CAPILANO has a sheltered outdoor area for foot passengers where you can enjoy the scenery even on a stormy day. The view of Howe Sound from the ferry's deck is one of the best reasons for making this journey. BC Ferries' *Queen of Capilano* carries 85 vehicles; the round-trip fee is $24 (peak) and $21 (off-peak). The round-trip fare for drivers and passengers is about $8 per person (slightly less off-peak). There is an extra charge of $1.50 for bicycles. *Note:* There are no reservations on the Bowen ferry; first come, first served.

of a wood-fired oven always draws me in, whether I'm hungry or not. Check the website for guest chef evenings.

Blue Eyes Marys Bistro (604-947-2583): Steps from the ferry, this restaurant, open for dinner only, Wednesday through Sunday, is as fresh as its flowery name implies and is worth a ferry ride even if you don't plan to overnight on Bowen. Reservations are recommended.

> **ACCOMMODATION**

Bowen Island boasts numerous bed and breakfasts, most tucked into the forest. Unfortunately, most of them require a vehicle to reach. Skip the bother and stay in Snug Cove.

Doc Morgan's Inn (604-947-0707; www.steamship-marina. bc.ca): This place offers a little bit of everything: floating and land-based cottages, suites, and even a guest house. Snug Cove doesn't get any cozier than this.

The Lodge at the Old Dorm (460 Melmore Road; 604-947-0947; www.lodgeattheolddorm.com): A walk beneath towering maples from the ferry is exactly the way to begin a visit. Dan Parkin restored this heritage lodge in the 1990s, and guests have been settling in comfortably ever since. For a good night's rest, leave your window open at night. A nearby waterfall infuses the air with a steady, soothing stream of healing ions.

South Pointe Luxury Cottages (310 Forest Ridge Road; 604-947-9343; www.southpointecottages.com): Two new cabins, the Napa and the Contemporary, were designed with couples in mind. If you're a thin-skinned '60s type, avoid the Contemporary with its "No Hippies Allowed" wall hanging. Breakfast is delivered to your door or poolside in summer. One caveat: depending on the route, the cottages lie 6 to 10 km from Snug Cove in the Forest Ridge neighbourhood.

> # 4

SQUAMISH

. . . . .

> **ACCESS:** Squamish is located 60 km north of Vancouver on Highway 99.

> **WHY GO:** Revel in the natural setting, mild climate year-round, abundant trails and water routes, and festivals.

> **KEEP IN MIND:** If you're planning to attend the Squamish Mountain Bike Festival in June or Squamish Loggers Days in August, make reservations well in advance.

WELCOME TO the self-proclaimed "Heart of the 2010 Winter Olympics." That may seem like a grandiose claim, especially since no Olympic events are actually scheduled in Squamish. However, a quick scan of the year-round options to get sporty in "Squish," as it's affectionately known, quickly validates its other claim as the outdoor recreation capital of Canada.

Squamish may gleam with a veneer of newness, but those in search of natural rejuvenation have been journeying to this town of 15,000 at the head of Howe Sound for well over a century. Come explore the river valleys, lakes and mountains that define this tightly knit community. It's not surprising that scores of recreational enthusiasts of all persuasions have left their footprints—and fingerprints—in and around Squamish. This is definitely a year-round destination, with a sea level location guaranteeing that its low-elevation trails remain snow-free much of the year.

For tourism information on Squamish, call 604-815-4994 or 1-866-333-2010 or visit www.tourismsquamish.com. To rent outdoor gear, check out Valhalla Pure Outfitters (805–1200 Hunter Place; 1-877-892-9092; www.squamishgear.com). Cyclists should check out Corsa Cycles (830–1200 Hunter Place; 604-892-3331; www. corsacycles.com) or Tantalus Bike Shop (40194 Glenalder Place; 604-898-2588; www.tantalusbikeshop.com) for parts and service. River's Edge Sportfishing Outfitters is a great place to get fishing licences, gear, guided tours, and tips on where the fish are biting (604-898-5656). Paddlers should consult SunWolf Outdoor Centre (604-898-1537 or 1-877-806-8046; www.sunwolf.net) or Canadian Outback Adventures (1-800-565-8735; www.canadianoutback.com) to book their Squamish adventure.

With over 1,200 routes put up locally, Squamish is a climbing mecca. Climbers drawn to the granite walls of Stawamus Chief Mountain and the Little Smoke Bluffs will find guide books and gear at Climb On Equipment (38165–2nd Avenue; 604-892-2243), Squamish Rock Guides (604-815-1750; www.squamishrockguides. com), and Vertical Reality (37835–2nd Avenue; 604-892-8248).

> ### ALICE LAKE PROVINCIAL PARK &

ACTIVITIES: *Camping, cycling, fishing, hiking, paddling, picnick-ing, running, swimming, walking*

This park is hugely popular, with summer camping chief among its attractions. Reservations are recommended May through September. Find it 12 km north of downtown Squamish to the east of Highway 99. I find the second-growth forest in which the campsites are set a bit gloomy except during the hottest weather when shade is a boon. Far better to day-trip here and explore any of the ten trails that loop past four charming mountain lakes, Alice being the largest and most approachable, and the surrounding slopes.

Alice is well suited for paddling, and it's not unusual to see pods of kayakers and canoeists taking lessons at one end while anglers quietly troll at the other. There's ample room for both, with a pier to fish from at the southern end and launch sites at each end of the lake beside the picnic areas. And although freshwater lake fishing from a dock may not be everyone's speed, there is a chance you'll hook a trout in these stocked waters, particularly in May and June. Rows of tables ring the lakeshore, each with its own barbecue. Find a grassy place to spread your blanket. The setting is enormously restful. Lakeshore Walk, shaded by cedar groves that thrive on the moisture that the lake provides, links picnic areas on both the northern and southern sides of the lake. The view from the lake's northern end of the peaks in nearby Garibaldi Park's Diamond Head region is one of the best in the park.

Chief among the walking and cycling routes is the 6-km Four Lakes Loop Trail. Note that this trail is closed to cycling May 1 to September 15. Jack's Trail is one of the best intermediate routes on which to experience the joy of mountain biking locally, as it rolls and winds between the park and the Garibaldi Highlands area. This 5-km trail—from which more numerous and challenging routes branch off—begins at the southern end of Alice Lake. The well-marked trailhead lies adjacent to the gravel road that leads up DeBeck's Hill (a demanding workout in its own right, with a broad view of Squamish and Howe Sound on top before a barrelhouse descent).

> ## BRACKENDALE EAGLES PROVINCIAL PARK &

ACTIVITIES: *Birding, nature observation, walking*
Follow Buckley Avenue and Government Road north of Cleveland Avenue in downtown Squamish for 7 km, or head west of Highway 99 in Brackendale on Depot Road where a large sign of an eagle is posted. Turn left (south) onto Government Road, which soon leads to the park's main trailhead.

One of North America's largest populations of bald eagles roosts in Squamish's Brackendale neighbourhood. Best viewing time is November to March, when the tall black cottonwoods lining the Squamish River stand bare. Each January, there is an annual tally of their numbers. In 1994, a world-record 3,769 were counted. The best viewing spot is from the top of the dike beside Government Road, directly across from the Easter Seals Camp, in Brackendale Eagles Park. In a good year, you may see thirty eagles or more at any one time from there. A wheelchair ramp leads up onto the dike from Government Road. Two benches, whimsically fashioned from driftwood, provide good perches for enjoying grand views of the river, valleys, and mountains. Information kiosks, including an inspirational Sko-mish First Nation display, are mounted on the dike and detail the natural history of eagles.

ACTIVITIES: *Cycling, driving, fishing, picnicking, rafting, viewpoints*
The Squamish Valley Road begins 16 km north of downtown Squamish. Follow the signs west from Highway 99 opposite the entrance to Alice Lake Provincial Park. A bridge crosses the Cheakamus River at Cheekye, and on its far side the road divides into the Squamish Valley Road to the left and the Paradise Valley Road to the right.

The Squamish and Paradise valleys are two of the most picturesque locations in the Sea to Sky corridor. The rewards for making the journey up either are manifold. In early summer, wildflowers colour the roadsides, while glaciers cloak the surrounding peaks—a reminder that parts of B.C. are still emerging from the most recent ice age.

The Squamish River accompanies the road in places but is hidden for the most part. The Squamish Valley Road is an easy place to cycle. A particularly good viewpoint of Tantalus and Zenith mountains occurs at the one-lane bridge across Pillchuck Creek, about 13 km from the Cheekye Bridge. The Squamish Valley and the Squamish River widen here for the next 20 km. By July, when water levels have usually dropped to their seasonal lows, sandbars appear and provide excellent picnicking, camping, and fishing locations. Dolly Varden char and cutthroat trout run in the silty grey river, which never warms up enough for more than a quick plunge, even on the hottest days.

The predominant feature in the Squamish Valley's south side is the dozen or more peaks and glaciers that comprise the Tantalus Range. A combination of snowmelt and rain feeds numerous waterfalls that tumble from such heights above the river that their contents are occasionally carried off by the wind before more than a few drops reach the ground. Distinctively snaggle-toothed Mount Cayley dominates the north side of the valley. Its ruptured summit bears telltale signs of volcanic activity that erupted here twelve thousand or so years ago.

The Squamish River benefits from its confluence with the Elaho near the north end of the valley. Drive a short distance up the Elaho Forest Service Road for a view of a stretch of the river whose name says it all: the Devil's Elbow. This 270-degree bend in the

Stawamus Chief Mountain, Squamish

Elaho provides a nerve-testing challenge for whitewater rafters and kayakers. The put-in spot for rafting companies lies in a quieter area just above the elbow.

Although less than half as long as nearby Squamish Valley, Paradise has a quiet beauty all its own. Paradise Valley Road is almost entirely level for much of its 11.3-km length, making for easy cycling. The rewards for making the journey are several good picnic and fishing spots on the banks of the Cheakamus River. There's good freshwater angling on the Cheakamus River almost year-round, though strictly catch and release, as fishing is on rivers and creeks in the Squamish region. Unlike the Squamish River into which it flows, water in the Cheakamus is clear year-round. Anglers cast from the banks of the Cheakamus for coho salmon in October and November, for steelhead from late February to April and for Dolly Varden char anytime. Best access to the banks is from the north end of Paradise Valley Road. The historic Pemberton Trail, now used almost exclusively as a hiking and biking trail through the Cheakamus Canyon, takes over where the road ends.

> ## SQUAMISH ESTUARY
ACTIVITIES: *Birding, cycling, walking*
Travelling north on Highway 99, turn west into downtown Squamish at the second traffic lights, where an Esso station is the anchor tenant. Drive south along Cleveland Avenue, the town's main drag, to Vancouver Street, then head three blocks west, to the trailhead to the Squamish estuary.

Meadow Loop Trail leads through the town's oceanfront estuary, making this a fine place to begin a wildlife-viewing walk. From the trailhead, the grassy dike trail rambles west past the channelled waterways, home to migratory waterfowl as well as an overwintering population of geese and raptors. Out on the estuary, uncluttered views open up, with the smooth granite walls of the Stawamus Chief displayed to great effect. Equally arresting when skies are clear is the dagger point of Atwell Peak and its broad-shouldered companion, the Dalton Dome. Together they dominate the skyline of Garibaldi Park to the north. Shannon Falls' snowy tresses can be seen cascading down the slopes to the south of the Chief. Spires of solitary, stunted Sitka spruce anchor the estuary's perimeter.

A cool breeze often blows across Howe Sound's shoreline, so dress accordingly. Bring binoculars to follow the flight of hawks or eagles over the marshland.

Meadow Trail turns south at a log-sorting yard, then follows the Central Channel atop the Heritage Dykes, the oldest man-made structures in Squamish. Strategically placed benches provide good viewing perches. (Allow 45 minutes to complete the loop.) Further inland, two additional estuary trails—Forest Loop and Swan Walk—lead through wooded areas to the west of the BC Rail Spur Line. The easiest way to reach both trails is to follow Bailey Street, an industrial gravel road that curves around the north end of Chieftan Mall off Cleveland Avenue near Highway 99. Several approaches to the estuary trails are clearly marked here. Take the Swan Walk for the best chance of spotting trumpeter swans that overwinter in the Central Channel. These majestic honkers sport the largest wingspan of all West Coast birds.

> ## STAWAMUS CHIEF PROVINCIAL PARK
ACTIVITIES: *Camping, climbing, hiking, viewpoints*
Welcome to Squamish's answer to North Vancouver's popular Grouse Grind. To reach the park drive to the base of the Chief via the designated turnoff at the viewing area on Highway 99 just north of Shannon Falls. Follow the road that leads up the embankment in the middle of the viewpoint and leads south to the provincial campsites and trailhead parking lot.

Stawamus Chief Mountain has three summits, each one progressively higher and separated by deep clefts. At the outset, a common trail leads upwards towards all three, then it divides into two separate routes. At this junction, the majority of hikers, particularly those with children, head for the South (or First) Summit, a 7-km round trip.

You'll find numerous benefits—such as some modest rock climbing and a great view of a notch on the Chief's north face—if you choose the slightly more challenging route to the Centre (Second) and North (Third) Summits, an 11-km round trip. In fact, one of the most pleasant options, particularly if you have an extra hour's time, is to follow the loop that links both.

No matter which summit you choose, be prepared for an unrelenting regime of up, up, and up (and the resultant knee-knackering corollary of down, down, and down). Take the time to enjoy your surroundings beneath tall stands of ramrod-straight Douglas-fir, which provide shade as welcome as the steady breeze that funnels round the mountain off Howe Sound. *Note:* There is little shade on much of the trail, so pack plenty of fluids for the higher sections of the climb.

> ## OTHER ATTRACTIONS
Festivals: Thanks to the trail-building efforts of volunteer groups such as the Squamish Off-Road Cycling Association (www.sorca.ca), new mountain bike routes appear each year. The town that was once

solely identified with logging now hosts two of the major events on the Canadian mountain bike calendar—the Test of Metal (www.testof metal.com) in June and the Cheakamus Challenge (www.cheakamus challenge.ca) in September—both of which are cross-country rides of epic proportions. Much easier for spectators to enjoy is the five-day Squamish Days Loggers Sports Festival held in early August (www.squamishdays.org), which features hearty pancake breakfasts, bed races along the town's main street, and manly events such as log rolling, speed bucking, and tree felling.

Shannon Falls Provincial Park: The well-marked entrance to Shannon Falls Provincial Park is on the east side of Highway 99 at the southern end of town. The Shannon Falls' parking lot is usually full by noon on weekends from May through September. There are two large picnic areas suited to families and groups who like room to stretch out and play.

Squamish Adventure Centre (38551 Loggers Lane; 604-815-5084; www.adventurecentre.com): Squamish styles itself as the outdoor capital of Canada, and that's what its boldly designed, 880-square-metre Adventure Centre silently proclaims to passersby on Highway 99 at the entrance to the city's downtown core. Designed to emulate a bald eagle spreading its wings, the soaring glass structure is composed of 210 panels of half-inch tempered glass, one of the few building materials not sourced locally. The building's main columns were milled from Douglas-fir, which, along with the crushed basalt granite pad, came from the Squamish Valley. The centre promotes the joys of kayaking, river rafting, mountain biking, eagle viewing, windsurfing, kiteboarding, skateboarding, camping, and above all else, rock climbing, a sport that first put Squamish on the adventure radar in the 1960s. Book a guided outdoor adventure trip here while enjoying a snack at the centre's Pause Café or shopping for guidebooks, maps, and souvenirs. As well, a series of carved wooden panels details the history of Squamish, particularly the events of the twentieth century.

It's not simply coincidence that the Adventure Centre overlooks Stawamus Chief Mountain and backs onto a rockface called the Smoke Bluffs. Almost as famous as the Stawamus Chief, the Smoke Bluffs feature dozens of short but challenging routes where climbers can scramble like monkeys.

West Coast Railway Heritage Park (39645 Government Road; 604-898-9336; www.wcra.org): All aboard. This train is bound for glory, or at least the West Coast Railway Heritage Park, where rolling stock from steam and diesel rail transportation's past, including the treasured 1940s-era Royal Hudson locomotive, has found a resting place. An ambitious $4 million development project is currently underway. Plans include a turntable linked to an open-air exhibit facility that will house seven pieces of heritage railway equipment, including the Royal Hudson, the restored 1890s business car, British Columbia, as well as the 1905 Colonist sleeping car. Take a stroll along the park's seven tracks and decide for yourself which cars or engines might make suitable candidates to exhibit on the new plaza. The diminutive 1910 Baldwin 2 steam locomotive sits on a siding beside the massive wood-frame BC Rail Car Shop. Climb into the cab and ring the engine's bell. The clanging will reverberate in the mountain air, recalling the day in 1915 when the first train headed north with a carload of anglers on board bound for Rainbow Lodge on Alta Lake in what is now Whistler. At the West Coast Heritage Railway Park, history is not only being preserved, but it's also still being made.

> **DINING**

Brackendale Café Art Gallery, Theatre, and Teahouse (41950 Government Road; 604-898-3333; www.brackendaleartgallery.com): Open weekends and holidays from noon to 10 PM, the Brackendale Art Gallery is a good stop to learn more about bald eagles; it hosts a variety of artistic, musical, and dramatic productions and serves up warm bowls of soup—perfect on a cold day. Sculptor Thor Froslev, who began building this sprawling space in 1969, is also responsible for publicizing Brackendale as the winter home of the bald eagle. The distinctive wooden signs on Highway 99, dominated by the profile of an eagle, are his creation.

Wild Wood Bistro and Bar (38922 Progress Way; 604-815-4424): A fixture in the Sea to Sky corridor with sister locations in Whistler and Pemberton, the Wild Wood offers all the goods.

North Shore Grill & Brew Pub (37801 Cleveland Ave in the Howe Sound Inn; 604-892-2603 or 1-800-919-2537; www.howesound. com): The Howe Sound Inn's restaurant and microbrew pub offer the best of both worlds. Spiffy up or just hang loose; it's your choice. One creative kitchen serves both. The grill's casual decor matches the indoor-outdoor feel of the inn, minus the sports fare featured on the pub's macro-televisions. Crusty beer breads are baked in a wood-fired oven; loaves and pastries are sold in the inn's small bakery.

> ## ACCOMMODATION

Although there are a number of fine bed and breakfasts locally, chief among which is the *Nu-Salya B&B Chalet* (2014 Glacier Heights Place; 1-877-604-9005; www.nusalya.com), when I overnight in Squish I lean towards an inn or a cabin.

Sea to Sky Hotel (40330 Tantalus Way; 604-898-4874 or 1-800-531-1530; www.seatoskyhotel.com): The best place in Squamish to restore your composure once you're done birding, hiking, mountain biking, paddling, picnicking, or walking is the hotel's Birchwood Spa, complete with swimming pool, hot tub, sauna, steam room, and fitness centre.

Howe Sound Inn & Brewing Company (37801 Cleveland Ave; 604-892-2603 or 1-800-919-2537; www.howesound.com &): Set in the shadow of Stawamus Chief Mountain, this pub, restaurant, and hotel is a good staging ground for exploring the nearby estuary. Good nights' sleeps are a better bet in rooms 13 to 20 on the inn's quieter side off Cleveland Avenue.

SunWolf Outdoor Centre (70002 Squamish Valley Road; 604-898-1537 or 1-877-806-8046; www.sunwolf.net): Live the woody life to the tune of a rushing river in a cabin nestled beside the Cheakamus and Cheekye rivers. If you feel like cloistering yourself, reserve one with a kitchenette. If you want to get outside, guided whitewater rafting and eagle-viewing float trips are on tap. Check out the maps and guidebooks in the main lodge. For tips on where to go and what to do, quiz the knowledgeable staff.

> 5

WHISTLER

. . . . .

> **ACCESS:** Head 115 km north of Vancouver on Highway 99.

> **WHY GO:** Whistler is North America's premier resort—and it's right in our own backyard.

> **KEEP IN MIND:** Whistler has a reputation for being expensive. As most accommodations come with kitchens, one of the best ways to stay on budget, at least as far as meals, is good old DIY.

WHEN I brought out my first guidebooks to Whistler in the 1990s, it was already evident that the "little resort that could" had begun to cast a welcoming halo well beyond its municipal boundaries. Since then, growth in neighbouring Squamish and Pemberton has born out that promise and given rise to subsequent editions, including *The Whistler Book* in 2005. For detailed information on outdoor activities throughout the region, pick up a copy.

The selections in this chapter reflect my favourite attractions and amenities garnered from years spent overnighting at the renowned resort municipality. Information on outdoor activities as well as detailed recreation maps of Whistler are available from the Whistler Visitor Info Centre (4230 Gateway Drive; 604-932-5922; www.whistler chamber.com) and the Whistler Activity Centre (4010 Whistler Way; 604-938-2769 or 1-877-991-9988; www.tourismwhistler.com).

For guided tours check out Backroads Adventure Tours (604-932-3111; www.backroadswhistler.com), which offers guided and independent canoe and kayak trips on the River of Golden Dreams with the option of a pedal ride back; the Whistler Outdoor Experience Centre (604-932-3389) offers canoe and kayak rentals and guided tours at Lakeside Park on Alta Lake and the Edgewater

Lodge on Green Lake (www.whistleroutdoor.com). Cyclists may want to visit Evolution Bike Service (604-932-2967; www.evolution whistler.com), Fanatyk Co Ski and Cycle (604-938-9455; www. fanatykco.com), Katmandu Sports (604-932-6381), or Wild Willie's Ski Club (604-938-8036; www.wildwillies.com) for rentals, trail maps and repairs.

> **COUGAR MOUNTAIN**

ACTIVITIES: *Cross-country skiing, fishing, hiking, horseback riding, mountain biking, nature observation, picnicking, sky-lining, snowshoeing, walking*

Follow Highway 99 north from the heart of the resort as it curves along the western shore of Green Lake. Watch for 16 Mile Creek Forest Service Road (also called Cougar Mountain Road on some maps), a well-marked, two-lane road that rises uphill on the left (west) side of Highway 99, 1 km north of the Emerald Estates neighbourhood. After a short distance you will pass a brown Forest Service sign marking the beginning of the road along 16 Mile Creek. Just past the sign is a widening on the right (north) side of the road, base for the Cougar Mountain at Whistler adventure centre (604-932-4086; www.cougarmountain.ca). A wide range of motorized and self-propelled guided activities is offered here year-round, from horseback riding to dog sledding. This is also where snowmobilers, snowshoers, and cross-country skiers congregate in winter, since snow is not cleared past this point. In summer, drive 4 km and park at the entrance to the Showh Lakes recreation area. A detailed map posted at the information kiosk here outlines trail choices, all well marked. A 1.6-km hiking trail (no bikes) leads uphill on the right and links with the Ancient Cedars Loop Trail, a 5 km round-trip. Allow 2 hours to make the complete journey, and take plenty of fluids on warm days.

Also from the kiosk a rough road leads 1 km uphill to the Showh Lakes trailhead and parking lot. Hike or bike 2 km to the lakes and the Ancient Cedars trailhead. Halfway along, the larger of the two lakes appears below. A trail leads down through stumps and berry bushes heavy with fruit in late summer to a giant log half-submerged in the shallow water. Walk out on it to fly-cast, picnic, or swim.

Cheakamus Lake from Whistler Mountain

The Ancient Cedars Trail is worth waiting for. After the dust and open sky along 16 Mile Creek Road, the forest seems gloomy. White snowberries and the red fruits of devil's club stand out vividly among the evergreens by late August. (Beware the rhubarb-like leaves and spiny stems of devil's club, which can leave you with painful, inflamed scratches.) This rocky, root-filled trail is surprisingly soft in spots from the years of cedar needles that have accumulated on the forest floor.

A small wooden bridge spans a creek beside a waterfall near the outset of the loop trail. You can tell when you've reached the ancient cedars: trunk diameters suddenly swell to 3 m. On a hot day, the shade cast by these spires blessedly lowers the temperature a degree or two. The hush among these spires is remarkable. Take your time. Breathe deeply. Reconnect with wild nature, Cougar Mountain style.

> ## WHISTLER INTERPRETIVE FOREST

ACTIVITIES: *Cycling, picnicking, running, viewpoints, walking*
Head south on Highway 99 to Function Junction, then east at the traffic lights on Cheakamus Lake Road. A good place to begin is the 4.5-km Riverside Trail, which runs along both sides of the Cheakamus. It's easy to find and, aside from several short, steep stretches, suited to all ability levels, whether you're exploring on foot or by bike. You can also pick up the trail at any number of points along its route. One drawback is that on the trail's eastern side there's only limited access to the fast-flowing Cheakamus River, which frequently channels through steep-sided granite walls. Flowing out of Garibaldi Park, the river passes through the Whistler Interpretive Forest. Find one of the dozens of riverbank picnic spots to relax at, either before or after a ride, run, or walk, and let the throaty river wrap its wall of sound around your mind.

The Whistler Interpretive Forest's star feature is its extensive 13-km network of narrow trails, especially suited to mountain biking and running, that criss-cross the main roads. The trails have garnered a reputation as some of the best built and, therefore, most enjoyable in Whistler. Helpful signs indicate time, distance and elevation gain.

A suspension bridge links the trails on both sides of the Cheakamus. Named MacLaurin's Crossing, it lies several kilometres upstream from the entrance to the forest. Paired with BC Park's Helm Creek Trail bridge, about 6 km farther upstream in Garibaldi Park near Cheakamus Lake (well worth a visit in its own right), the bridge allows for adventuring along both sides of the river.

> ## LOST LAKE TRAILS

ACTIVITIES: *Cycling, picnicking, running, viewpoints, walking*
Here's something you can do without straying far from your hotel or condo. A network of trails ring the shoreline and hillsides above diminutive Lost Lake, as popular in summer with cyclists, runners, and walkers as with cross-country skiers in winter.

A detailed map of the Lost Lake trail system is posted beside the Valley Trail as it leads from day parking lot (Lot 3) beside Blackcomb Way in Whistler Village, towards Lost Lake. Free maps of the Lost Lake trail system are available from Cross Country Connection (604-905-0071; www.crosscountryconnection.bc.ca), where you can also rent bikes and get repairs and advice. A more detailed bike trail map for both Whistler and Pemberton, published by Terrapro, is available for $12.95 from most bike shops and bookstores in Whistler.

One of the most appealing things about the Lost Lake trails is that trailhead signs graphically detail the level of difficulty of each. The Lost Lake trails are also generally wider than most of the cross-country bike routes that have been constructed throughout the valley. Rocks-and-roots single-track trails as well are harder to find; keep an eye out for these unmarked gems as they lead away from the main trail system. You'll recognize them on sight.

My favourite is Tin Pants, a multi-use 9.7-km route that leads uphill from the Centennial Trail just east of the cross-country skiers' ticket booth (closed in summer). The well-marked trail winds back and forth above the west side of Lost Lake.

Rarely explored on foot, Tin Pants' smooth, hard-packed construction will appeal just as much to runners or cyclists looking for a good place to stretch their legs. Stylish touches, such as bridges built from lodge pole pines, abound, giving Tin Pants the look of a twig furniture showroom in places. This is particularly true at several prominent viewpoints where Tin Pants intersects with the expert-rated Centennial Trail. One of its best vantage points overlooks Rainbow Mountain as it rises on the west side of valley to its 2,314-m summit.

Tin Pants takes its quirky name from bug-proof apparel worn by loggers.

After your ride through the woods above the lake, make your way around the shoreline on the Lost Lake Loop to seek out sections of other trails. A particularly enjoyable stretch of easy-rated Lower Panorama leads away from the north end of the lake past an observation deck overlooking the Lost Lake wetlands restoration project. This very tranquil spot is a great place to sit and watch the wind make

Blackcomb Peak from Whistler Mountain

patterns on a small pond in front of the deck while you decide where to head next. With more than a hundred cross-country mountain bike trails to choose from, Whistler does not lack for options. For starters, a wooden bridge links the intermediate-rated Molly Hogan Trail at the north end of Lost Lake with Tin Pants where it crosses the Old Mill Road Trail. Now that you've gotten your second wind, get going.

> **ZIPTREK ECOTOURS** *(Carleton Lodge; 1-866-935-0001; www.ziptrek.com)*

ACTIVITIES: *Nature observation, skylining, walking*

As harebrained as harnessing yourself to a steel cable and sailing through Whistler's ancient forest might sound—especially in winter—visitors looking for a new vantage point on adventure have gravitated to this high-flying experience since Ziptrek Ecotours first debuted in 2002.

Given that you're floating 75 metres or more above the ground, there's a surprisingly peaceful feeling in the forest canopy high above Fitzsimmons Creek whose boulder-filled bed forms the natural dividing line between Whistler and Blackcomb. Since the initial five cables were installed, Ziptrek has doubled in size and become one of Whistler's most popular year-round activities.

White noise from Fitzsimmons Creek's rushing water fills the air. It helps calm your nerves as you make ready to step off the platform into midair. After your first flight along the inch-thick cable you wonder what the big whoop was all about. This delightfully easy adventure is far less extreme than it first appears. Unlike a roller-coaster ride or a swing on a trapeze, your stomach doesn't feel like its fallen down around your knees. And even if you never take flight, simply exploring the forest canopy via a series of suspension bridges on a Ziptrek's companion TreeTrek tour is giddying enough.

Much of the forest on the lower slopes of both Whistler and Blackcomb mountains was logged in the 1940s and again in the 1970s. A perimeter of old growth was left along each side of Fitzsimmons Creek. That's where Ziptrek Ecotours constructed its natural cedar platforms, all of which are connected by cables strong enough to handle the weight of 20 Volkswagen Beetles—if they had to.

Ziptrek Ecotours is the brainchild of a pair of adventurers who developed this eco-friendly technology to suit the coastal temperate rainforest. Not a single tree was harmed in the construction—a good thing, since there are precious few trees left. This adventure is more than just another walk in the woods: over the course of a 3-hour tour you'll learn as much about the forest and the variety of life forms it sustains as you will about confronting your fear of flying—a double bonus.

> **OTHER ATTRACTIONS**

Golf: Four top-ranked golf courses make Whistler, according to *Golf Digest*, one of the "Top 20 Greatest Golf Destinations in the World." The oldest course, which holds its charm after twenty-five years, is the centrally located Whistler Golf Club (4001 Whistler Way, 1-800-376-1777 or 604-932-3280, www.whistlergolf.com). Striking scenery and abundant wildlife (including the occasional black bear) may take your eye off the ball, but whatever your level, you're guaranteed to have a memorable round at this 6,722-yard course, the first in Canada designed by Arnold Palmer. The season lasts from May to October. If you don't golf but your partner does, you may "ride along" for $20—or walk the course for free. Alternatively, it's surrounded by a walking/cycling path with benches and lookouts that doubles as a cross-country ski trail in winter.

Soo Valley Wildlife Reserve: Snowmobiling may have its fans, but when it comes to exploring the frozen countryside, particularly in the Soo Valley Wildlife Reserve 20 minutes north of Whistler, there's no more authentic way than by dogsled. To book a tour, contact Whistler Dogsledding Adventures (www.cougarmountain.ca), which also runs dogs on nearby Cougar Mountain and in the Callaghan Valley, site of the 2010 Olympic Nordic events. Although full tours must be reserved in advance, visitors are welcome to drop by Whistler Dogsledding Adventures' base in Soo Valley to watch the dogs in action and cross-country ski the trails.

On the trail, you can either snuggle into the coziness of the sled bag or stand astride the runners and, with help from your guide, drive the sled yourself. One of dogsledding's life lessons is that there is a freedom out on the trail that you just won't find at home, and it is far more environmentally friendly than snowmobiling. These days Whistler visitors prefer to go to the dogs, so to speak.

Whistler Mountain Bike Park: Blackcomb Mountain's Magic Park is a place where novice skiers and snowboarders typically overcome their jitters in winter. If you've ever been tempted to give freeride-style pedalling a try, this is the place. Rent a helmet fitted with full-face protection, plus padded arm, leg, and hand pads. Then mount up on a dual-suspension bike and wheel on over to the Magic chair-lift. It's also worth spending a few dollars more for a guide to brief

> **BEST MAKE-OUT SPOT**

HOT MAKE-OUT SESSIONS don't come any finer than high in the air beneath snow-covered peaks. No wonder the gondolas are the top make-out places in Whistler. I highly recommend this warm-up as a great way to begin your day on the mountains. Top marks to those who hit all three gondolas on the same day.

you on some basics, starting with how to load your bike onto the lift. Given the bike's hefty size, this can be a challenging workout all on its own. About the only thing one can categorize as "small" about a freeride bike is its seat—as insignificant as a flea on an elephant. That's because freeriders don't spend much time sitting down. Like skiing and snowboarding, this style of cycling is done almost entirely from a standing position.

Spa Time: The Taman Sari Royal Heritage Spa (4359 Main Street, 604-938-5982, www.tamansarispa.com) provides an exotic tropical paradise where all your senses are stimulated after a full-body Javanese Massage. You won't soon forget the personal pampering this spa provides or the pungent scent of Jamu, a herbal concoction that perfumes the warm air. The Taman Sari is part of the Summit Lodge (www.summitlodge.com; 1-888-913-8811), which offers special two-night stay-and-spa packages. Other first-class day spas in Whistler with more of a West Coast feel (think cedar, seaweed, and glacial clay) include Vida Wellness Spa, in the Fairmont Chateau Whistler (4599 Chateau Boulevard, 1-800-401-4098 or 604-938-2086, www.fairmont.com/Whistler) and the Spa at the Four Seasons Whistler (4591 Blackcomb Way, 604-966-2620, www.fourseasons.com/whistler). The Solarice Wellness Centre + Spa (two locations, 604-935-1222 or 1-888-935-1222, www.solarice.com), which has a bright studio above the Whistler Info Centre, offers drop-in yoga classes and various therapeutic treatments.

> ## DINING

Elements Urban Tapas Parlour (4359 Main Street; 604-932-2778; www.summitlodge.com): Enjoy casual tapas-style menu choices. Très yummy.

Fifty Two 80 Bistro (4591 Blackcomb Way; 604-935-3400; www.fourseasons.com/whistler): Everything harmonizes in this bistro's relaxed atmosphere where creativity abounds, right down to the tinkle of piano keys.

Araxi Restaurant and Bar (4222 Whistler Village Square; 604-932-4540; www.araxi.com): One of the best places to enjoy seafood and a glass of the Okanagan's finest wine is atop a bar stool at Araxi's unique eighty-seat patio with heated outdoor bar, the perfect place for people-watching in the hub of the village year-round, or in the wood-panelled lounge adjacent to the entrance.

> **ACCOMMODATION**

To ensure a good night's sleep, when booking in the heart of town request a room that doesn't face on Village Stroll. In Village North, avoid rooms that face on Northlands Boulevard.

Edgewater Lodge (8020 Alpine Way; 604-932-0688 or 1-888-870-9065; www.edgewater-lodge.com): This lodge offers the best views, hands down, of Whistler and Blackcomb mountains from any property in the resort short of the hostel on West Side Road. It has rooms only, but breakfast is included, and it features an excellent dining room and outdoor adventure centre.

Sundial Boutique Hotel (4340 Sundial Crescent; 604-932-2321 or 1-800-661-2321; www.sundialhotel.com): Boutique at its best, this hotel comes complete with private balcony hot tubs plus a rooftop one for stargazing. East-facing rooms have front-row seats for whatever is going off on the slopes above Skier Plaza, such as big air stunts executed by skiers and snowboarders launching through a flaming hoop. Also check out weekly "Welcome to Whistler" presentation on Sundays throughout the winter, complete with fireworks.

The Westin Resort and Spa (4090 Whistler Way; 1-888-634-5577; www.westinwhistler.com): Sounds of a waterfall calm the air in the suites that rise beside the Whistler Mountain gondola. Fall out of bed and onto the lifts—it doesn't get much better than that. In-room kitchens and a quiet location (opposite the equally charming Hilton) help assuage the user-fee charged for use of the pool and fitness centre.

PEMBERTON

. . . . .

> ACCESS: Head 175 km north of Vancouver on Highway 99.

> WHY GO: Enjoy mountains and meadows with a small-town flair.

> KEEP IN MIND: In summer mosquitoes can be as fierce as the action at the Pemberton Hotel.

PEMBERTON, PLAYFULLY nicknamed Spud Valley for the world-famous seed potatoes cultivated there, is a little village in a steep-sided mountain valley, parts of which never receive sun in winter. The silty-grey Lillooet River rolls stealthily south past farm fields, walled by dikes that double as greenways for horseback riders, cyclists, and runners. Unlike the Okanagan, this is not where folks come to retire. Just the opposite. The majority of its 4,000 or so residents live by the same adventure-driven credo as nearby Whistler, 35 km south.

Pemberton's centuries-old farm roots and millennia-long First Nations history distinguish it from its upstart neighbour. Storefront hitching racks are something you're definitely not going to find anywhere else along the Sea to Sky corridor. A growing trend sees chefs from Whistler restaurants cutting deals with local growers for specialty crops. In turn, that same green bounty draws crowds to summer food festivals and inspires urban refugees to put down roots and start small businesses catering to those who—like themselves—opt to live at a slower pace, if only for a weekend.

For details on Pemberton, visit tourismpembertonbc.com or call 604-894-2000. The Pemberton Visitor Info Centre (604-894-6175) operates May to September at the intersection of Highway 99 and Portage Road, the entrance to the village.

For local cycling tips, maps, and service, visit Pemberton Bike Co. (1392 Portage Road; 604-894-6625). Staff will helpfully sketch in trails that haven't yet shown up on any maps. They'll also offer advice on travel times and ability levels on various routes and point the way to the nearest trailhead. The shop is an integral part of the village's cycling community and sponsors the annual Tour de Soo cross-country mountain bike race between Whistler and Pemberton.

Anglers should check out Spud Valley Sporting Goods (1380 Birch Street; 604-894-6630), a well-stocked place to purchase all things outdoors related, including fishing licences. Knowledgeable sources to consult about angling in Pemberton's waters include Valley Fishing Guides (604-935-3474 or 1-888-932-9998) and Whistler Fishing Guides (604-932-4267).

One of the best ways to see the Pemberton Valley is atop a horse. Places to do just that include the Lazy Crow Ranch (Poole Creek; 604-966-8412; www.lazycrowranch.com), the Adventure Ranch (604-894-5200; www.adventureranch.net), Adventures on Horseback (604-894-6269), Punch Creek Trail Rides (604-894-6086), and Pemberton Stables (604-894-6615). Equifest (September; pember tonequifest.com) and the Lillooet Lake Rodeo (Mount Currie fairgrounds, May long weekend) offer plenty of horsey action too.

Thermals propel those keen on soaring, gliding, or parasailing high above the Pemberton Soaring Centre (Pemberton Airport; 1-800-831-2611 or 1-800-894-5727; www.pembertonsoaring.com).

> **PEMBERTON VALLEY ROAD**

ACTIVITIES: *Cycling, driving*

Pemberton and environs make for ideal day-tripping for cyclists, given that most of the roads are paved and level. The shoulders on these country roads are not broad, but traffic doesn't pass by with the same intensity as on Highway 99. You can relax as you pedal around, checking out the old homesteads and exploring the back roads.

To get to the Pemberton Valley Road follow Prospect Street for a short distance north from the heart of town to the intersection with Camus Street. Just around the corner, Prospect Street turns into the Pemberton Valley Road. Head northwest along the Pemberton Valley Road, which links downtown with Pemberton Meadows. This

Mosquito Lake Park, Pemberton

road runs up the valley for 46 km and winds its way gently past cleared acreage. The names on many of the mailboxes you pass— Ronayne, Hartzell, Ryan, Miller, Garling—are those of settlers who arrived generations ago. Many of these family names grace mountains and waterways throughout the valley. One example is Miller Creek, 5 km north of Pemberton. A bridge crosses the creek here, and another crosses the Ryan River where it joins the broad Lillooet River, 2.5 km north of Miller Creek.

You have now entered the heart of the valley. North of Ryan River, for the next 18 km, you pass through the Pemberton Meadows. Mount Ronayne rises above on your right; imposing Mount Samson lies straight ahead to the northwest. The meadows stretch north to where the valley narrows and farm cultivation ends.

Spring is an ideal time to explore both the upper Pemberton Valley and the shores of the Lillooet River, when wide, grey sandbars lie exposed. Water in the river reflects the pale olive and yellow hues of the tall alder and cottonwood trees that are just beginning to come into leaf. In the river's oxbows, tree trunks washed down during flood season lie jackstrawed together. Paw prints in the soft sand betray the presence of wildlife that otherwise remains entirely unseen. Black-tailed deer, which occasionally stray out to feed in fields where winter crops were sowed, are the exceptions.

It's easy to make your way out onto the sandbars, particularly in the upper stretches of the valley where the Pemberton Valley Road and the Lillooet River run side by side. You can park beside the river and walk out on the wide sandy expanses, or walk or cycle along one of the dike trails leading to the river. Both approaches are possible from the Pemberton Valley Road's intersection with the Lillooet River Road, about 26 km northwest of Pemberton. As you approach this junction, watch for two wooden gates shaped like hitching rails opposite Shaw Creek Farms. Leave your vehicle here and follow the dike trail that leads several kilometres through the forest beyond the gates to the river.

> ### ONE MILE LAKE

ACTIVITIES: *Cycling, picnicking, swimming*
The Village of Pemberton maintains a small day-use park beside One Mile Lake, which you can reach via the east side of Highway 99 at the southern entrance to town. There are four picnic tables beside a large stone fireplace and a pit toilet set back in the woods. A small beach with a floating dock invites visitors to take a plunge in the warm waters. In a region where the glacier-fed creeks are too cold for comfort, One Mile Lake is an exception. From the dock you look north over the broad Pemberton Valley to the tops of the Cayoosh Range. A gentle trail circles most of the lake, with a boardwalk across the marshy north end where a small stream drains north into nearby Pemberton Creek. Another dock is located halfway along the lake's eastern side. Beside it is a small rock bench, a good place to rest with a pair of binoculars; there's plenty of waterfowl activity on the lake during spring and fall migration. By midsummer, much of the lake is covered with lily pads.

> ### MOUNT CURRIE AND THE D'ARCY-ANDERSON LAKE ROAD (PEMBERTON PORTAGE ROAD)

ACTIVITIES: *Driving, fishing, picnicking*
The 40-km road that links Mount Currie with D'Arcy was once an important section of the old Gold Rush Trail. When travellers had made their way up the river and lake system to Mount Currie, they still had to clear the Pemberton Pass before reaching the shores of

Anderson Lake. Today, this paved road is a pleasant, albeit winding, journey by car. Surprisingly, the total driving time from Mount Currie to D'Arcy is an easy 30 minutes—not long when you consider how much history lines the way. This quiet, rolling stretch of road has a unique personality, perhaps because of the nature of the narrow Birkenhead River Valley through which much of it passes. The road to D'Arcy covers the same ground originally surveyed by Britain's Royal Engineers in 1860. The Birkenhead River Valley is so narrow that there isn't room for more than one trail. The existing road and the railroad bed have been laid over the old road.

As you drive north of Mount Currie towards D'Arcy, the road climbs briefly after it crosses the railway tracks, then begins to level. At approximately 7 km watch for a bridge over Owl Creek, followed immediately by a clearing on the right where a hydro substation is located. It is marked by a Forest Service sign that indicates the Owl Creek recreation site at the confluence of Owl Creek and the Birkenhead River. Picnic tables spread with white petals await travellers in May, although they are just as appealing at other times, and particularly when the sun shines and the river sings. In September the Birkenhead River runs red with spawning chinook and coho salmon.

> ## CAYOOSH PASS AND JOFFRE LAKES PROVINCIAL PARK
ACTIVITIES: *Driving, hiking, paddling, picnicking, walking*
Three small turquoise lakes lie cradled at the top of Cayoosh Pass, 31 km north of Pemberton on Highway 99. The largest of the trio is minutes from the parking lot—close enough to portage a canoe or kayak—while the upper two lakes are a strenuous 12-km hike away. Cayoosh Pass is a drop-dead-beautiful location with massive icefields on high. Duffey Lake Provincial Park lies a short drive north towards Lillooet—well worth the effort to further appreciate the enchanting views.

> ## MOSQUITO LAKE PARK
ACTIVITIES: *Fishing, hiking, mountain biking, swimming, walking*
To reach Mosquito Lake Park follow Reid Road west from the Pemberton Portage Road near Owl Creek to Ivey Lake Road. Turn left on Linda Road and watch for a trail kiosk on your right. Turn here on a

secondary road that climbs for 1 km to a parking lot beside diminutive Mosquito Lake. Vehicle traffic is blocked beyond here. An old logging road and a lakeside trail ring the diminutive lake.

A pause at one of the three docks anchored at Mosquito Lake's shoreline is a must. By June, the water temperature is warm enough to hop in. The lake welcomes all comers. A black bear may make a silent appearance on one of the downed logs that juts out from the forest, while a vividly coloured western tanager alights on a nearby branch, its wing feathers the same shade of fluorescent yellow-green as the lichen on the forest floor. The longer and quieter you sit, the more this tableau—including a passing family of loons—will unfold before you.

> ### NAIRN FALLS PROVINCIAL PARK
ACTIVITIES: *Walking*
The trail to Nairn Falls is only 1.8 km long, a comfortable 20- to 30-minute walk that begins at the visitor parking lot just inside the park gates on Highway 99 just south of One Mile Lake. You'll feel the ground trembling and hear the roar of the water before the falls come into view. The Green River boils over Nairn Falls, swirls around boulders, then rushes past before dropping again with a roar, and finally joins the Lillooet River. When the river's action is heightened by an above-average run-off, pieces of driftwood shoot from the top of the falls as if from a cannon.

> ### OTHER ATTRACTIONS
Pemberton Barn Dance (Root House on Pemberton Meadows Road): The Barn Dance is one of the biggest events of the year as farmers, ranchers, and partygoers gather for a community-sponsored hoedown in an old root house still used to store spuds, which lends a distinctively farmyard flair. The event, held in July, is complete with beer garden, mechanical bull, and barbecue.

Canada Day (Pemberton Recreation Centre): Marching bands gather in the centre of town; vintage automobiles and horse-drawn carriages roll side by side; bicycles and ponies bedecked with ribbons carry excited youngsters, and sports teams stand resplendent in fresh uniforms. To find the recreation centre, follow Portage Road in downtown Pemberton to its intersection with Prospect Street. Follow Prospect to Pemberton Meadows Road.

Pemberton Pioneer Museum (corner of Prospect and Camus streets): The pioneer museum, one of Pemberton's prime attractions, occupies a two-storey log cabin fronted by a garden of herbs, geraniums, and hollyhocks. Inside, the cabin has been lovingly restored and furnished with antiques, a decor that makes it easy to imagine living here under the peaked roof. It is open daily during summer months; at other times of the year peer in the windows at the old rattan rocker next to the pump organ in the living room or the oilcloth-covered table and hand pump in the kitchen. Several more cabins, a collection of antique farm and logging equipment, an Aboriginal dugout canoe, and a vintage democrat (horse-drawn wagon) stand adjacent to the museum. A metal rooster surmounts the weathervane atop Sam Jim's old cabin. The Barney house, built in the 1920s, was once the cozy home of a family of six. Its interior is now outfitted as a classroom.

> ## DINING

Pony Espresso (1392 Portage Road; 604-894-5700; www.ponyespresso.ca): From dawn to dark, the Pony satisfies everyone's needs, a fact that explains why it's the landmark dining place with locals. It features organic ingredients, friendly staff, a solid beer and wine list, and a laid-back atmosphere—the best value for the money.

Wild Wood Bistro and Bar (1436 Portage Road; 604-894-0114; www.wildwoodrestaurants.ca): Reliably good food all day—and night—long. This chain of four started in Whistler's Function Junction neighbourhood and enjoyed such success with its Pacific Northwest flavours that the concept has expanded to Pemberton and Squamish.

Pemberton Valley Vineyard Restaurant and Inn (1427 Collins Road; 604-894-5857; www.whistlerwine.com): Chef Ryan Leitch draws on local culinary artisans and farmers to create unique dishes for his guests, many of whom choose to spend the night in one of the auberge's three suites.

Sturdy's North Arm Farm (1888 Sea to Sky Highway, 604-894-5379): Jordan and Trish Sturdy's North Arm Farm sells spuds in quantities more manageable than 45-kilo (100-pound) bags available at farmgates, as well as baked goodies and a host of seasonal fruits and veggies. Mind the geese that guard the farm's entrance, located on the south side of the highway between Pemberton and Mount Currie. In August, the farm also hosts the annual Feast of Fields.

> ### ACCOMMODATION

Nairn Falls Provincial Park (Highway 99, 2 km south of town): In the park you'll find eighty-eight well-spaced campsites, seven of them designed as doubles for visitors who are travelling in a group. The campground is open from late May to October, when there is a $14 charge for overnight visitors; at other times of the year no-fee camping is possible if you are prepared to walk in from the gated entrance. You may reserve a campsite in advance through Discover Camping (604-689-9025 or 1-800-689-9025; www.discovercamping.ca).

Ivey Lake Lodge (1702 Reid Road; 604-894-6456; www.ivey lake.ca): Three self-contained log cabins set in the woods north of Mount Currie offer quick access to Mosquito Lake Park and oodles of mountain bike trails.

Pemberton Valley Lodge (1490 Portage Road; 1-877-894-2800; www.pembertonvalleylodge.com): Set back off Highway 99 beneath Mount Currie's imposing north face at the entrance to Pemberton, this lodge features several suites that come complete with kitchens and fireplaces. Additional perks include outdoor pool and hot tub, plus complimentary shuttle service to Whistler.

> ## THIS SPUD'S FOR YOU

Visitors in search of potatoes will find Yukon Gold, Magenta red, Kennebec, and Norchip (a variety recently developed for french fries but that has also found a wider audience with its all-round good flavour). Sacks of white and red varieties are advertised for sale at some farms in Pemberton Meadows for as little as $20. The Yukon Gold variety is so flavourful that the potatoes taste as though they've been grown in butter.

> 7

LILLOOET

. . . . .

> **ACCESS:** Lillooet is 253 km from Vancouver on Highway 99 via
> Pemberton; 321 km on Highways 1 and 12 via Lytton; 431 km on
> Highways 1, 97, and 99 via Cache Creek.

> **WHY GO:** Trade in the rainforest for sagebrush.

> **KEEP IN MIND:** Get an early start on summer days, as this region
> is one of the hottest and driest in B.C. Drink plenty of fluids as you
> explore.

EMERGING FROM behind a wall of Coast Mountain greenery
into Lillooet's sagebrush-dotted landscape always triggers a
release in me. It's not everywhere that you can travel between
two such contrasting ecosystems in the course of a half-day drive.
That's exactly why I always look forward to making the journey
to "Mile 0," whether through Whistler and the Duffey Lake Road
section of the Sea to Sky Highway or through the Fraser Canyon.
Whichever route you choose, plan on five hours to make the journey.
There's little point in trying to make time along either of the steep-
sided approaches to this historic river town. Instead, stop and enjoy
the views at every opportunity. This is indeed one of the most scenic circle tours in the province, and that's saying something. Rather
than retracing your steps, head up one way and return the other.
Make the drive itself an integral part of your getaway plan, with Lillooet at its heart.

Much as Lillooet anchored the Gold Rush Trail, today it serves
as the gateway to the South Chilcotin Mountains, which at some
seasons of the year turn shades of gold themselves. Trails there have
drawn me back time and again, just as they have with mountain
bikers, hikers, and horse packers. Often, either before or after an

Spruce Lake Protected Area near Lillooet

extended foray into the backcountry, I overnight in Lillooet in order to stock up on goodies or take advantage of a soaker tub to freshen up before heading home. Either way, I always feel at ease breathing in the rich scent of sage that infuses the air.

A good place to gain an inside perspective on Lillooet, both past and present, is the town's Visitor Info Centre (790 Main Street; 250-256-4308; www.lillooetbc.com), also home to the Lillooet Museum. Cyclists and anglers will want to visit Camelsfoot Sports (633 Main Street; 250-256-7757) or Winner's Edge (644 Main Street; 250-256-4848) for licences, gear, and advice. For trail rides contact Chilcotin Holidays (250-238-2274; www.chilcotinholidays. com), Red Rock Trail Ride (250-256-4495), or Spruce Lake Wilderness Adventures (250-283-2375; www.sprucelaketours.com).

> **BRIDGE RIVER VALLEY**
ACTIVITIES: *Driving, picnicking, swimming*
Highway 40 runs for 95 km through the Bridge River Valley, which begins just north of Lillooet. You don't have to drive the entire

distance on this paved road to appreciate its special grandeur. Even if you only make it as far as Carpenter Lake, the halfway point, you will have had more than an eyeful as your reward. The pastel shades in the arid landscape are in a constant state of flux, depending on the time of day and angle of the sun. One thing that doesn't change is the blue-hued Bridge River. East of the Bridge's confluence with the Moha River, find a spot along the river bank to relax and revel in the cooling breezes that waft between the canyon walls that overhang the road. Swimming holes offer the sweet temptation of a dip.

> **FOUNTAIN VALLEY**

ACTIVITIES: *Driving, picnicking, viewpoints*
Here's a route in keeping with B.C.'s pioneer past. Drive the Fountain Valley Road which runs northeast between Highway 12 (about 20 km south of Lillooet) and Highway 99 (about 13 km north of Lillooet) through Xaxl'ip First Nation territory. This is definitely sagebrush and cowboy country, with hay fields and corrals spread beside the road. Barns adorned with antlers add a frontier touch. Fountain Valley Road's most scenic stretch occurs north of Kwotlenemo (Fountain) Lake on an open benchland above the Fraser Canyon near Highway 99, where fields of organic produce, such as carrots and tomatoes, are grown for shipment to Vancouver. Forest Service recreation sites at either end of Fountain Lake are your best bet for picnicking. (For a preview of Fountain Valley and its history, visit www.cayoosh.net/fountain.html.)

> **MARBLE CANYON PROVINCIAL PARK**

ACTIVITIES: *Camping, climbing, picnicking, swimming*
Like three jewels in a limestone setting, Turquoise, Crown, and Pavilion lakes adorn the cliffed shoreline of Marble Canyon, a geological relic that over the millennia strayed inland from the Pacific Ocean and became stranded in the Pavilion Ranges, where it now sits 35 km northeast of Lillooet on Highway 99. There's no mistaking Chimney Rock—also called Coyote Rock by members of the Fountain First Nation—which dominates the craggy skyline. Unlike the darkly granitic Coast Mountains, these crumbling white-faced peaks stand as mute testimony to a more ancient time in a land far

from here. Below the surface of the lakes, freshwater coral grows in ways unseen anywhere else on earth. Pause for a picnic, and you might be tempted to spend the night, although campsites here are somewhat confined between the lake and the highway.

> ### SETON LAKE
ACTIVITIES: *Fishing, picnicking, nature observation, swimming*
BC Hydro's Seton Lake Reservoir recreation site sits 6 km west on Highway 99, on the north shore of Seton Lake. A trail leads beside the upper parking lot to a group of smooth, round depressions in the earth. Called *kekuli*, these ancient excavations were once the foundations of homes constructed with poles and hides by the ancestors of the local St'at'imc people. They provided not only shelter from the strong winds that frequently blow across the lake but also an excellent vantage point from which to view the surrounding countryside. A service road leads below the viewpoint to the chilly lake's eastern end. Here you'll find a broad stretch of sandy beach and picnic tables, with a drive-in boat launch and change rooms.

A leafy row of acacia trees planted in 1942 by Lillooet residents to honour their war dead shades the shoreline, a welcome relief in summer. Typically, a strong on-shore wind helps moderate the heat, which in this region routinely tops the daily Canada-wide high temperature readings in July and August. The rough splendour of the Seton Bluffs dominates the skyline on the shore opposite the beach, where they tower above the lake. (To see for yourself, visit www.cayoosh.net/mcneils.)

> ### SETON RIVER FISH HATCHERY CHANNELS
ACTIVITIES: *Nature observation, picnicking*
Fishing is one of the most popular pastimes around Lillooet. Rainbow trout dominate the forty-odd lakes, rivers, and streams just as salmon and sturgeon rule the Fraser. Carpenter and Gun are big lakes with strategically placed boat ramps located along Highway 40 west of Lillooet. The most easily accessible place is the dock at the BC Hydro recreation site on Seton Lake beside Highway 99, where you can cast for rainbow trout, steelhead trout, and Dolly Varden char up to 6 kilos. A network of fish-hatchery channels and a

reservoir lie just east of the lake beside the highway where rainbow trout, mountain whitefish, sturgeon, and kokanee school. Angling is best during spring and fall. Pink, chinook, coho, and steelhead salmon are all found in the Seton River. Spawning channels near the south side of the river allow spawning salmon to bypass Seton Dam. If nothing else, stop at the Naxwit picnic area and enjoy the riverside gardens.

> ## SPRUCE LAKE PROTECTED AREA

ACTIVITIES: *Camping, driving, hiking, horseback riding, mountain biking, viewpoints*

One of the most extensive networks of hiking, mountain biking and horseback riding trails in the Lillooet region is the 160 km of routes in the Spruce Lake Protected Area in the South Chilcotin Mountains. Find it 95 km west of Lillooet via Highway 40 near the village of Gold Bridge. The Slim Creek Forest Service Road begins at the eastern end of Gun Lake, 10 km west of Gold Bridge and climbs 12 km to the start of the Spruce Lake Trail at Jewel Creek. Jumping off points to popular areas in the 565-sq.-km park, such as Spruce Lake and Tyaughton Creek, lie little more than a one-hour drive from Lillooet. Well-worn game and horse trails lead past mountain lakes, across mid-elevation grasslands and timbered slopes, and up into alpine meadows surrounded by spectacular mountains, a testament to the length of time both humans and wildlife have journeyed through here. Above the treeline lies a stunning visual panorama of rainbow-hued Chilcotin Range peaks that bump up against the more familiar glaciated forms of the Coast Mountains. For detailed information, visit www.bcparks.ca.

> ## OTHER ATTRACTIONS

Festivals: In January the town hosts an annual ice-climbing festival that celebrates the joys of clinging to frozen waterfalls. In winter Marble Canyon Park (see above) has one of the best and most easily accessed icefalls in the region. On the Victoria Day long weekend in May, Lillooet stages its annual May Day celebrations, complete with the crowning of a fresh-faced Queen of the May who rules throughout the following year.

The Fraser River: The mighty Fraser River flows past the town in a wide, muddy swath. Lillooet is just the right size town for a leisurely stroll that not only leads past mementoes of the 1850s gold rush but also touches on more recent accomplishments, such as the old 1913 suspension bridge spanning the Fraser River at the northern end of town. The bridge hasn't seen vehicle traffic since 1981, when the modern Bridge of 23 Camels opened downstream, and hence it is ideally suited to walking. In fact, do a loop from the heart of Lillooet over one bridge and cross back on the other. Both bridges provide splendid views of the roiling river. In summer look for First Nations anglers drying salmon on smoke racks beside the river.

Hat Creek Ranch (Junction of Highway 99 and 97, 75 km east of Lillooet and 11 km north of Cache Creek; 1-800-782-0922; www.hatcreekranch.com): A lovingly restored heritage site, the Hat Creek Ranch was once a stage coach roadhouse stop on the original Cariboo Wagon Road. Take in the guided tours and a host of special events, including hay rides and gold panning, offered May through September, or just stop in and mosey around on your own.

> ## DINING

Horsting's Farm Market (Highway 97, 2 km north of Cache Creek; 250-457-6546; www.horstingfarms.com): This market is a must-see as part of a circle tour and features fresh produce, preserves, and local crafts out front and daily soups, breads, and berry pies at the small restaurant in back. Ultra-yummy.

Lillooet Bakery (717 Main Street; 250-256-4889): Savour superb goodies from a master German baker. It's small wonder that bus tours make this one of their must-see stops. Several inside tables are augmented by an outdoor patio with picnic tables. Order the German breakfast special, and you'll have enough bread, cheese, cold cuts, tomatoes, and pretzels left over for your picnic lunch as well.

Dina's Place (690 Main Street; 250-256-4264): This whitewashed northern Greek restaurant suits Lillooet's often scorchy summer days. Come evening, when air temperatures become tolerable, the patio is the place to watch shadows overtake the eroded hillsides above the Fraser River. Two wood-fired ovens impart a toasted flavour to a wide variety of vegetarian, meat, and seafood entrees.

> ## ACCOMMODATION

Seton Dam Campground (Highway 99, 6 km west of Lillooet): There's no charge to stay at any of the forty-five pleasantly shaded sites, open May to September, at this BC Hydro campground. One of the more unusual features here is an old Chinese stone oven, a remnant of the gold rush days in the late 1800s. A marker points to its location near the east end of the campsite. Trails link with the beach on Seton Lake.

The 4 Pines Motel (108–8th Avenue; 250-256-4247 or 1-800-753-2576; www.4pinesmotel.com): Here is a good, clean place to rest your head. If you're saddle weary from a day on the range, either on horseback or a bike, or just from sitting behind the wheel, request a room with a jet tub. Kitchenettes are available for DIYers.

Tyax Mountain Lake Resort (Tyaughton Lake Road, Gold Bridge; 250-238-2221; www.tyax.com): The largest log structure on the West Coast sits beside Tyaughton Lake with the vast Spruce Lake Protected Area at its doorstep. Twenty-nine suites in the lodge, 90 km west of Lillooet on Highway 40, then 5 km north on Tyaughton Lake Road, are complemented by five self-contained chalets. Action at the lodge centres on the sauna, outdoor Jacuzzi, games and workout rooms, a restaurant, and western-themed lounge with a towering fieldstone fireplace. Paddle or explore the lake by sailboat or sailboard. The lodge's own float planes fly anglers to the nearby Trophy Lakes. Come winter the lodge is home base for TLH Heli-skiing (www.tlhheliskiing.com).

SUNSHINE COAST

GIBSONS AND ROBERTS CREEK

SECHELT AND HALFMOON BAY

PENDER HARBOUR AND EGMONT

POWELL RIVER AND LUND

> ## 8

GIBSONS AND
ROBERTS CREEK

. . . . .

> ACCESS: Gibsons is a 40-minute ferry ride between BC Ferries ter-
minals in Horseshoe Bay in West Vancouver and Langdale on the
Sechelt Peninsula on the Sunshine Coast. For information on sailing
times, fares, and reservations, contact BC Ferries (1-888-223-3779;
www.bcferries.com). Lower Gibsons (Gibsons Landing) is 3 km west
from the Langdale terminal on Marine Drive, an enjoyable cycle
with only one hill climb.

> WHY GO: Experience the Beachcombers, live.

> KEEP IN MIND: A cascade of festivals between June and August
means busy times; plan ahead and leave impromptu visits for other
months.

EVEN RESIDENTS of the world's most livable city occasionally
need to sneak out of town to a little hideaway. Summer or
winter, Gibsons provides just that. When the weather report
doesn't sound promising, I reason that if anywhere close to Vancouver might get a break from storms, it would be the Sunshine Coast.
To ensure I have a place to dry off and warm up after an outdoor
adventure, I book into a little place—there are no resorts in these
parts—preferably with a good restaurant nearby.

You don't have work hard at hiding out on the Sunshine Coast.
Much of it is naturally hidden. Just branch off the main roads
between Gibsons and Roberts Creeks and see for yourself. In winter,
beneath bare tree branches, the landscape lies winded, as if catching
its breath. Look around. You've practically got the place to yourself.
And it's only a short ferry ride away.

62

Much like in the television series *The Beachcombers*, which was filmed in Gibsons, the townsfolk are a little grizzled and decidedly blue collar, a reflection of the fact that many work in either the fishing or logging industry. The Howe Sound Pulp and Paper mill in Port Mellon, 10 km east of Langdale, is a major producer of newsprint. In the late 1960s and accelerating through the following two decades, artists and craftspeople moved to the more-affordable Sunshine Coast to build studios. The first wave settled in the Gibsons–Roberts Creek area, and subsequent newcomers gradually found cheap land as far north as Pender Harbour. These days their influence is reflected in the numerous festivals, fairs, markets, and gallery openings held throughout the year. What remains as consistent now as then is the sense of community.

Year round, contact Sunshine Kayaking (Gibsons Landing; 604-886-9760; www.sunshinekayaking.com) for rentals, sales, and tours. In winter Alpha Adventures (1057 Roberts Creek Road; 604-885-8838; www.outdooradventurestore.ca) offers ski and snowshoe rentals, lessons, and guided tours of Dakota Ridge.

For tours of the area contact Gibsons Landing Harbour Tours (604-886-4910) for nature and wildlife tours or Navigator Marine Service (604-886-7602 or 604-290-4095) for water taxi services.

For general tourism information, visit the Gibsons Visitor Info Centre (417 Marine Drive; 604-886-2374 or 1-866-222-3806; www.gibsonsbc.ca) or the Town of Gibsons Offices (474 South Fletcher Road; 604-886-2274; www.gibsons.ca). For information on festivals, events, shops, and services, visit www.gibsonslandingbc.com.

> **BONNIEBROOK BEACH**

ACTIVITIES: *Cycling, paddling, picnicking, swimming, viewpoints, walking*

No matter what time of year, my favourite place to head around Gibsons is Bonniebrook Beach, found via Gower Point Road and Ocean Beach Esplanade. Only locals will know what you're talking about, as the name doesn't appear on maps. This long stretch of pebble beach eventually turns sandy where Ocean Beach Esplanade dead ends. Judging from the numerous paw prints, this is a popular destination for dog owners.

My preferred way to get there is by bike from Lower Gibsons. Budget 30 to 45 minutes to cycle the 5-km route one way. The return journey presents a much stiffer challenge, as there are two hill climbs (enjoy the descent on the way out). The first occurs just east of Bonniebrook Lodge (see below). For safety, I suggest walking your bike up the second stretch for a short distance around a tight corner. *Note:* To avoid an unnecessary uphill climb along Gower Point Road in lower Gibsons, follow Glassford Road for three blocks to where it intersects with Gower Point Road and head west and north from there. Detailed street maps of Gibsons are available at the Gibsons Visitor Info Centre (see above).

A cairn in Chaster Park honours the arival of Captain George Vancouver who overnighted here in June, 1792. Ironically, camping is not allowed here these days.

Points of interest along the way include the Gospel Rock viewpoint overlooking the mouth of Howe Sound from Gower Point. A large granite bluff fringed with arbutus marks the point. There's room for two cars to pull off. Farther west, Chaster Regional Park begins opposite Bonniebrook Lodge and signals the beginning of a long, sweeping arch of beach that stretches far to the north near Roberts Creek. After the hilly approach, it's a delight to pedal this stretch of level road. Numerous beach access trails present themselves, including a set of stairs beside the esplanades' cul-de-sac. A profound sense of peace and quiet prevails along this beach, seemingly just for your pleasure.

> **GIBSONS LANDING**

ACTIVITIES: *Cycling, paddling, viewpoints, walking*
Drag your heels without making any sound and you'll be right in keeping with the sleepy pace around Gibsons' harbour, known officially as Gibsons Landing until the name was shortened to Gibsons at the request of locals in the late 1940s. Take your time to explore what's on offer on this stretch, little more than several blocks long: shops, restaurants, galleries, and B&Bs sit cheek by jowl. The town's tourism office (see above) anchors the main intersection of Marine Drive and School Road at Pioneer Park, kitty corner to the

iconic Molly's Reach Restaurant (see below). A statue commemorates the arrival of George Gibson and his two sons here in May 1886. The trio came ashore from the family boat, the *Swamp Angel*, and promptly took up residence.

On paper the route west between Armours Beach, popular with swimmers in summer, and a protective breakwater, looks longer at first glance than in reality. An astonishing number of businesses, points of interest, and parks and beaches cluster around the harbour. Exploring all sixty or so could easily absorb your attention during the course of a weekend stay.

I sometimes ride my bike along the seawalk, but there's so much to see in so little space that walking is the better approach. When you need a little breathing room, head out to the gazebo at the end of the town pier both for a perspective on the town's quaint setting and for the overwhelming experience of appreciating Howe Sound from this perspective. I've never found a better place to size up the Lions (the Sisters) or Mount Garibaldi, which dominates the skyline above Squamish. A short distance south lies Keats Island, a natural destination for paddlers. Launch either at the Gibsons Marina or several blocks west of the harbour at Pebble Beach on Headlands Road, or take a guided tour with Sunshine Kayaking (see above) from a wharf on the seawalk below Molly's Lane.

When it comes time to give your feet a rest, Winegarden Waterfront Park is a good place to plan what's next or take in one of the frequent free Music in the Landing concerts given May to October. In summer, during festivities such as the multi-day Sea Cavalcade (www.seacavalcade.ca), the streets around the harbour are blocked off as Gibsons goes car free.

> **ROBERTS CREEK PIER REGIONAL PARK** &

ACTIVITIES: *Picnicking, swimming, viewpoints, walking*
A sandy crescent fans out where Roberts Creek meets the ocean. Early in the last century, Harry Roberts, son of the patriarch who established the town, operated a freight shed here. On its side he painted "Sunshine Belt." It struck a chord with visitors who ever since have been referring to the Sechelt and Malaspina peninsulas as the Sunshine Coast. A wide promenade leads out into the Strait

of Georgia from where you can look back at the homes, old and new, that line the shore. Storms pile driftwood high up along the shore. From out on the breakwater you look north towards the sandy beaches at Roberts Creek Provincial Park, a wildly popular place to picnic in summer. Uphill lies the heart of Roberts Creek, with the Gumboot Garden Complex to further entertain you.

> **OTHER ATTRACTIONS**

Creekside Salon and Spa (1041 Roberts Creek Road; 604-885-8856; www.creeksidessentials.com): These folks follow the petrochemical-free Aveda concept in their treatments. My preference is for a one-hour massage and infrared sauna session, particularly after a day on the water or Nordic skiing on Dakota Ridge (see below).

Dakota Ridge (www.dakotaridge.ca): To get to Dakota Ridge turn right off Highway 101 on Field Road at Wilson Creek Plaza north of Roberts Creek, then right onto a logging road for 10 km to a parking area. From there, a 3-km tail leads uphill to a network of cross-country trails. For current road and snow conditions, visit www. suncoastcentral.com/outdoor-reports.asp. For updates on events and road upgrades, visit www.scrd.bc.ca/rec_dakota_ridge.html. The tops of ridges above Gibsons benefit from surprisingly large snow-falls triggered by the Arctic outflow winds that funnel out to the coast from the Interior. Dakota Ridge is maintained by local skiers. Alpha Adventures (see above) offers guided tours, especially helpful if you're not comfortable driving to the trailhead.

Gift of the Eagle Gallery (689 Gibsons Way; 604-886-4899; www.giftoftheeagle.com): The works of a variety of local artists are on display here, from wooden bowls to blown glass to ceramics and fabric art. Good selection and prices make this one of the shopping highlights in Gibsons.

The Sunshine Coast Museum and Archives (716 Winn Road; 604-886-8232; www.sunshinecoastmuseum.ca &): Displays about the life and times of the Sunshine Coast with a maritime theme are on display here. Wooden boat aficionados will enjoy the "Salt on the Wind" exhibit, which features local boat builders Allen and Sharie Farrell who make sturdy wooden sailing ships with only hand tools. The couple have used the boats for their home and to travel

Gumboot Garden, Roberts Creek

from local waters to the South Pacific. Local inventions, such as a submersible camera used to explore the underwater world of the Sunshine Coast, are mounted beside Union Steamship memorabilia from the days before BC Ferries brought vacationers to Gibsons. Natural history, First Nations and pioneer relics, butterflies, woven baskets, and logging and farm tools augment the collection. Several rooms have been furnished with early-twentieth-century furniture and accessories to bring pioneer stories to life. The museum also houses the photographic artifacts of Helen McCall, a professional photographer who lived on the Sunshine Coast from the 1930s to 1950s and supported her family through the sale of postcards. Her extensive collection creates a unique snapshot of the Sunshine Coast during her lifetime. Of course, the museum wouldn't be complete without relics from *The Beachcombers*, a fixture on CBC TV for nineteen years.

> **DINING**

Molly's Reach Restaurant (647 School Road; 604-886-9710): I avoided this place for years, convinced the diner with its oversized yellow marquee must be trading on past glory as the set for *The*

Beachcombers television series. What a surprise to discover otherwise. All it took was a table with a harbour view, a glass of local draught beer, a hefty shrimp sandwich, low-key ambience, and friendly service to win me over.

Wild Bistro and Bakery (682 Gibsons Way; 604-886-1917; www. wildbistro.com): Famous for both their grain and gluten-free goodies, this is a good place to get take-out picnic lunches.

Chez Phillipe (1532 Ocean Beach Esplanade; 604-886-2188): For a small town, Gibsons offers consistently good restaurant value, nowhere more so than at Bonniebrook Lodge (see below). French-trained Phillipe Lacoste runs a classic seasonal auberge dining room. I take the easy route and order the daily four-course set meal, but there is a wealth of à la carte choices as well.

Haus Uropa Restaurant (426 Gower Point Road; 604-886-8326): The Swiss have a word for it: fondue. That's the only thing cheesy about this warm, bright dining room. Moonlight reflects off the water in Shoal Channel and lights up the restaurant's harbourside patio. The slow-food philosophy is honoured here, Zurich-style. Order up an Okanagan wine personally sourced by the owners on one of their frequent buying trips, toast your blessings, sit back and let the evening unfold on island time, or in Gibson's case, at peninsula pace.

> ## ACCOMMODATION

Bonniebrook Lodge (1532 Ocean Beach Esplanade; 604-886-2887 or 1-877-290-9916; www.bonniebrook.com): Long before the current era of monster homes, this three-storey, butter-yellow lodge was a landmark on the coast between Gibsons Landing and Roberts Creek. Sunshine streams down on Bonniebrook's bright location fronted by a beachfront lawn. The updated interior features four deluxe suites spread over the top two floors of the manor house plus three cabin-themed suites set at ground level in the forest behind the lodge. To my mind, it's a toss-up between the upstairs ocean views and the soothing voice of Chaster Creek, which bubbles through the forest. Either way, breakfast is delivered to your door, cooked up in the lodge's French restaurant (see above). Chef Phillipe is an ardent kayaker, happy to share pointers from the luxury of the lodge's own launch site on Bonniebrook Beach.

Country Cottage Bed and Breakfast (1183 Roberts Creek Road; 604-885-7448; www.countrycottagebb.ca): In the mid-1980s, Philip and Loragene Gaulin opened Country Cottage, one of the first bed-and-breakfast lodgings on the Sunshine Coast. Their dog-friendly farm includes the vintage Rose Cottage and the more recently constructed Cedar Lodge. As soon you arrive you'll want to kick off you shoes, put on the kettle, and roll onto the quilt-covered bed. Philip is an ardent cross-country skier. In winter, guests are welcome to accompany him on his Sunday jaunts. Whether you choose to head off to explore the trails or just chill at nearby Roberts Creek Pier Regional Park (see above) you'll be fortified by a farm breakfast that Loragene creates on her wood-burning stove. *Note:* Reserve six months in advance for statutory holidays and at least two months in advance for weekends. Weekdays are the best times to drop in on short notice. Arm yourself with cash, because this B&B doesn't take credit cards.

> 9

SECHELT AND HALFMOON BAY

. . . . .

> **ACCESS:** Sechelt lies 27 km north of the BC Ferries Langdale terminal on Highway 101 (Sunshine Coast Highway). For information on sailing times, fares, and reservations, contact BC Ferries (1-888-223-3779; www.bcferries.com). West Coast Air operates daily service between Vancouver and Sechelt (604-606-6888 or 1-800-347-2222; www.westcoastair.com).

> **WHY GO:** Experience a paddler's paradise.

> **KEEP IN MIND:** The town swells with visitors in summer and overnight accommodation is often in short supply, particularly in early August during the annual Sunshine Coast Festival of the Written Arts (www.writersfestival.ca), the largest and longest-running summer gathering of Canadian writers and readers.

THE 87-KM-LONG Sunshine Coast narrows like an hourglass's waist at Sechelt, where a 1-km-wide isthmus separates Trail Bay in the Strait of Georgia to the west from Porpoise Bay in Sechelt Inlet to the east. For a town of 8,500, there's a lot of waterfront to go around. In all likelihood, there are just as many kilometres of biking and hiking trails in the surrounding hills as there are coastal paddling routes. Sechelt's charms are best appreciated when exploring a host of regional and provincial parks. Although the downtown core offers a little of everything, including summer night markets with food and live music, out in nature is where the real action happens. If you're tentative about heading off on your own, no excuses. Guided trips of various stripes are on offer to take you behind the scenes for an insider's perspective on Sechelt's rich history. Mermaid Boat Tours

(5764 Wharf Street; 604-989-0068; www.mermaidboattours.com), for example, features Porpoise Bay excursions, including full moon rides, with Captain Michelle at the helm. And once you've had a taste of adventure, go solo next time—with your buddy, of course.

If you're looking to explore the land by bike, pay a visit to On the Edge Bike Shop (5642 Cowrie Street; 604-885-4888; www.ontheedgebiking.com). If you'd rather get out on the water, head to Davis Bay Sports Fishing (604-885-7046; www.fishingsechelt.com and click on "Fishing Charters") or Trail Bay Sports (5504 Trail Avenue; 604-885-2512) for fishing gear and licences and Halfmoon Sea Kayaks (Two locations: 5356 Ole's Cove Road, Halfmoon Bay, and 5644 Cowrie Street; 604-885-2948) or Pedals and Paddles (Tillicum Bay Marina, Porpoise Bay Road; 604-885-6440 or 1-866-885-6440; www.pedalspaddles.com) for paddling gear and rentals. Additionally, Talaysay Kayaking and Cultural Adventures (Porpoise Bay Provincial Park; 604-628-8555 or 1-800-605-4643; www.talaysaytours.com) offers rentals, lessons, and Shishalh First Nation tours.

For general visitor information, contact the Sechelt Visitor Info Centre (5790 Teredo Street; 604-885-1036 or 1-877-885-1036; www.secheltvisitorinfo.com).

> **PORPOISE BAY PROVINCIAL PARK** &

ACTIVITIES: *Camping, nature observation, paddling, picnicking, swimming, walking*

Porpoise Bay is 4 km east of downtown Sechelt on Sechelt Inlet Road and is a perennial camping magnet for families from late May to early September. There are three main reasons why I like this park: a wide, shallow beach for swimming; handy access for launching a kayak or canoe to explore Sechelt Inlet; and a shady forest trail for walking and nature viewing in an estuary that teems with wildlife. If pressed, I'd add people watching to my list. So much activity takes place here, the same as ever over the past millennia. For a unique perspective, take a Shishalh First Nation tours with Talaysay Kayaking and Cultural Adventures (see above). You may see a Pacific white-sided dolphin or two. *Note:* In addition to 84 vehicle-access campsites, a grassy field solely for cyclists and backpackers is set aside for tenting.

> **SARGEANT BAY PROVINCIAL PAR** &

ACTIVITIES: *Picnicking, nature observation, swimming, walking*
To get to Sargeant Bay Park, head 7.5 km west of Sechelt. Turn west
off Highway 101 onto Redrooffs Road and follow signs 1 km to the
entrance. I stop here time and again to explore Sargeant Bay's long
cobblestone and sand beach. Pick out a suitable driftwood log to use
as a backrest or picnic table, then sit back and drink in the scenery.
With a southern exposure, cool breezes often coax whitecaps out on
the bay. If you're in need of shelter, head into the surrounding forest and find a spot beneath tall Douglas-fir intermixed with shiny-
skinned arbutus. During spring and fall migrations, a wetland behind
the beach provides a protective habitat for over a hundred bird species. Loons, grebes, cormorants, herons, swans, geese, ducks, eagles,
hawks, and perhaps even a straggling turkey vulture are some of the
larger, more easily detected ones. Sit quietly, and smaller birds such
as killdeer and nuthatch will reveal themselves among the thickly
bunched cattails. A walking trail leads through the lower park, while
an intermediate-level bike trail as well as a hiking trail leads from the
east side of Redrooffs Road to Trout Lake from where a single-track
mountain bike trail loops further off into the hills. Detailed trail
maps are available at On the Edge Bike Shop in Sechelt (see above).

> **SECHELT INLETS PROVINCIAL MARINE PARK**

ACTIVITIES: *Camping, paddling, picnicking, swimming*
The easiest and quickest access to this park is the boat launch at Porpoise Bay Provincial Park or the marina at Tuwanek, both located
on East Porpoise Bay Road, which begins in downtown Sechelt.

Take a paddle on the wild side of Sechelt. You'll need a boat to
explore this necklace of seven sites dotted along both sides of Sechelt
Inlet. (The reason for the park's plural name is that two secondary
inlets, Salmon and Narrows, branch off on the east side of the main
inlet.) Not that you have to visit them all. I find that once ashore,
each has a way of working on my mind so that I'm content to sit
on the beach taking in the views. Then it's time to stretch my arms
again and off I go to the next site. One caveat: in summer, a predictably strong wind funnels out from the inlets to the strait. Early risers
benefit from calm conditions that change abruptly by mid-morning.

Halfmoon Bay

Stick close to shore and be wary when crossing the mouth of Salmon Inlet to reach Kunchin Point, the most northerly of the sites. A good approach for a half-day paddle would be to decide which side of the inlet to explore and stick to those sites. I prefer the three north of the Tuwanek marina on the east side of the inlet. Pick up some picnic fare and head out. Then if you find yourself hunkered down because of wind and whitecaps, you can relax while enjoying lunch and a swim. Whatever happens, don't risk launching until calm returns, as it inevitably does. *Note*: Since drinking water is not available, pack plenty along.

> **SMUGGLER COVE PROVINCIAL MARINE PARK** ♿

ACTIVITIES: *Camping, cycling, picnicking, swimming, walking*
This exquisite marine park, 16 km north of Sechelt on Highway 101, then 5 km west on Brooks Road, appeals as much to those who approach by land as to boaters who carefully pick their way into the cove through Welcome Passage at low tide when an obstacle course

of reefs and rocks are revealed. The decision is up to you. Launch at the trailhead and paddle around an exposed point of land at the mouth of Halfmoon Bay to reach the hidden cove, or hike in 1 km along a forested trail. The trail provides smooth access for those on foot or in wheelchairs. Three kilometres of trails lead from the cove's basin through an enchanting stand of old-growth forest and around the indented shoreline.

> **OTHER ATTRACTIONS**

House of hewhiwus (5555 Sunshine Coast Highway; 604-885-4592): Ceremonial poles mounted in front of the House of hewhiwus (House of Chiefs), in the Sechelt Indian Band's central complex at the east entrance to Sechelt on Highway 101, are a visible reminder that the Shishalh First Nations have anchored the isthmus for millennia. As the largest landowners in Sechelt, the Shishalh run several businesses, including a lucrative gravel operation. When mainstreeting, check out the tems swiya museum and tsain-ko gift shop, especially the extensive display of woven baskets for which shishalh women are justifiably renowned. *Note:* The museum is closed on Sundays.

> **Halfmoon Bay once featured a resort with rental cabins distinguished by their red roofs. As a marketing gimmick, the owner took poetic liberty and named the property "Redrooffs."**

Redrooffs Road: This scenic back road loops west of Highway 101 for 10 km from Sargeant Bay (see above) to Halfmoon Bay, a popular summer destination decades ago. Drive slowly and enjoy the rolling sensation while doing a little looky-looing. Red roofs or not, many dream homes characterize this charming neighbourhood. Be careful—you might see a "For Sale" sign with your name on it.

A flavour of yesteryear flashes by at places like the Welcome Bay Community Hall as the loop-de-loop route hugs the coast and passes a mittful of parks, including Sargeant Bay, Redrooffs, and Coopers Green. Pull in at Coopers Green Park for one of the warmest swimming holes on the coast, although you will need beach shoes to avoid an owie on the pebble beach. Divers and snorkellers practise in the park's shallow waters. Giant octopuses lurk nearby. A boat launch provides an opportune way to paddle out to their offshore habitat as well as to the Merry Island Lighthouse just south of the bay. There's plenty of grass lawn on which to spread a blanket and soak up the region's fabled rays. If you need something to toast the sunsets for which Halfmoon Bay is renowned, check out the nearby general store.

Snickett Park &: Although the strand and pier at Davis Bay, 5 km south of town on Highway 101, grabs most people's attention, I enjoy the waterfront panorama on Sechelt's south side just as much. The oceanfront esplanade's hardpacked pathway lines Trail Bay and leads a short distance west to Pebble Beach in Snickett Park, a wave-polished granite jewel box with views stretching out across the Strait of Georgia to Nanaimo on Vancouver Island. This is an ideal place to watch cruise ships lit up like pleasure palaces glide past in summer.

> **DINING**

Pebbles Restaurant (5454 Trail Avenue; 604-885-5811; www.drift woodmotorinn.com): One of the best views in town accentuates this seafood-themed menu. No matter what the time of day, I recommend the chowder, followed by a stroll along Trail Bay to Snickett Park (see above).

Spence on the Coast Restaurant and Lounge (202–5500 Sunshine Coast Highway; 604-740-8221; spenceonthecoast.com): Every town needs a new kid on the block, and Spencer Watts is the one in Sechelt. Don't let the fact that his restaurant lives in a mall fool you. Although location was once the key to success, these days creativity attracts customers and service keeps them coming back. Spence has both in spades. The dining room is bright and airy. And since the restaurant is in a mall, parking isn't an issue. Neither is sourcing Sunshine Coast seafood, which Watts buys fresh off the boat whenever possible. Shellfish is a specialty. Lunch is a bargain, which accounts for the lineups that began forming almost as soon as the doors opened. If Spencer's face looks familiar, it's because he's a regularly featured guest on Vancouver's CityTV *CityCooks* show, where he won the Master Chef competition in 2006.

Blue Heron Inn (5591 Delta Road; 604-885-3847 or 1-800-818-8977): Intimately set on the east side of Porpoise Bay, the Blue

Straight of Georgia, Sechelt

Heron's track record of satisfied customers, including me, is impressive. The romantic location, both inside and out, has spawned many a lovestruck evening. In summer, stroll out onto the inn's private dock to savour the sunset as your first or last course. When making reservations in cooler months, request a table near the dining room's massive stone fireplace. Whether or not money is an object, this place is a bargain with its generous portions of Mediterranean-themed recipes. I go for the Caesar salad and bouillabaisse, although not always both on the same visit.

> **ACCOMMODATION**

In addition to camping at Porpoise Bay and Sechelt Inlets parks (see above) here are two more pampered suggestions:

A Place by the Sea Bed and Breakfast and Spa (5810 Marine Way; 604-885-2745 or 1-866-885-2746; www.aplacebythesea.com):

Romance, thy name is A Place by the Sea. When it's time to rest your head, then wake up to breakfast in bed, one of Shay and Nancy's three individually themed suites is where you want to bet. The dream location on the west side of Sechelt Inlet is enough by itself to put this place over the top. During summer months, complimentary sea kayaks are on offer at the private dock. An in-house spa, complete with sauna, will help straighten out any kinks.

Rockwater Secret Cove Resort (5356 Ole's Cove Road, Halfmoon Bay; 604-885-7038 or 1-877-296-4593; rockwatersecret coveresort.com): If you recall Lord Jim's Resort Hotel, a fixture in Halfmoon Bay over the past three decades, a stay at the expanded and rebranded property will ring a few bells. Cozy one- and two-bedroom cabins, smartly refurbished, still dot the rocky shoreline beneath spreading arbutus trees. The main lodge, which houses a variety of suites, a consistently good restaurant, and a day spa, blends into the hillside. There's much to be said for stepping out of a ground-floor suite into the lodge's heated swimming pool. A winding boardwalk leads off through a shore pine and arbutus forest to clusters of executive tents, furnished with heated floors, shoji screens, fireplaces, soaker tubs, the works. Unique, upscale, though not soundproof, the best of the lot is tent 65, followed by 60 and 59; all three are anchored to the rocky slope above the tideline. Sleeping in the treetops, you'll feel like a big game hunter on safari. There's still a little of Lord Jim's spirit left here. In summer, Halfmoon Sea Kayaks operates from a boathouse beside the resort's wharf and offers rentals, tours, and lessons to guests and visitors alike. *Note:* Make spa appointments in advance. I suggest the couples massage given on adjoining tables in a tent beside the ocean.

> 10

PENDER HARBOUR
AND EGMONT

. . . . .

> ACCESS: Pender Harbour lies 59 km north of Langdale on Highway 101 via Sechelt. Egmont lies 16 km farther north.

> WHY GO: Experience the Venice of the North.

> KEEP IN MIND: Pender Harbour is just that—a body of water whose name defines the indented coastline.

PENDER HARBOUR is a world removed from anywhere else on the Sunshine Coast. Up and down, round and round. That sums up how you'll feel after driving the roads in this hilly neck of the rainforest. You're never far from water, both fresh and salty. Big lakes and cozy ocean coves lie within sight of each other. The water blends together like a network of canals—try to guess where one ends and another begins as you roll along.

A jigsaw puzzle of straits, channels, inlets, narrows, bays, points and peninsulas define a patchwork of neighbourhoods—Madeira Park, Garden Bay, Irvine's Landing, Kleindale—collectively called Pender Harbour. Tucked away to the west of the Sunshine Coast Highway, you'd hardly know anyone lived there until you start sleuthing around. Take your time and enjoy the loving attention given to gardens and landscaping, evident in picture-perfect locales such as Garden Bay. In 2004 Pender Harbour won the Communities in Bloom gold medal. From Pender Harbour, slowly make your way along the northern tip of the Sechelt Peninsula. Don't blink or you'll miss Ruby Lake, Earls Cove (home to BC Ferries and not much else), and the harbour hamlet of Egmont.

I journey here to explore outstanding natural attractions that inspire investigation on foot, by bike, or with a paddle firmly gripped in both hands. Depending on my mood, I'm either up for adventure or simply content to sit beneath an arbutus tree and wait for a curious harbour seal or a bald eagle to check me out. Just like the tides that charge through Skookumchuk Narrows one minute then go slack the next, there's so little pressure to do anything that it's scary. Or massively sexy. Take your pick.

With so much around, Pender Harbour is the perfect place to go angling or paddling. Both Bargain Harbour Charters (604-883-9858) and Pender Harbour Charters (604-883-1181; www.salmonfishingbc.ca) offer fishing charters. Paddlers may want to visit Alpha Adventures (Garden Bay Marina; 604-741-1007; www.outdoor adventurestore.ca; open in spring and summer) for kayak and canoe rentals, Rising Sun Kayak Adventures (Egmont Marina Resort; 604-883-2062 or 1-800-632-0722; www.egmont-marina.com) for tours, lessons, and rentals, as well as climbing, diving, hiking, mountain biking tours, or Sunshine Coast Resort (12695 Sunshine Coast Highway, Madeira Park; 604-883-9177; www.sunshinecoastresort.com) for motorboat and kayak rentals.

For tours contact High Tide Tours and Water Taxi (16660 Backeddy Road, Egmont; 604-883-9220; 1-866-500-9220; www.hightidetours.com), which will take you to Skookumchuck Rapids and Princess Louisa and Jervis inlets, or Malaspina Water Taxi (Government Dock, Madeira Park; 604-740-2486; www.malaspina watertaxi.com), which stops at Jedediah Island Marine Provincial Park and offers canoe and kayak rentals.

For general travel information, find detailed maps of the Sunshine Coast at the Travel Info Centre in Madeira Park (12895 Madeira Park Road; 604-883-2561; www.penderharbour.ca). The online magazine *Bigpacific.com* also features a comprehensive listing of activities and accommodations.

> **FRANCIS POINT PROVINCIAL PARK** &

ACTIVITIES: *Picnicking, nature observation, swimming, walking*
To get to Francis Point Park, travel 3 km west of Highway 101 on Francis Peninsula Road to Merrill Road. Turn left, and follow it to reach to the park boundary.

There's no better place to appreciate the natural beauty of the coast than Francis Point on Pender Harbour's lower peninsula. As well as being a relatively new provincial park, Francis Point is also one of the most obscure. Few signs of its existence appear until you reach the trailhead. From there, a sturdily constructed, 2-km trail traces the rocky shoreline. Imposing stands of old-growth forest shelter visitors, a welcoming environment whether on a sunny day when arbutus hang heavy with clusters of red berries or during a downpour when towering Douglas-firs offer verdant shelter. A strategically placed split-rail fence restricts access to the fragile moss-draped surface at a viewpoint overlooking Middle Bay.

Francis Point Park offers telling testimony to the determination of some Pender Harbour residents. In 1998, the Francis Point Marine Park Society was formed to purchased this 81-ha property. Early efforts to raise the $4 million asking price accounted for little until the Seattle-based Paul G. Allen Forest Protection Foundation, a philanthropic organization dedicated to preserving old growth forests, donated $1.6 million. With help from the Nature Conservancy of Canada, the society eventually raised $100,000 more than their objective. This surplus is secured in a trust fund, and interest is earmarked for future park improvements.

Captain Vancouver and his crew spent a night in Middle Bay, riding out a storm on June 16, 1792 (the feast day of St. Francis, hence the name Vancouver gave the point).

With this level of stewardship in mind, tread lightly as you explore as far south as the Francis Point Beacon. In summer, bring your bathing suit as Middle Bay features the best saltwater swimming spot in the region. Rock bluffs above the bay soak up the sun and make a good place to dry off or have a picnic.

> **SKOOKUMCHUCK NARROWS PROVINCIAL PARK** &

ACTIVITIES: *Nature observation, running, walking*
Skookumchuck Narrows Park's well-marked trail begins on the south side of Highway 101 opposite the Egmont Heritage Centre and leads 4 km to Roland Point. Allow one hour each way.

Timing is everything when planning a visit to see the most spectacular tidal rapids east of the Bay of Fundy. To catch the action at

Suncoaster Trail near Egmont

full bore, consult a tide chart in advance to know exactly when to be there. Best times are posted online or listed in many Sunshine Coast publications. High and low tides trigger the action. At their extremes in June and December, currents run as fast as 14 knots (26 km/h). Although experienced whitewater kayakers seem to handle the standing waves with deceptive ease, sudden whirlpools may sweep up unwary boaters and toss them about like corks. All great fun to watch while praying no one gets into trouble. The gentle path that leads to the viewpoint at Roland Point offers an unremarkable forest walk or jog. At the halfway point, Brown Lake provides a diversion to check for birds. If you arrive at slack tide, be prepared to be under-whelmed. This is simply where the north end of Sechelt Inlet nar-rows. It's pretty enough, particularly at low tide when marine life is on display. Otherwise, what's the big whoop? Don't let this happen. Take a guided water tour instead. Then again, one-note trails offer more opportunities for conversation as you amble along. A good place to begin or end a visit to the park is the newly-minted Egmont

Heritage Centre (6671 Egmont Road; 604-883-9994). *Note:* Bring insect repellent in summer.

> **SUNCOASTER TRAIL** &

ACTIVITIES: *Cycling, picnicking, running, walking*
This multi-use trail, accessible at various points along the east side of the Sunshine Coast Highway, is one of my favourite ways to explore the Sunshine Coast between Halfmoon Bay and Egmont. Since trailwork began in 1996, I returned often to explore different sections as the project gradually took shape. In a region where there's not much room to squeeze a recreation trail between the ocean and the steeply sloped Caren Range, the owners of the Ruby Lake Resort bought a crucial piece of property, which connected the resort with Sakinaw Creek and avoids the narrow Sunshine Coast Highway. Much of the trail follows BC Hydro rights-of-way. The public utility also financed information kiosks posted at several places along the highway.

One of the most pleasant features on the Suncoaster Trail is a bridge that spans Sakinaw Creek about 14 km north of Pender Harbour. A tall roadside marker with distinctive yellow icons depicting a hiker and a wheelchair indicates where this section of the trail begins. Turn uphill to reach a parking area. Depending on your appetite for exercise, six side trails lead away from the main hard-packed, wheelchair-accessible gravelled pathway. Beside the bridge, an oval picnic table sits amid an understorey of waist-high sword ferns and spindly salmonberry bushes. A forest of towering red alder rises above the creek. Mosses, lichens, liverworts, and ferns coat their limbs and sprout from branches like hanging gardens.

Those who enjoy exploring by mountain bike will especially appreciate the work of trail builders who designed a series of switch-backs along the south side of Sakinaw Creek where it splashes downhill towards the highway. This is a fine example of the easy to intermediate-level challenges found along the Suncoaster's midsection and one that cyclists will eagerly retrace as their knowledge of its twists and turns grows in tandem with their confidence.

Another section links with McNeil Lake Forest Road, which leads east from Highway 101 near the Kleindale neighbourhood. As you ascend this road you are greeted with good views north towards the Coast Mountain peaks that rise above Jervis Inlet. Follow McNeil Lake Road for 3 km to the signed trailhead. From here the trail leads north through second-growth forest and along a BC Hydro right-of-way service road. Kleindale is worth a stop to pay your respects at the old cemetery on the hillside that overlooks the shallow neck of the bay below the Malaspina Ranch Stables, a great place to do some horseback riding. An enormous dugout, the *Orenda*, carved from a tree felled in Stanley Park and sailed to Hawaii in the 1970s, lies at rest in a grassy field.

> ## OTHER ATTRACTIONS

Dogwoods: Pacific dogwoods bloom from April to June. Also called western flowering dogwood, B.C.'s floral emblem achieves champion heights in gullies and streams beside Highway 101 as it winds along the Sechelt Peninsula between Halfmoon Bay and Egmont. Travellers get a canopy-level view of the white-mantled trees in places such as Sakinaw Lake, where the landscape drops away sharply from the highway. An enjoyable way to explore the forests is along one of several public pathways, such as the Suncoaster Trail (see above), that run for 33 km between Klein Lake and Homesite Creek.

Katherine Lake Regional Park: Katherine Lake Park, located 4 km west of Highway 101 on Garden Bay Road, is a freshwater treat in a region dominated by saltwater locales. The sandy beach at this small lake will appeal to swimmers, picnickers, and campers. If you like to take an early-morning plunge after a night spent sleeping under the stars, this is it.

Klein Lake Regional Park: To get to Klein Lake Park, head south from Egmont Road on rough-but-passable North Lake Road for 3.6 km. Make your way here to start a mountain bike or hiking exploration of the Suncoaster Trail (see above), to paddle the modest-sized lake, or simply to check into one of the postcard-perfect campsites, almost all of which feature makeshift docks, except for the sites at the southwest side at the end of the access road where a float dock of milled wood puts the rest to shame. The makeshift ones formed of driftwood, rope, nails, and, occasionally, plywood decking speak of hot summer days when time is well spent occupied with fashioning a dock, some of which jut a fair ways offshore and have the appearance of an unfolded folding yardstick. The lake sports a healthy fish population as attested to by the efforts of kingfishers at work scouting the movement of fry and adult stock.

> ## DINING

Whether you choose to stay at Ruby Lake Resort or the West Coast Wilderness Lodge (see below) or just drop by for a meal, the best dining experiences locally are found there. Three other good catches are:

Off the Hook Seafoods (12376 Sunshine Coast Highway; 604-883-9593): This perfect place for DIY action features live, fresh, and frozen fruits of the sea, with sushi for good measure.

Garden Bay Hotel (Garden Bay; 604-883-9919; www.gardenbay pub.com): Park your boat at the hotel's marina or just wander in off the road. There are enough choices on offer from the hotel's pub-and-restaurant galley to satisfy the hungriest salty dog.

Backeddy Marine Pub (16660 Backeddy Road, Egmont; 604-883-2298 or 1-800-626-0599): Good pub grub served up on the Egmont waterfront.

> ## ACCOMMODATION

It's worth enduring the rough access road to camp at Klein Lake Regional Park (see above). But if you're looking for something more luxurious, these two resorts are worth a trip in themselves:

Ruby Lake Resort and Rainforest Spa (15426 Sunshine Coast Highway; 604-883-2269; www.rubylakeresort.com): Over the past decade a libretto of operatic proportions has played out at Ruby Lake since the Cogrossi family arrived from Milan, Italy, and converted this staid resort into a wildlife-viewing sanctuary complete with Italian trattoria restaurant (seafood, wild game, natural foods, with artwork by neighbour Joni Mitchell), spa, and outdoor amphitheatre. Ten adjoining waterfront cottages, a deluxe cabin, and a safari-tent village overlook the resort's lagoon, where bald eagles drop by at dusk for their regular feeding. In addition to the Suncoaster Trail, a gentle walking trail leads around Ruby Lake's diminutive lagoon and connects with the recently established Iris Griffith Field Studies and

Interpretive Centre (15386 Sunshine Coast Highway; 604-883-9201; www.lagoonsociety.com). Canoe and kayak rentals are available for those wishing to explore the expansive waters of Ruby Lake.

West Coast Wilderness Lodge (Egmont; 1-877-988-3838; www.wcwl.com): The West Coast Wilderness Lodge perches above the entrance to Jervis Inlet. A stay here in one of twenty suites spread among five guest lodges is like a one-stop shopping trip. The WCWL caters to ocean and whitewater kayakers, mountain bikers, rock climbers, and those who simply enjoy an outdoor experience coupled with great food served at the lodge's Inlets Restaurant. My favourite place to watch dolphins cavort with sea lions as swans and eagles soar overhead is in the wood-fired oceanside sauna, complete with picture window. Certified guides are available to work with guests to sharpen skills in sea kayaking and whitewater paddling, in route finding on the lodge's two outdoor climbing walls, and in mountain biking along trails in the nearby Caren Range.

POWELL RIVER AND LUND

. . . . .

> ACCESS: Powell River sits 177 km north of Vancouver on High-ways 1 and 101 via BC Ferries between Horseshoe Bay and Langdale, and between Earls Cove and Saltery Bay. Allow 5 hours. For infor-mation on sailing times, fares, and reservations, contact BC Fer-ries (1-888-223-3779; www.bcferries.com). Pacific Coastal Airlines (1-800-663-2872; www.pacificcoastal.com) offers daily service from Vancouver International Airport. Powell River Taxi (6105 Lund Street; 604-483-3666) serves the Malaspina Peninsula, and Lund Water Taxi (604-483-9749; www.lundwatertaxi.com) connects Lund with various Gulf Islands.

> WHY GO: Desolation never looked so good.

> KEEP IN MIND: Lighter traffic in off-season months means almost never having to wait for a ferry sailing.

IF YOU enjoy the smooth, sedate pace of ferries, this extended jour-ney along the Sechelt and Malaspina peninsulas is for you. Fer-ries are a convenient and rewarding part of this adventure package, especially the hour-long sailing between Earls Cove and Saltery Bay aboard the *Queen of Tsawwassen*. Give the weathered ferry's outside seating a try for a mini–Inside Passage experience. Pack a pair of binoculars, since much of the pleasure simply involves "seeing B.C.," as Emily Carr once put it. The painter, author, and veteran coast traveller concluded that sightseeing was the single most powerful unifying force in a province filled with geographical diversity.

Don't feel that you're in such a hurry as you travel from one ferry slip to the next that you can't stop at one of the farms along the way where fresh fruit and vegetables are for sale. Ferry connections are scheduled so that there is an adequate amount of time to make the drive from one to the next.

Beyond the Sechelt Peninsula, particularly the settled portion between Gibsons and Sechelt, there's a palpable remoteness. The Malaspina Peninsula feels more like an island than part of the coastal mainland. The pace of life at the northern end of the Sunshine Coast is decidedly less adrenal than in Metro Vancouver. Even so, over the past decade I've seen an up-tick in the pace of life in Powell River and its much smaller neighbour, Lund. Tourism options are tremendous: Malaspina Strait provides a water link to nearby islands such as Texada, Savary, and the Copelands, while Okeover Arm leads to the entrance of Desolation Sound.

Powell River's mill has been the peninsula's economic engine for a century. The thirst for fibre to feed the mill, coupled with a catastrophic fire that incinerated much of the forest decades ago have reshaped the landscape, as has the flooding of numerous low-lying valleys to provide hydroelectric power.

Powell River's rejuvenated townsite, a national historic region consisting of some four hundred homes and several dozen commercial businesses built adjacent to the Powell River Paper Company between 1909 and 1930, was one of the world's first planned communities (www.powellrivermuseum.ca). Together with the neighbourhoods of Westview, which houses the downtown core, and Cranberry, set back above the waterfront, the spirit that saw the original townsite designed with the welfare of the workers and their families in mind thrives with an ongoing concern for community well-being. Access for disabled persons is foremost among these concerns, best exemplified by the town staging the BC Disability Games in 2007. Couple this with a cultural zeal that sees the town host a biennial international choral festival, Kathaumixw (Ka-thou-mew), a Sliammon name for "a gathering together of different peoples" (www.kathaumixw.org), and you can see why Powell River is special. *Note:* If you're planning to visit during that time, reserve accommodation well in advance.

Visitors hoping to explore the area by bike may want to check out Savary Island Bike Shop (Lund; 604-483-7771), Suncoast Cycles (9440 Highway 101; 604-487-1111; www.suncoastcycles.com) for rentals and service), or Taw's Cycle & Sports (4597 Marine Avenue; 604-485-2555; www.tawsonline.com).

Visit Powell River Outdoors (4597 Marine Avenue; 604-485-2555 or 1-877-481-2555; www.proutdoors.com) for fishing gear, advice, licences, and rentals. Paddlers will want to contact Alpha Adventures (6812 Alberni Street; 604-485-7529; www.outdooradventure store.ca) for kayak and canoe tours, rentals, and lessons, Skeeter Jack's Outback Shack (9398 Highway 101; 604-487-1997; www.skeeter jacks.com) for canoe and kayak rentals, transportation to lakes, as well as camping gear, fishing tackle, and cold beer, or Powell River Sea Kayak (Lund; 1-866-617-4444; www.bcseakayak.com) for rentals, lessons, and tours.

Desolation Sound Boat Tours (7066 Parksville Street, Powell River; 1-877-551-2628; www.desolation.ca) offers eco and bear-watching excursions), Footprint Nature Explorations (6429 Sutherland Avenue; 604-414-6884; www.footprint-natureexplorations. ca) gives kayaking, hiking, and biking tours, Sunshine Coast Tours (1-800-870-9055; www.sunshinecoasttours.ca) offers daily summer tours of Princess Louise Inlet and Skookumchuck Narrows, and Terracentric Coastal Adventures (Lund Harbour; 604-483-7900; www.terracentricadventures.com) features Zodiac, sea kayak, and Tla'Amin First Nation cultural tours.

For a comprehensive list of activities, attractions, accommodations, and dining on the Malaspina Peninsula, contact Tourism Powell River (111–4871 Joyce Avenue; 1-877-817-8669; www.discover powellriver.com).

> **INLAND LAKE FOREST PROVINCIAL PARK** &

ACTIVITIES: *Camping, cycling, picnicking, running, swimming, walking*

The Powell Forest Canoe Route (see below) and the 180-km Sunshine Coast Trail, Haywire Bay Regional Park, and Inland Lake Forest Park all converge a short drive east of Powell River via Cranberry Street, Haslam Street, and Inland Lake Road. Mountain biking and hiking trails lead past waterfalls and across wooden bridges at every turn. The place I savour is the forested 13-km, multi-use trail that encircles 5.5-km-long Inland Lake. Designed with wheelchair riders

Lund's harbour

in mind, the hardpacked, level trail includes stretches of boardwalk
that overhang the picturesque lake in places. This is a great place
to spend a half-day enjoying a leisurely bike ride or paddle coupled
with a swim and a picnic. A moderate 4.5-km section of the Sunshine Coast hiking trail leads between Inland Lake and Haywire
Bay. At night, the heartfelt bass croaks of Louisiana bullfrogs fills
the bowl of stars above.

> **POWELL FOREST CANOE ROUTE**
ACTIVITIES: *Camping, paddling, picnicking, swimming*
Freshwater lakes aren't a rarity around Vancouver, but large, warm
ones certainly are. With a couple of notable exceptions—Cultus
and Alouette lakes—most of local ones are too small for an extended
paddle trip and too cold for a leisurely dip. For an extended trek,
explore the Powell Forest Canoe Route, 5 km north of Highway 101
on well-marked logging roads to Lois Lake. It is one of the more sig-
nificant paddle treks in the province, right up there with the Bowron
Lakes in the Cariboo. The full-on, twelve-lake, 57-km trip requires

five to seven days to complete and includes almost 11 km of portages. A shorter 12.5-km route takes three days and includes about 5 km of portages. Canoe racks are provided in many places along the portages to rest your shoulders while admiring a succession of snow-mantled peaks above the rolling hillsides. For starters, I suggest a day paddle on Lois Lake, more than enough to give you ideas for a longer excursion.

A predictable wind rises from the west around mid-morning and strengthens throughout the day. By mid-afternoon those in light-weight boats will be scrambling for shore to escape its fury. Enforced landings are made more difficult by the accumulations of driftwood, which occasionally choke the shallows.

Bleached, spear-tipped spires of old-growth forest protrude as much as 10 metres above the surfaces of several flooded lakes such as Lois. In parts of the lake, the treetops look like the sunken masts at a marina that has succumbed to a rise in sea level. I like to stick close to shore and drift among the aromatic sweet gale and willow shrubs. Purple wild flag and Oregon iris push their lacy flowering tops above the surface in places where only those in a canoe or kayak can admire them at close range. Similarly, by drifting silently among the tall snags you can approach osprey nests, where the downy heads of cheeping young can be seen peaking above their twig homes. When it comes time to stretch your legs on shore, walk the 1 km portage trail that links with Horseshoe Lake through a sheltering stand of original-growth Douglas-fir forest.

> **SHELTER POINT REGIONAL PARK**
ACTIVITIES: *Camping, cycling, paddling, picnicking, swimming, walking*
If you can handle another ferry, head offshore from Powell River to the Rock, or more formally, Texada Island. Frequent BC Ferries sailings link Powell River to Blubber Bay. Crossing time is 35 minutes. Shelter Point, a jewel of a park, lies 27 km south of Blubber Bay. (For fees and information, contact 604-483-3231; www.powellriverrd. bc.ca.) A magnificent stand of old-growth forest lines the park's shoreline. Douglas-firs and western red cedars provide a fitting accompaniment to the beauty of the nearby beach with its exotic-looking sand

dollars, sea anemones, and oversized moon snail shells. Eagles and ospreys rest in the tallest boughs when not cruising the coastline for a meal. Look west across the Strait of Georgia at the Comox Glacier's broad white expanse for one of the best views of Vancouver Island. Lasqueti Island lies to the southwest. A breeze blows almost constantly across the strait and it's easy to see that Shelter Point comes by its name honestly. *Note:* Avoid Shelter Point on the Canada Day long weekend when the annual baseball tournament is in full swing and the park's forty-seven campsites booked out.

> ## OTHER ATTRACTIONS

Savary Island: Savary Island is a 15-minute water taxi ride or a one-hour paddle west from Lund's boat ramp. The Savary Island Land Trust (604-483-4743; www.silt.ca) publishes a detailed map of the island that is widely distributed in Lund and Powell River. This 7.5-km-long island is long and skinny as a string bean and ringed by an unbroken strand of white shell, pebble, and sand beach; count on taking a full day to walk around its shoreline. (*Note:* There are no services of any kind on the island.) Although yours may be the only footprints you see on the beach, you won't lack for company. Eagles by the dozen swoop and cry on the breeze. At low tide, seals haul up offshore on glacial erratics. Keep your eyes peeled for one of the tallest arbutus trees on the West Coast. The copper-coloured giant anchors Garnet Point on the southeastern side of the island; at 24.4 metres, it's hard to miss. Just as prominent is a hulking piece of rusted logging equipment abandoned at the tideline decades ago further west in Duck Bay.

Copeland Islands Marine Provincial Park: For paddlers, a short water taxi ride is an easy way to reach the entrance to Desolation Sound and avoid the bother of large-hulled power boats, which, unlike the smooth-planing water taxis, leave substantial wakes. Emergency landing spots along the peninsula north of Lund are in short supply until the low-slung Copelands begin to offer shelter. By themselves, the Copelands—or Raggeds as this chain of four islands and fourteen islets is known locally—are an exquisite place to explore by canoe or kayak. Marine life abounds, as does a sense of cloistered stillness. Unlike on Savary Island (see above), which, with the exception of its beaches, is privately owned, two separate camp-sites on the Copelands offer a chance to comfortably overnight. Just make sure to haul your boat high enough above the tideline. Otherwise, like a thief in the night, the ocean might silently make off with your sole link to the mainland while you snooze. *Note:* Shellfish harvesting is not permitted in the park.

Lund (www.lundbc.ca): You can't get more well and truly hidden than the little port of Lund, 20 km north of Powell River on Highway 101. The Malaspina Peninsula narrows to a thin finger of land here, wedged between Malaspina Strait on the west and Okeover Arm to the east. Desolation Sound, a paddler's paradise, lies just to the north. Anchored by a historical hotel, a boardwalk, plus several art galleries and restaurants, low-key Lund enjoys one of the prettiest locations on the Sunshine Coast.

If you're feeling drawn to explore offshore, a good way to appreciate the waters of Malaspina Strait and Desolation Sound is aboard a sturdy water taxi as it forays from Lund around the northern Sunshine Coast. Got a bike or a kayak? Toss it on. Only brought your swimsuit and a picnic hamper? That'll do just fine. There's really only one thing that matters before setting off: score some blackberry cinnamon buns at Nancy's Bakery (see below). And keep in mind that the *Raggedy Anne*, or companion boats in the Lund Water Taxi fleet, typically drop off passengers where few, if any, supplies or services are available. Unless, of course, you count the plentiful colonies of shellfish for which this stretch of the Strait of Georgia is renowned. Just be sure to check for any red tide or paralytic shellfish poisoning closures posted at the federal dock. Have a tidal waters sport fishing licence handy, too. *Note:* Leave your vehicle at Dave's Parking (604-483-3667); the first two hours are free.

> **DINING**

Nancy's Bakery (1431 Highway 101; 604-483-4180): Nancy's anchors Lund's boardwalk-lined cove from a stylish, two-storey adventure centre, restaurant, and crafts store. Visitors may arrive for a host of reasons, including concerts on summer evenings, but eventually everyone gravitates to Nancy's, which has rightfully earned its moniker, Lund of the Rising Bun.

The Alchemist Restaurant (4680 Marine Avenue; 604-485-4141; www.alchemistrestaurant.com): Fresh from the Burrowing Owl Estate restaurant in Oliver (see chapter 28) the culinary team of Erin and François specialize in French Mediterranean cuisine, admirably suited to the local growing environment, exactly what the Powell River dining scene needs. Small wonder there are nightly lineups at this heritage house's door.

The Laughing Oyster Restaurant (C4 Vandermaeden Road, RR #2; 604-483-9775; www.laughingoyster.ca): Worth a trip in itself, the Laughing Oyster's green lawn rolls down to Okeover Arm, one of the prime oyster grounds on the coast, large portions of which are featured on the menu. My choice is the West Coast Seafood Harvest.

> ## ACCOMMODATION

Lund Hotel (604-414-0474 or 1-877-569-3999; www.lundhotel.com): The local Tla'Amin First Nation now operates the historical Lund Hotel, which has been admirably renovated. Room 216 provides a particularly scenic corner from which to overlook the snug harbour. A pub, restaurant, art gallery, and grocery and liquor store share the ground floor.

Desolation Resort (2694 Dawson Road; 604-483-3592; www.desolationresort.com): Okeover Arm is a sheltered inlet drenched in an unearthly silence. On the steep hillside that rises above the inlet sit twelve fully equipped, imaginatively designed wood chalets, some with outdoor hot tubs. Complimentary canoes and kayaks are moored on a floating dock that juts far enough out into Okeover Arm that you could easily fish for your supper. If not, the Laughing Oyster Restaurant (see above) is only a short walk away.

Sevilla Island Resort (Lund; 604-414-6880; www.sevillaislandresort.ca): Owner Ian Hobbs picks up guests at the town dock and motors them across the harbour to this resort, perched on an island in Finn Bay. Water views on three sides guarantee everyone gets the best bed in the house in one of four suites. The kitchen serves up breakfasts and dinners as well as brown bag lunches for paddlers taking part in one of the resort's eco-tours to local hot spots such as the Copeland and Savary islands (see above) and Desolation Sound.

GULF ISLANDS

GALIANO ISLAND

MAYNE ISLAND

NORTH AND SOUTH
PENDER ISLANDS

SALT SPRING ISLAND

SATURNA ISLAND

> 12

GALIANO ISLAND

. . . . .

> ACCESS: Galiano Island is a 55-minute ferry ride from BC Ferries' Tsawwassen terminal, 40 km south of Vancouver, to Sturdies Bay at the eastern end of the island. For sailing times, fares, and reservations, visit www.bcferries.com or call 1-888-223-3779. For transportation on Galiano, including shuttle service from Sturdies Bay, contact Fly'n Riun's Taxi Galiano (250-539-0202; www.taxigaliano.com).

> WHY GO: On this closest southern Gulf Island to Vancouver you'll find rolling countryside reminiscent of Quebec's Eastern Townships and abundant accommodation.

> KEEP IN MIND: Getting off Galiano can be as tricky in peak season as arranging space on the ferry from Vancouver. Don't make the mistake of travelling without a reservation, especially since there is no charge for this service on Gulf Island routes.

GALIANO ISLAND has a century-old reputation as a leisure destination. Several island businesses cater to outdoors pursuits, such as ocean kayaking and mountain biking. Three provincial parks complement two equally impressive community land trusts. Forest-lined roadways lead to white sand and shell beaches. Sheltered waters welcome boaters, and back roads beckon cyclists. You can come prepared for just about anything—and find it here.

Galiano Island is divided into two separate jurisdictions—an administrative split that also points to a difference in lifestyle at each end. Whereas those on North Galiano are more likely to value their solitude, residents in the south are more active socially. As a whole, Galiano's community is one of the most artistic and environmentally progressive in the Gulf Islands.

Active Pass from Mount Galiano

Almost as soon as you disembark from the ferry at Sturdies Bay, you are in the heart of one of two small commercial districts on the island. Galiano's only gas station is just uphill, across Sturdies Bay Road from the visitor information booth. Galleries featuring work by island artists are also nestled into this intersection, as is a grocery and liquor store, the post office, and a bakery and deli. A short distance farther up island lies another grocery and liquor store, as well as a hardware store, at the intersection of Porlier Pass and Georgeson Bay roads. When planning your trip be aware that most businesses close at 5 or 6 PM.

It's 35 km from Sturdies Bay to Dionisio Point at the island's north end—quite a stretch for those on bicycles. Of all the southern islands, Galiano has the most well-organized mountain bike trail system. Bluffs Park is the site of some spectacular views and the beginning of a network of trails and roads around Mount Galiano.

You may not want to head up island beyond Montague Harbour, where steep cliffs line most of Galiano's west side and Porlier Pass Road rises and falls through densely wooded areas without much to enchant the eye. (If you are approaching from Sturdies Bay by bike, take Porlier Pass Road to avoid the steeper climb from Montague Harbour on Clanton Road, which merges with Porlier at the top of the hill above Montague.) It takes four to five hours to cover the undulating road on two wheels, less than an hour by car. Wayfinding is easy, as Porlier Pass Road is the only one that runs the full length of the island. As you move around the island clockwise, you'll enjoy a procession of parks and viewpoints. Bellhouse Provincial Park, Montague Harbour Provincial Marine Park, Mount Galiano, and Bluffs Park are all within easy range of the ferry terminal.

Since there's more to do here than will fit into a weekend visit, plan whether you'll come with a car or on foot, riding a bike or pulling a boat. You can often arrange to rent equipment and have it waiting for you when you arrive.

To explore the island by bike pay a visit to Galiano Bicycle Rental and Repairs (Sturdies Bay; 250-539-9906) or Toadie's Roadies (Montague Harbour Marina; 250-539-3443), which also offers moped and boat rentals. Paddlers can consult Gulf Island Kayaking (Montague Harbour Marina; 250-539-2442; www.seakayak.ca) for guided tours and rentals.

For general travel information visit the Galiano Info Booth (Sturdies Bay Road; www.galianoisland.com).

> **BELLHOUSE PROVINCIAL PARK**

ACTIVITIES: *Viewpoints, walking*
To get to Bellhouse Park head past the commercial district near the ferry terminal, turn left off Sturdies Bay Road onto Burrill Road, then turn left again onto Jack Drive.

Bellhouse has been a public day-use site since 1964, when the Bellhouse family deeded it to the province. The Bellhouses, who have resided at Burrill Point since 1904, operated the Farmhouse Inn (located in what is now the park) from the 1920s to the 1960s. Over the years, guests at the inn enjoyed watching the marine traffic in Active Pass, and it was Leonard Bellhouse's wish in bequeathing the land to the public that it remain for this purpose. Certainly the park's magnificent location far outweighs its modest 2-ha size. A small beach lies along its eastern shoreline, and around the point on the west side are some of the most animated shapes of eroded limestone on the island. This park is a photographer's dream, both for its natural setting and for the scale of human activity when large ferry boats churn by.

> **BLUFFS PARK**

ACTIVITIES: *Cycling, picnicking, walking, viewpoints*

Bluffs Park, south off Sturdies Bay Road onto Jack Drive, then east on Burrill Road, is the perfect partner for Bellhouse Park, with its views overlooking what you experienced at shoreline. You will pass a number of old homesteads as Burrill Road leads southeast, then turns uphill onto Bluff Road. Whether you're walking or cycling, the short climb from here to Bluffs Park will have you puffing in no time. Bluff Road becomes gravel-surfaced just past Warbler Road. A large wooden sign announces that you have entered the Bluffs. Watch for a road leading off to the left a short distance beyond this sign. It leads to the spectacular viewpoint on the Bluffs, one of the best in the islands. From here you can see all of Active Pass below, including Bellhouse Provincial Park on one side and Georgeson Bay to the south. Follow the trail that runs along the bluffs past an old wooden shelter for the best views of Mayne, Saturna, North Pender, Salt Spring, and Vancouver islands before descending through the woods on the loop trail to meet up with Bluff Road once more. There are numerous spots on the bluffs for a picnic, but please, no fires. If you're on a bike, make the thrilling descent down Bluff Road to Georgeson Bay Road through a tall stand of cedar trees. Don't hurtle by too quickly or you'll miss the special feeling of passing among them. On an island that's been as heavily logged as Galiano, such first-growth groves are rare indeed.

Max and Marion Enke, who lived on Galiano from 1902 to 1913, donated the land that made Bluffs Park possible in 1972. A plaque honouring their gift of 136 ha stands beside the parking area.

Pebble Beach Reserve, Galiano Island

> **DIONISIO POINT PROVINCIAL PARK**

ACTIVITIES: *Boating, camping, paddling, swimming, walking*

Dionisio Point bears the first of Captain Galiano's several Christian names. Until a disputed right-of-way on Cook Road reopens, visitors must use a boat to reach Dionisio Point Provincial Park. Dionisio Point is a sandy finger of land—with a beach on each side—that stretches east towards the Strait of Georgia before branching to the north and south. The north branch of sandstone, its small cliffs and ledges topped with a thin coating of soil that supports grass cover, arbutus trees and Garry oaks, provides protection for a popular anchorage in a small cove. The bare southern branch partially encloses shallow Coon Bay, which empties completely at lowest tides. Quietly exploring the shoreline on foot or by boat is one of the most interesting ways to spend a visit to Dionisio. The water of Porlier Pass (also known as the Cowichan Gap), running between Galiano and Valdes Island to the north, churns through at changing tide. You can actually hear the ripping sound as the surface of the pass becomes ruffled by waves and whirlpools. The only time you'd want to be out here in a small, open boat would be at slack tide.

You can do almost all the exploring you wish by hiking the trails that connect the four bays between Dionisio Point and the lighthouse at Virago Point. Each leads to a small point and is invested with a charm of its own. The red lighthouse at Race Point and its companion nearby on Virago Point were completed in 1902.

One bonus if you do explore by water is that you bypass the Indian reserve that encompasses Lighthouse Bay, a protected body lying between the two lights. Although no one lives on the reserve any longer, Indian reserves are private property, posted as restricted areas, and require permission from the band office to enter.

> ## MONTAGUE HARBOUR PROVINCIAL MARINE PARK &

ACTIVITIES: *Boating, camping, paddling, picnicking, swimming, walking*

The sheltered west side of Galiano is much different from its exposed eastern counterpart with far fewer signs of logging. Heading for Montague Harbour, 8 km north of Sturdies Bay, you will enter a narrow, fertile valley that has been home to humans for thousands of years. Evidence of millennia of feasting here by Cowichan and Straits First Nations people can be seen in the middens—massive mounds of bleached seashells—that cover several of the beaches next to the harbour, including Shell Beach, a perfect place for swimming.

This park caters to visitors who arrive in their own boats, as well as those who came by ferry. Immediately as you enter is the marine park marina (250-539-5733; www.montagueharbour.com) and public dock. A nature house, moored beside the dock, is open during the summer. Interpretive displays of sea life are among its features. The beach on this side of the park is one of the better ones.

From the park's parking lot, follow the road that leads to the day-use picnic area, which fronts long curving Shell Beach. The view from here up the west side of Galiano is what the Gulf Islands are all about: sheltered waterways; islands of all sizes; wildlife in the form of birds, seals and otters; boats of all kinds passing by, and high cliffs that rise straight up out of the sea. Shell Beach slopes gently off on both sides of a concrete boat ramp from where a steady stream of kayakers and power boaters head off towards more remote settings, such as Dionisio Point on Galiano's northern end (see above).

Walk the trails that lead out onto Gray Peninsula. Ancient arbutus, Douglas-fir, hemlock, and Garry oak shelter thick underbrush, restricting walkers to the winding trail along the peninsula's east side. On the western exposure the forest thins, beaches spread before you, and you're sure to disturb a heron as you round one of the points. The hour needed to explore the beaches and promontories of Gray Peninsula will be one of the most enjoyable of your visit to Galiano.

> ## MOUNT GALIANO PARK

ACTIVITIES: *Hiking, viewpoints*

There are three approaches to this park. The steepest ascent begins from the well-marked parking area at the west end of Active Pass Drive, whereas entrances at Grace Trail on Georgeson Road and the Lord Park Trail at the intersection of Lord and Morgan roads offer gentler approaches. All three trails merge into an old logging road.

Allow 30 to 60 minutes to reach Mount Galiano's round summit, a 6-km round trip, where a Garry oak forest anchors the south facing bluffs overlooking Mayne Island's Village and Miners bays as the entire tableau of islands stretches before you. On a clear day, sunlight blazes off the glaciated peaks of the Olympic Mountains in Washington state. Ferry horns trumpeting in Active Pass are reminiscent of rutting season in bull moose country. Eagles arc in the updraft in front of the bluff as the waters below are alive with boats of all shapes and sizes. In summer, watch for delicate, reedy phantom orchids blooming beside the trail—their tiny buds are frequently accompanied by Indian pipe.

> ## PEBBLE BEACH RESERVE

ACTIVITIES: *Beachcombing, swimming, walking*

In 1998, the Galiano Conservancy Association (www.galianoconservancy.ca) purchased the Pebble Beach Reserve, a large tract of previously clear-cut land that is now regenerating. To get there, head to mid-island on Porlier Pass Road and turn east for a short distance on McCoskrie Road to the well-marked trailhead. A 3-km loop trail links Pebble Beach and Cable Bay. From the trailhead, most visitors take the short, gentle approach to Cable Bay for quick access to the ocean. Those leaning towards the "pleasure postponed is pleasure enhanced" philosophy should consider the slightly lengthier single-track route to Pebble Beach, which leads through a western red-cedar forest. An easily negotiated sandstone shoreline stretches from there north to Cable Cove, a 20-minute scramble.

Pebble Beach is covered with jellybean- to egg-sized stones with nary a flat-sided skipper to be found. Look carefully and you might just spy one of the agates for which this strand is renowned. Off in the distance to the east is the familiar profile of the Lions, a reminder that, although it may feel a world away, Galiano is almost close enough to be home.

> **OTHER ATTRACTIONS**

Canada Day Jamboree: This festival, held at North Island hall, comes complete with a parade, where typically half the citizenry is in the procession of floats and fire reels while the other half cheers them on from the roadside. Amid the hula hoop and cake decorating contests, the biggest draw is the Lions Club barbeque. The lineup for burgers—veggie, beef, or salmon—stretches out beneath a leafy forest canopy of maples. Finish your meal with a visit to the dessert tent, where you'll find home-made fruit and berry pies.

Galiano Golf and Country Club (24 St. Andrews Drive; 250-539-5533 or 1-877-909-7888; www.galianoisland.com/galianogolf): Everyone is welcome to swing by this challenging nine-hole, 1,936-yard course, if only for a light meal at the club's café lounge.

> **PLACE NAMES**
. . . .

IN 1792, the British and Spanish fleets were both exploring and laying claim to new territory along the B.C. coast. Galiano Island was caught in the crossfire of this competitive name game and, as a result, English and Spanish place names vie for importance along its shoreline and promontories. Montague Harbour is named for a British ship, Mount Sutil for Captain Galiano's schooner, Active Pass after an American paddle steamer, and Porlier Pass, at the island's north end, for a bureaucrat in Madrid. What a tussle.

Madrona del Mar Spa (134 Madrona Drive; 1-877-530-3939; www.galianoinn.com): My favourite way to visit a spa is with a special someone else. Treatments for two at this waterfront spa include one of my favourite features: a heated float pool, as salinated as Polynesian waters, where you just float.

> ## DINING

Takeout: When there's time to kill before the ferry, I head to either of two good takeout diners: *Mariem's Thai Food* (250-539-3171)—try the tum yum soup with chicken or prawns; a guaranteed heat killer is her Thai iced coffee—or *Max and Moritz Spicy Island* (250-539-5888), which offers an eclectic mix of Indonesian and German food and good coffee.

> **Galiano is far younger geologically than the other Gulf Islands, and because it has very little arable land it was one of the last islands settled by Europeans and Asians.**

Grand Central (2740 Sturdies Bay Road; 250-539-9885; www.grandcentral.ca): Funky and fresh, this place reminds me of one of my all-time favourite ski town haunts, Graham's in Glacier at the foot of Mount Baker, and is complete with live music and wireless Internet. No shirt? No shoes? No problem.

Woodstone Country Inn (250-539-2022; www.woodstoneinn.com): There's nothing that pleases me more than putting myself in the hands of chef (and owner) Gail Nielsen-Pich with her nightly prix fixe three-course menu. Desserts are optional, as are selections from the limited but thoughtfully selected wine list. I say opt for both and stay at this cozy, reasonably priced country inn, too. Reservations are required.

> ## ACCOMMODATION

Montague Harbour Marine Provincial Park: On the hillside above Montague Harbour sit twenty-one walk-in campsites, half of which have commanding views of the water. Sites 31 to 38 are the best locations in the park. There is a small nightly charge for use of these campsites. Nearby are nineteen drive-in campsites, sheltered by the forest. There is a charge of about $15 per night for their use from April to October. Given a choice, I'd rather stay at a walk-in site. Several drive-in sites, notably 3 and 7, are reached by climbing a short set of flagstone steps. Their position above the roadway spares sleeping campers from the headlights of vehicles arriving after dark. Call Discover Camping (1-800-689-9025; www.discovercamping. ca) to reserve both vehicle/tent and walk-in sites.

Active Pass Caboose (250-539-2316; www.cedarplace.com/ caboose): This unique and private waterfront retreat puts you to bed in a fully equipped restored heritage CPR railcar, complete with kitchen facilities. The first ferry through Active Pass in the morning will give you a complimentary wake-up call with its horn.

Island Time Bed and Breakfast (952 Sticks Allison Road; 250-539-3506; 1-877-588-3506; www.islandtimebc.com): Overlooking the Strait of Georgia, the three suites on offer are the top pick of bed and breakfasts on the island. Bring your tennis rackets, since court's in session. The hot tub in the gazebo is where you'll find me.

Woodstone Country Inn (250-539-2022; www.woodstoneinn. com &): This is one of my favourite Gulf Islands retreats, probably because of the exquisite silence that hangs over the small valley in which the inn is cupped at the foot of Mount Galiano. Park yourself under the catalpa tree and enjoy afternoon tea with homemade ginger snaps and Nanaimo bars, which is included along with a gourmet breakfast. Whether you're in a wheelchair or not, my pick is the Lilac Room. A unique touch is the complimentary rubber boots for guests wishing to walk to the wildlife viewing platform in the nearby meadow.

MAYNE ISLAND

· · · · ·

> ACCESS: Mayne Island is a 90-minute ferry ride from BC Ferries'
Tsawwassen terminal, 40 km south of Vancouver, to Village Bay. For
detailed sailing times, fares, and no-charge reservations (crucial in
summer months), visit www.bcferries.com or call 1-888-223-3779.
Alternatively, Seair (1-800-447-3247; www.seairseaplanes.com)
offers twice-daily float plane service to Miners Bay. For transportation on Mayne, including shuttle service from Village Bay, contact
MIDAS Taxi (1-250-539-3132).

> WHY GO: Mellow out with Active Pass.

> KEEP IN MIND: There is no public campground on Mayne Island.

LIGHTS. FERRIES. ACTION. Yes, activities swirl around Mayne Island
with the intensity of ocean currents in Active Pass, which forms
the northern boundary of the second-smallest Gulf Island
served by BC Ferries. Mayne is truly worthy of a quick getaway,
either by car, bike, or kayak. As the original community centre for
the southern Gulf Islands, Mayne was once the social hub, quaintly
nicknamed Little Hell because of the tolerance accorded public con-
sumption of alcohol by its citizenry—the other islands in the Gulf
chain were "dry." Despite dire railings that rained from the pulpit
at St. Mary Magdalene Anglican Church, nothing dampened this
spirit of tolerance. These days the scent of cannabis frequently wafts
on island breezes, a sign that prohibition is as futile now as ever.

In a province where everything seems to have materialized just
yesterday, Mayne's visible historical roots are a refreshing change.
The Active Pass lighthouse at its northeastern tip was erected more

Georgina Point Heritage Park, Mayne Island

then a century ago. Many of the buildings in Miners Bay, including the Springwater Lodge, date from the same period. The lodge is the province's oldest operating hotel, where you may find yourself keeping company with a microbrewery's finest as part of a long-standing island tradition. The cliffs of Galiano Island rise up on the opposite side of Active Pass and are best viewed from the federal dock on Miners Bay that fronts the Springwater.

The emergence of a new national park in 2003 at the opposite end of the island at Bennett Bay has heightened Mayne's appeal. Whether you explore this portion of Gulf Islands National Park Reserve on foot or by boat, there's an unspoiled atmosphere to the place that lends the island an even greater magnetism. Like the gold rush stampeders, I'm drawn to Mayne to unearth hidden treasure and create precious memories, something that's much easier to accomplish with a camera and binoculars than a pick and shovel.

To get a full appreciation for the island, consider exploring it by sea kayaking. For tours, lessons, and rentals, check out Mayne Island Kayaking (563 Arbutus Drive; 250-539-5599; www.kayakmayne island.com).

For general information about Mayne Island, consult the Mayne Island Chamber of Commerce (www.mayneislandchamber.ca).

> ### BENNETT BAY (GULF ISLANDS NATIONAL PARK RESERVE)
ACTIVITIES: *Cycling, paddling, picnicking, swimming, viewpoints, walking*

Bennett Bay, 7 km south of Village Bay on Fernhill Road via Miners Bay, is by far the most impressive park on Mayne and boasts the sandiest beach in the southern Gulf Islands. Part of the fledgling national park assembled through a joint initiative of the federal and B.C. governments, it is an ideal cycling destination. Once there, explore nearby Campbell Point (called Wilkes Point locally after the family that once owned it) on foot. I welcome opportunities like this, particularly if I'm cycling with friends, since it's hard to socialize and pedal at the same time. Now's the chance to chat while following the gentle trail that leads out to the point through a forest in which the boughs of ramrod-straight fir and loosey-goosey arbutus dance around each other.

From Campbell Point you can visualize how stampeders in the 1850s would row across the strait from there to Point Roberts, the closest spot on the Lower Mainland, on their way to the Cariboo goldfields in the central interior. In colonial times prospectors streamed into Victoria from around the world, then leapfrogged from Vancouver Island to Miners Bay and from there to the Lower Mainland. Unlike today's ramblers, they must have been in one hell of a hurry.

> **CAMPBELL BAY**

ACTIVITIES: *Picnicking, swimming, walking*

My runner-up favourite beach on the island features a long swath of sand and pebbles framed by well-worn driftwood logs mired to their knots, perfect backrests for taking in the expansive views due east across the Salish Sea. In summer, a tangle of overhanging salmonberry and snowbrush shrubs provide shade. As tempting as it is to just chill out, I recommend taking time to explore the intricately carved sandstone caves on the bay's north side. Reach Campbell Bay via a well-marked narrow trail that leads down an embankment on Waugh Road.

> **MAYNE ISLAND CIRCLE TOUR**

ACTIVITIES: *Cycling, driving*

Of all the southern Gulf Islands, Mayne is best suited for exploration by bike. Its hills are much less daunting than those on Galiano and its roads far less trafficked than on busy Salt Spring. You could circle Mayne in the course of a day trip, although I recommend that you extend your visit over at least one night in order to fully savour the experience. That way you can let elements of chance discovery influence the pace of your journey, such as an impromptu visit to the Mayne Island Glass Foundry, one of three art galleries near the Georgina Point Heritage Park on the northeastern tip of the island.

Most of the other Gulf Islands are long, skinny strips of land, but Mayne is somewhat circular, more like an amoeba in shape. Six major bays make inroads on its circumference at neat intervals. For cyclists, there's just enough distance between each to provide a break before taking up the journey once more. The same can be

> **THE ROYAL TREE**

. . . .

AN OCTAGONAL bench surrounds a tree, planted by King George VI and Queen Elizabeth on May 12, 1937, beside the federal dock in Miners Bay, a regal perch indeed from which to review the fleet in Active Pass.

said of the hills, although there are few tough climbs and mostly an equitable balance between ascents and descents. Many of the roads are shaded throughout the day, with the exception of those on the south coast, where open fields testify that farming was once the calling that brought many of the early settlers to Mayne. Overall riding distance around the island is about 30 km. Plan on taking five hours to accomplish this (easily half that by car). *Note:* Fresh water is a rare roadside commodity on all Gulf Islands, so you should conserve your resources. Places where you can top up your canteen include the public day-use park at Dinner Bay near the ferry terminal and several commercial locations in Miners Bay. Finding these places is not difficult. If you haven't already picked up a map of the island aboard the ferry that brought you to Mayne, get an island guide at the real-estate office next to the terminal as soon as you dock, or pick one up at the Village Mall in Miners Bay. At first, it's difficult to judge the scale of the distances between points on the map, but the short ride from the ferry dock at Village Bay to the historic settlement at Miners Bay helps put them in perspective. Once you've headed uphill from the ferry dock onto Village Bay Road, it's mostly downhill to Miners Bay. On your left as you go is the Helen Point Indian reserve, standing in tranquil contrast to development elsewhere on the island.

> **MOUNT PARKE REGIONAL PARK**
ACTIVITIES: *Hiking, viewpoints*
One of several protected areas on the island, this park offers a moderately strenuous, 2.2 kilometre, 45-minute hike to the top that's well worth it for the Gulf Island geography lesson provided at the summit's viewpoint. Find the park mid-island off Fernhill Road on Montrose Road. *Note:* Cyclists must leave their bikes at the trailed rack on Montrose Road.

> **OTHER ATTRACTIONS**
Georgina Point Heritage Park: Located 2.5 km east of Miners Bay on Georgina Point Road, this regional park's centrepiece is the Active Pass Light Station. Automated in the 1990s, the light keeper's home is now used for public functions. What remains undiminished

is the panoramic view across the Strait of Georgia. With the aid of binoculars you can easily pick out the Wall Centre in downtown Vancouver. If you come by too early to have a look out inside the lighthouse you can still enjoy inspecting the tide pools that dot the sandstone ledges beside the park's small but pristine beach.

Mayne Island Glass Foundry (563 Aya Point Road; 250-539-2002; www.mayneislandglass.com): Whimsical moulded starfish, seahorses, and slugs line the pathway to Mark Lauckner's glass studio, home to one of the largest collections of glass telegraph insulators in Canada. The foundry is open weekends between 11 AM and 4 PM. Find it near Georgina Point Heritage Park on the northeastern tip of the island.

Miners Bay: Flanking the Springwater Lodge for several blocks are numerous period homes with lovingly tended gardens, some of which also offer lodging. A garage, several grocery and hardware stores, a bakery, and an agency liquor store make Miners Bay an indispensable place to begin (and end) a visit to Mayne. Take some time to explore before moving on. If you're here in July or August, visit the former jail that now houses the Mayne Island Museum, open from 11 AM to 3 PM Friday to Sunday. It's two blocks up Fernhill Road from the Springwater, across from the Mayne Island Agricultural Hall, which hosts regular performances. In mid-August, the hall also hosts the oldest Fall Fair in the Gulf Islands.

St. Mary Magdalene Anglican Church: This 1897 church on Georgina Point Road is picturesque and worth a look inside. Explorer and author Warburton Pike gave a 180-kilogram boulder that he found on nearby Saturna Island to St. Mary Magdalene Church for use as a baptismal font. It wasn't his first such ecclesiastical gesture. Five years earlier, Pike had donated land on Mayne Island for the church. The sandstone marvel, consecrated on Easter Sunday, 1901, stands mounted on a cruciform pedestal inside the entrance to the church. Although sandstone formations characterize shorelines throughout the southern Gulf Islands, this boulder is unlike any I've ever seen. Embedded pebbles necklace its base, while its top is neatly defined by four wave-sculpted indentations, each as big as my cupped hands. You don't need to attend a service in order to view the font, although you'll certainly find yourself made welcome if you do. The pulpit has seen a lot of fire and brimstone pour forth, though that's not the way it's done any longer. Still, attending church on so-called Little Hell holds a certain burning irony, especially as Mayne Island's Anglican community named their house of worship after Christendom's penitent prostitute, Saint Mary Magdalene. On clear days, a warm red glow infuses the church interior as sunshine pours through a large, circular rose window. If nothing else, take time to sit on a strategically located bench beneath a pointed archway below the hill on which the wood-framed church presides, and watch the parade of boats and the occasional pod of killer whales through Active Pass.

> **DINING**

Sunny Mayne Bakery Café (Village Bay Road at the Mayne Street Mall; 250-539-2323; www.sunnymaynebakery.com): This cozy café is a good place to garner inside information on the island while ordering up some picnic goodies.

Springwater Lodge (400 Fernhill Road; 250-539-5521; www.springwaterlodge.com): Miners Bay is truly Mayne's centre, anchored by the Springwater Lodge beside the federal wharf. The lodge started life as the Collinson family's boarding house, was upgraded to the Grandview Lodge in the 1910s, and only later became the Springwater. In continuous operation for all this time, it now vies with the Lund Hotel on the Malaspina Peninsula for the distinction as the oldest on the B.C. coast north of Victoria. You can still get a pub meal, a drink, and, if needed in summer, a bed at the Springwater.

Oceanwood Country Inn (630 Dinner Bay Road; 250-539-5074; www.oceanwood.com): See the listing under Accommodation.

> **ACCOMMODATION**

Mayne has no public campground, but it boasts more highly rated bed and breakfasts (featuring, in many cases, much more than breakfast) than any other Gulf Island. When it comes time to rest your head (not to mention your tender keister if you've been cycle touring) there are over a dozen inns, cottages, and bed and breakfasts on the island, some of which provide bikes and kayaks for their guests, including:

Tinkerers' Retreat (417 Sunset Place; 250-539-2280; www.bb canada.com/133.html): Open May through October this B&B's modest appearance is overshadowed by awesome views of Active Pass from its flowery medicinal garden. This superb location in Miners Bay makes for a good starting point to explore nearby parks and beaches. Bike rentals available as well as oodles of free advice from the charming couple who have operated Tinkerers' for the past three decades.

Blue Vista Resort & Sea Kayaking (563 Arbutus Drive; 250-539-2463 or 1-877-535-2424; www.bluevistaresort.com): One of the rewards of staying here is that you can journey to Mayne car-free and arrange a complimentary ferry pickup courtesy of the Blue Vista whose cottages nestle in the forest above Bennett Bay Beach. As well as being the island's kayak centre, the resort also offers bike rentals.

Oceanwood Country Inn (630 Dinner Bay Road; 250-539-5074; www.oceanwood.com): The Oceanwood has a dozen guest rooms, many with soaker tubs and some with fireplaces. Enjoy country-style breakfasts plus an on-premises restaurant that serves elegant four-course meals. Two-day pedal-and-paddle packages are a specialty.

> ## 14

NORTH AND SOUTH
PENDER ISLANDS

· · · · ·

> **ACCESS:** The Penders are a 90-minute to 3-hour ferry ride from BC Ferries' Tsawwassen terminal, 40 km south of Vancouver, direct or via a transfer at Mayne Island or Swartz Bay on Vancouver Island. Most trips are a little more than two hours. For detailed sailing times, fares, and reservations, visit www.bcferries.com or call 1-888-223-3779.

> Seair Seaplanes (1-800-447-3247) offers three scheduled flights per day from Vancouver International Airport at $82 per person each way, arriving at North Pender's Port Washington government dock. Harbour Air (1-800-665-0212) offers three flights daily in summer and one in winter from downtown Vancouver ($89) or the airport ($78) to Poets Cove at Bedwell Harbour on South Pender.

> For transportation on the islands Pender Island Cab Company (250-629-2222) offers service by pre-arrangement, including trips to and from the ferry terminal.

> **WHY GO:** Unwind amid a mix of relaxed spas, restaurants, galleries, lodges, and B&Bs, and explore the islands' numerous scenic byways, pleasant forest trails, and quiet coves.

> **KEEP IN MIND:** There are just two ferry departures a day from Vancouver, so travel reservations are essential, and you should book accommodation well ahead to ensure you get what you want.

THE PENDER ISLANDS were split by a canal dredged across a narrow isthmus in 1902–03 and were only reconnected in 1955 by a one-lane wooden bridge. Many parts of North Pender are quite developed, with a golf course, an island-style strip mall, and the incongruous Magic Lake Estates subdivision. South Pender

Gowlland Point, South Pender Island

offers more farmland and forest and windswept headlands, but it's also home to the extravagant Poets Cove resort. Both islands have a fair amount of parkland and publicly accessible waterfront, and both have serious luxury comforts. Because of their central location, the Pender Canal's importance as a waterway, and the longstanding Canada Customs facility at the marina in Bedwell Harbour, the islands also have a strong boating tradition.

Visitors can take what they want from all the islands have to offer. If your desire is a little piece of Whistler Village in the Gulf Islands, Poets Cove is for you. If you want something that's out of the Islands' past, visit the funky cottages of Arcadia by the Sea. There are quiet luxury B&Bs, and there are campgrounds. If you want a fancy hotel lounge, there's Syrens at Poets Cove. If you want a basic working-class bar, there's the pub at Port Browning Marina Resort, known with affection by locals as the Brown Spot.

You can go hiking, cycling or kayaking during the day, get a massage at one of many spas before dinner, and then eat a fancy meal at the increasingly chic island restaurants. Or you can eat a leisurely brunch, go disc golfing in the afternoon, then grab a bottle of estate schonberger from the local winery, a picnic dinner from the bakery, and watch a summer evening's slow and quiet arrival at Thieves Bay, where killer whales frequently pass offshore in the late afternoon. Spend a whole day visiting the islands' many galleries and studios, or let many of them come to you at Hope Bay's Red Tree Gallery. Artists are also abundant at the Saturday morning Pender Island Farmers' Market, which takes place April through November amid a sparse forest of old-growth trees next to North Pender's beautiful barnlike timber community hall.

If you are simply not predisposed to exercise simply drive slowly along the intricate network of roads, past heritage churches and quiet cottages, to any number of quite welcome dead ends at the ocean. Despite the recent rush of development, much of Pender remains a bucolic throwback to the Gulf Islands' early colonial settlement.

The first scheduled ferry service to Pender began in the early 1900s on the *Iroquois*, which capsized in 1911, killing twenty-two.

In marked contrast to the quiet byways is the $40 million Poets Cove Resort and Spa, which opened in 2004. Depending on whom you ask, it's either the high-end tourist magnet the Penders require or an overly manicured blight on the landscape that should never have been permitted by the Islands Trust, the regional Gulf Islands government that has a special mandate to preserve and protect the area's unique character. The trust has lauded Poets Cove as a model of sensitive development. Aboriginal leaders have called it one of the worst desecrations of an Aboriginal burial ground in recent Canadian history. More than fifty corpses were disinterred during the development, and the Alberta-based developer was eventually charged violating the Heritage and Conservation Act.

On the one hand, the resort has helped create much-needed local employment. On the other, many residents throughout the Gulf Islands feel the increasing number of fancy time-share cottages and fractional ownership resorts like Poets Cove degrade the laid-back architectural character of the islands and undermine the community-minded volunteerism that helped sustain the islands through the twentieth century. For the original inhabitants of the Salish Sea, however, talk of preserving old colonial Gulf Island values has its own hollow ring. No matter whom you ask, it seems, the luxurious Poets Cove resort comes with a very high price tag.

The Pender Islands Handbook offers exhaustive detail on the islands' history and activities, such as hiking. The book's website, containing only updates and links, is at www.penderhandbook.com. Much information, including detailed printable maps, can be found online at the Pender Island Guide website: www.penderisland.info.

To explore the islands on two wheels, visit the Otter Bay Marina (250-629-3579), a short walk south of the ferry terminal, where you can rent bicycles and scooters for $12 and $25 per hour, respectively, with discounts for extended periods. Bicycles can also be rented at Poets Cove (250-629-2116; www.poetscove.com) for $10 per hour or $40 for eight hours.

If you'd rather get out on the water Kayak Pender Island (1-877-683-1746, www.kayakpenderisland.com), with locations at Poets Cove and Otter Bay marinas, offers three-hour guided tours for $55 and customizable full-day tours for $95 (three-person minimum). Rentals are available only to trained individuals. Additionally Poets Cove Marina (250-629-2111 or 1-866-888-2683) rents a variety of small sail-, paddle- and motor boats.

> **GULF ISLANDS NATIONAL PARK RESERVE**

ACTIVITIES: *Beachcombing, boating/paddling, camping, hiking, swimming, viewpoints, walking*

The Pender Islands didn't get a vast swath of new parkland when the Gulf Islands National Park Reserve (www.pc.gc.ca/pn-np/bc/gulf/index_e.asp) was officially created in 2003. Much of the Pender portion of the reserve came from the transfer of provincial parks, in lieu of the province's cash commitment to acquire new land. But that land has been consolidated, with the potential for further growth, and areas such as Loretta's Wood, Greenburn Lake, and Roesland have been added. There are seventeen vehicle campsites at the Prior Centennial portion of the reserve and eleven water-access or walk-in sites in the Beaumont/Mount Norman area.

The Beaumont waterfront campsite has old-growth timber and a beautiful spit, which can be reached in 30 minutes along a lovely and not-too-strenuous shoreline trail from Ainslie Point Road, on South Pender's northwestern tip. As well, three trails lead to the Mount Norman summit, which, at 244 metres is the highest point on Pender. One branches off from the trail to the Beaumont campsite and offers a strenuous 40-minute hike to the top. Another, more spectacular, trail is the first of two that rise from Canal Road along South Pender's northern shore. It's a 45-minute hike each way and involves a wee bit of clambering, but the views through old-growth trees across Plumper Sound to Saturna's Brown Ridge are spectacular.

More sedate walking can be found in the Roesland area, site of a former farm and a cottage resort that dates back to the 1920s. The 1908 Roe House is now home to the Pender Islands Museum. From the parking lot on South Otter Bay Road, it's a 10-minute walk down to the footbridge that leads to Roe Islet. A network of mainly gentle forest trails surrounds nearby Roe Lake.

> **SPAS**

Pender is spa-crazy. Poets Cove, of course, has the Susurrus Spa, with its outdoor sandstone steam cave behind a waterfall ($15, if that's all you partake in), as well as peels, waxes, and the like. The Shangri-la Oceanfront Bed and Breakfast (5909 Pirates Road; 1-877-629-2800; www.penderislandshangrila.com/spa.html) has a spa that offers massage for infants (10 minutes, $25), healing touch, past-life regression therapy, and treatments for animals. If you don't want to intrude on someone else's idiosyncratic resort experience, there's the well-appointed Spa at the Driftwood (24–4605 Bedwell Harbour Road; 250-629-9969), which offers more conventional treatments like deep-tissue massage (at a reasonable $80 per hour), as well as pedicures and tanning.

> **GALLERIES AND SHOPS**

The Penders may have little more than 2,000 permanent residents, but they manage among them to offer nearly 30 galleries and studios. For the one-stop shopper, there's the Red Tree Gallery, one of the attractions at Hope Bay, where community investors funded the redevelopment of the site of the historical Corbett and Son General

Store, which was destroyed by fire in 1998. (Hope Bay also features the home knick-knacks boutique Sladen's, as well as the bay's namesake café.) The Renaissance Gallery (3302 Port Washington Road) features glass, jewellery, and eclectic antiques, while the Blissmania Studio and Blood Star Gallery, near Gowlland Point at South Pender's eastern tip (9907 and 9909 Jennens Road, respectively) features glass, wood, painted and folk art. Studio hours vary, and many are closed during winter. For up-to-date info on the special events that take place during the year, look for the Pender Island Artists' Guide on ferries and at local stores.

> ## ARCHAEOLOGICAL HISTORY

The Penders have a rich history that is increasingly accessible to casual visitors. Archaeological work near the Pender Canal in the 1980s exposed an Aboriginal artifact that was dated as 5,170 years old. In 1993 the Pender Island Museum Society erected a plaque on the North Pender side of the bridge. The plaque explains that the isthmus was known as Xelisen, meaning *lying between*. What's now Poets Cove was a site known as Ste'yus, a name derived from the verb *to dry*, likely a reference to the practice of drying salmon at Hay Point, where an unoccupied Tsawout and Tseycum reserve is located. Bedwell Harbour was a preferred location for shellfish harvesting, and huge middens of crushed shells are a testament to the area's Aboriginal past. Both Aboriginal and more recent history are on display at the Pender Islands Museum (250-629-6935), which opened in 2005 on the Roesland portion of the Gulf Islands National Park Reserve. The museum created a permanent display of Aboriginal artifacts at the Pender Island Library (4407 Bedwell Harbour Road). As well, the *Self-Guided Historic Tour of the Pender Islands* is available at the museum and at the Driftwood Centre's Talisman Books and Gallery.

> ## OTHER ATTRACTIONS

Medicine Beach/Mortimer Spit: Take Canal Road south towards the bridge to South Pender, bear right at the junction with Aldridge Road, and continue along Aldridge until it joins Schooner Way and Wallace Road, where secondary access roads are visible to the left. Medicine Beach, on the south side of the canal, is a pleasant place for a picnic or a stroll when the tide isn't too high. Public access is prohibited to the adjoining protected marsh, but its presence adds to the interest for bird watchers. On the South Pender side of the bridge to the left of Canal Road is Mortimer Spit. Currents are strong, and the water's cold, but that doesn't stop kayakers and swimmers from joining the sunbathers at this unique, popular location. Both areas were important to the Aboriginal people, for medicinal plants and shellfish, and should be treated with care and respect.

Gowlland Point: At the very end of Gowlland Point Road, at South Pender's eastern tip, the beach and rocky outcroppings offer spectacular views of Saturna's Monarch Head and Mount Baker to the southeast, the U.S. San Juans to the south, the ships passing through busy Boundary Passage, harbour seals, perhaps an otter, and if you're lucky, some killer whales or even a Dall's porpoise. As you're heading towards the road's end, just before the junction with Jennens Road, there's an access to the Brooks Point Regional Park Reserve, for those who want to further explore the area.

Morning Bay Vineyard and Estate Winery (6621 Harbour Hill Drive, North Pender; 250-629-8351; www.morningbay.ca): This nascent operation is quickly establishing a good reputation for its wines. Bottles are in some of the best Vancouver and Victoria restaurants, and the brand-new winery facility, designed by Vancouver architect Walter Francl, is a very stylish modern building. Tastings are often available by appointment when the tasting room isn't formally open. Morning Bay is also making a tradition of Winestock, an afternoon music festival of excellent rock, folk, and blues on the Labour Day weekend.

Golf Island Disc Park (250-629-6494; www.discgolfisland.com): Frisbee golf's devotees see it as a serious sport, not merely a hippie pastime. Visitors to the challenging twenty-seven-hole course on Pender, which is regarded as one of the best in Canada and hosts numerous tournaments, may well agree. They can form their own opinion for the price of a Frisbee on this otherwise free course in a public park.

Pender Island Golf and Country Club (2305 Otter Bay Road, North Pender; 250-629-6659; www.penderislandgolf.com): A pleasant and very affordable nine-hole public golf course, established in 1937, simulates an eighteen-hole course with the help of alternative tee boxes. There are power carts and rental clubs, the nineteenth-hole Chippers Café and Lounge, and a little stone bridge that echoes golf's most famous bridge at St. Andrews.

> ## DINING

The Hope Bay Café (7–4301 Bedwell Harbour Road; 250-629-6668; www.hopebaycafe.com): This oceanfront eatery offers lunch, dinner, and weekend brunch in a warm room with huge windows that put high tide right at your feet. Savour excellent comfort food in a relaxed environment.

The Pistou Grill (Driftwood Centre, 4605 Bedwell Harbour Road; 250-629-3131; www.pistougrill.ca): Alsace-trained chef and owner Pierre Delacôte ran the kitchen at Vancouver's Seasons in the Park and has cooked for Pierre Trudeau, Bill Clinton, and Boris Yeltsin. Come here for casual lunches and more serious dinners, both at reasonable prices.

Poet's Cove Resort and Spa (9801 Spalding Road, South Pender; 250-629-2100 or 1-888-512-7638; www.poetscove.com): Both the Aurora Restaurant and Syrens Lounge serve upscale, West Coast–themed dishes—Gulf Islands lamb is a specialty—with views over Bedwell Bay. For those who wish to overnight at this resort, prices range from $169 for a room in the lodge to $619 for a three-bedroom executive cottage.

> ## ACCOMMODATION

Gulf Islands National Park Reserve: There are seventeen vehicle campsites at the Prior Centennial portion of the reserve, and eleven water access or walk-in sites at the Beaumont/Mount Norman area (see above).

Sahhali Bed & Breakfast (5915 Pirates Road, North Pender; 1-888-724-4254 or 250-629-3756; www.pender-island-bedandbreakfast.com): Two luxurious suites and a nearby cottage offer cliffside views from very private decks, outdoor hot tubs and in-room breakfasts for $145 to $345 depending on suite, season, and length of stay.

Oceanside Inn (4230 Armadale Road, North Pender; 1-800-601-3284 or 250-629-6691; www.penderisland.com): Enjoy large, well-appointed rooms, private hot tubs, shared breakfasts overlooking Navy Channel, and charming hosts. Expect to pay $159 to $239, plus $20 for one-night stays. This inn is open April to October only.

> ## 15

SALT SPRING ISLAND

· · · · ·

> ACCESS: Depending on whether you catch a non-stop or an extended one- to three-stop sailing, Salt Spring Island is a 90-minute to 3-hour ferry ride from BC Ferries' Tsawwassen terminal, 40 km south of Vancouver. For detailed sailing times, fares, and no-charge reservations (crucial in summer months), contact www.bcferries. com or call 1-888-223-3779. The ferry to Salt Spring from Vancouver arrives at Long Harbour. From Swartz Bay on Vancouver Island, the ferry arrives at Fulford Harbour on the island's south side. Yet a third ferry to Salt Spring sails from Crofton south of Nanaimo on Vancouver Island and lands at Vesuvius a short distance northwest of Ganges.

Alternatively both Saltspring Air (1-877-537-9880; www. saltspringair.com) and Seair (1-800-447-3247; www.seairseaplanes. com) offer three scheduled flights per day from Vancouver.

Ground transportation is available from Ganges Faerie (250-537-6758; www.gangesfaerie.com), which offers shuttle service between all three ferry terminals as well as several island points including Ruckle Provincial Park), Salt Spring Rentals (250-647-0058; www.saltpring.com/rentals), where you can rent cars, trucks and scooters, and Silver Shadow Taxi (250-537-3030).

> WHY GO: Sheltered by the rain shadow of the Vancouver Island Ranges, Salt Spring enjoys as much sunshine as the Okanagan and only half the yearly precipitation that falls on Vancouver.

> KEEP IN MIND: By the very nature of its size, Salt Spring provides opportunities for more adventuring than can easily fit into a weekend visit.

WELCOME TO the fat cat of the Gulf Islands. Because Salt Spring is the biggest, most populous of all—as well as possessed of arguably the most poetic name—its pace is busy for a Gulf Island, but at least you're still a ferry or float plane ride away from city life. Quietly riding along with no one to rush you, pausing beside a beach to sniff the air, exploring a heritage farm where trails lead down to the sea—this is Salt Spring Island. If you're looking to get a feel for the island's soul, the two provincial parks on the southern half of the island are must-sees: Mount Maxwell Provincial Park for its lofty views and Ruckle Provincial Park for its heritage seaside perspective.

Wendy Hartnett of Island Gourmet Safaris (250-537-4118; www. islandgourmetsafaris.com) leads 6-hour historical, artistic, and gourmet food-and-wine van tours of the island Wednesdays through Fridays from mid-June to mid-September.

Explore Salt Spring and a host of surrounding islands by sea kayak with Andale Kayaking (1484 North Beach Road; 250-537-0700), Island Escapades (163 Fulford-Ganges Road; 250-537-2553 or 1-888-529-2567; www.islandescapades.com), Salt Spring Kayaking (2923 Fulford-Ganges Road; 250-653-4222; www.saltspring kayaking.com), and Sea Otter Kayaking (Salt Spring Marina in Ganges; 1-877-537-5678; www.saltspring.com/kayaking), all of which offer tours and rentals. Sea Otter will even deliver kayaks anywhere on the island.

For a copy of the Salt Spring Island *Visitors Guide*, visit www. saltspringtourism.com. Make the Salt Spring Island Visitor Info Centre your first stop on arrival in Ganges (121 Lower Ganges Road; 250-537-5252 or 1-866-216-2936). You'll also find good maps in the *Gulf Islander* visitors' guide (Driftwood Publishing; www.gulf islands.net).

> **BEDDIS BEACH**

ACTIVITIES: *Paddling, Swimming*
Beddis Beach, 10 km southeast of Ganges on Beddis Road at its intersection with Lionel Crescent, is one of my two favourite beaches on the island, along with Grandma's in Ruckle Park (see below). Part of the enjoyment of getting here by road is the rolling route that

Beddis Beach, Salt Spring Island

leads past farms and homes in a variety of styles, old and new. Once you've reached the beach, which simply involves a short walk along a treed lane, head to the north end for a glimpse of a grand property whose retaining wall lines the backshore. Although water temperatures on the west side of the island at Vesuvius are touted as warmer, nothing matches the view of Salt Spring's unspoiled extremities and surrounding waterways than from this sand, shell, and gravel beach. Offshore, a steady parade of boats enter and leave Ganges Harbour, making their way along Prevost and North Pender islands to the east. Those with paddling in mind will find Beddis a convenient place to launch or a prime destination to keep in mind when journeying from Ganges or Ruckle Park.

> **MOUNT MAXWELL PROVINCIAL PARK** &

ACTIVITIES: *Climbing, hiking, picnicking, viewpoints, walking*
To get to Mount Maxwell take Cranberry Road, which leads west from the Fulford-Ganges Road and follow the signs that point the way to the park. Cranberry Road feeds into Maxwell Road, and the

climb from here to the top of the mountain along a gravel road is challenging. Before you reach the summit the road passes through a stand of elegant old-growth grand fir and Garry oak that has been set aside as an ecological reserve.

From the top of Mount Maxwell the whole of the valley below on the south end of Salt Spring is revealed, running across the island from Fulford Harbour to Burgoyne Bay (named for the captain of the *Ganges* and included within park boundaries). With luck you'll arrive on a clear day when you can survey the other Gulf Islands, Vancouver Island, and the San Juans, capped off by the always astonishing sight of Mount Baker rising above the plains of western Washington.

Mind your step up here, as a series of cliffs drop straight down the south face of Mount Maxwell. Venturing out on them is dangerous without the proper climbing equipment, but there are a number of safe locations near the viewpoint here on Baynes Peak, the top of Mount Maxwell. Pick a ledge on which to stretch out for a picnic or to soak up some rays in the shelter of the stone walls. You may be treated to an aerial display by groups of ravens catching updrafts off the face of the mountain or turkey vultures circling above. Hanggliders are similarly inspired. Although it isn't the highest peak on Salt Spring (that distinction belongs to Bruce Peak to the south, at 709 m), Mount Maxwell combines easy accessibility with one of the best views of any on the Gulf Islands. There are 6 km of hiking trails here, many of them quite old and not all that well marked.

Note: There's also hiking on 602-m Mount Tuam and on Bruce Peak. From Fulford Harbour, take Musgrave Road to reach them both, although eventually by different trails leading north off Musgrave to Bruce and south to Tuam. You'll find great views from both down onto the Saanich Inlet and peninsula, and across Satellite Channel to Cowichan Bay.

> ## RUCKLE PROVINCIAL PARK &

ACTIVITIES: *Camping, cycling, hiking, picnicking, running, sea kayaking, swimming, viewpoints, walking, windsurfing*

At 486 ha (half the size of Stanley Park), Ruckle, located 25 km south of the BC Ferries terminal at Long Harbour, is the largest park on any of the Gulf Islands.

A popular conception of the early settlement of Canada by Europeans has them arriving on the Atlantic coast and steadily spreading westwards across the land. Although this scenario is largely true, certain impatient settlers couldn't wait. Long before the Canadian Pacific Railway was built 1886, they came on ahead by boat via the Pacific, some intending to seek their fortune in the Cariboo gold rush and others to establish present-day Victoria at the invitation of colonial governor James Douglas. By the 1850s several groups of settlers had moved to Salt Spring with the intention of farming. They were a mixed bunch, and their numbers included tapped-out miners returning from the Cariboo who had originally arrived from Australia, plus a group of black American families Douglas invited north from California to escape discrimination. (Although there had been permanent Native communities on some of the other Gulf Islands, Salt Spring was used on a purely seasonal basis by the Coast Salish travelling from their home bases on Vancouver Island.)

Among the new arrivals were Henry Ruckle and his young son Daniel. Together they put down roots on Salt Spring Island's southern tip, establishing the province's first family farm in 1872—or so says the information posted by BC Parks on the Ruckle property. Members of the family are still working 80 ha of cleared, rolling land surrounding the original buildings. Apple orchards dominate in places, testimony that this crop was a profitable one for the Ruckles long before the Okanagan Valley opened up. Produce was shipped to markets in Victoria and New Westminster from nearby Fulford Harbour. Generations of sheep have been keeping the ground below the trees free of windfalls; they still manicure the green growth in nearby pastures.

In June of 1974, a transfer agreement was reached whereby the provincial government received property from the Ruckle family to be used as public parkland. In the subsequent years, the 9-km road from Fulford Harbour has been paved and now presents an 30-minute ride by bicycle.

Salt Spring Island is the most popular Gulf Island with travellers, especially during summer months, and Ruckle is the largest park on any of these islands; as such, it draws a considerable number of visitors every year. Most of the 8 km of shoreline around the park is sloping rock, with only one major beach (on the bay in front of the Ruckle farm).

Ruckle is a surprising park in many ways. Arriving visitors enter what looks like a working farm. Vintage wooden buildings dot the clearing, including a beautifully preserved Queen Anne–style home still occupied by George Ruckle and his family. There are descriptive markers, some with historical photos, affixed to each building. It's easy to see how the spread grew from the original farmhouse to include a building for every use: creamery, chicken coop, machine shop, barn, and a host of other buildings served the farm. All have been well maintained. The cream-yellow paint on the old house and the reds on the barn wall have weathered so that in autumn they blend perfectly with the seasonal shades of the surrounding forest.

Another surprise is the tall stands of original Douglas-fir, arbutus, and Garry oak ringing the property. As you might expect on a century-old farm, trails lead off in many directions under the shelter of the forest. One long path leads from the orchards down to a small bay, where one of the island's best public beaches—Grandma's—lies. Prop yourself on a log while you marvel at the marine activity in Swanson Channel. North Pender Island lies directly across the waves. From the bay, a long winding path leads through the forest beside the ocean to the campsites, beach, and picnic areas. You can ride your bike for much of the distance and walk it over the rockier stretches. Pieces of curled arbutus bark litter the forest floor like a scattering of cinnamon sticks. The size of the trees is breathtaking, and their shaping by salt spray suggests the strength of winter storms.

> ## ST. MARY LAKE WATERSHED LANDS
ACTIVITIES: *Cycling, running, walking*
Drive up, up, up to Channel Ridge, as much for the enjoyment of the soft trails as for the viewpoints over St. Mary Lake and across Trincomali Channel to Galiano Island. An elaborate network of pathways, some better marked than others, interlace through the open woods. Study the trail map posted beside an imposing cement water tank, then strike out on either of the trails that lead past it. Allow an hour or more.

Blackburn Meadows Golf Club (269 Blackburn Road; 250-537-1707; www.blackburnmeadows.com): This nine-hole, executive target-style course bills itself as the numero uno organic golf course in Canada. What did you expect from the island that bills itself as the organic capital of B.C.?

Fall Colour: One of the most pleasant aspects of visiting here in autumn is not just the swaths of golds and reds but the fact that with so little road traffic you can take your time and leaf peep to your heart's content. Broadleaf and vine maple compete with arbutus heavily laden with clusters of red berries. All of this is augmented by garden hues that adorn roadside homes. Everywhere you look there are signs that residents take great care about the appearance of their properties. Although the most dramatic displays occur along Fulford-Ganges Road between Mount Maxwell and the southern harbour, just about any road will satisfy, including Walker Hook Road.

Salt Spring Island Cheese Company (285 Reynolds Road; 250-653-2300): David and Nancy Wood's goat and sheep cheeses run the gamut from soft to hard, including Camembert-style, feta, Marcella, and my personal favourite, thick-rinded, russet-hued Montaña. Take a self-guided tour of the farm and tasting room near Fulford Harbour, or stop by their stand at the Saturday Farmers' Market in Ganges.

> **DINING**

Embe Bakery (Ganges; 250-537-5611): The quality of a town is often reflected in its breads, not to mention cinnamon buns and chicken pies, which in this case deserve full marks.

Salt Spring Inn (132 Lower Ganges Road; 250-537-9339 &): There are numerous good places to choose from in Ganges. I like this place's pedigree. Although the inn is relatively new, the owner's roots run deep in the local dining scene.

Seaside Restaurant (795 Vesuvius Bay Road; 250-537-2249): Hands down, the Seaside offers the best tableside views of the Salish Sea on the island. Intimate, even romantic, in a locals kind of way, the modestly fronted exterior sits adjacent to both the Crofton ferry slip and the island's warmest beach.

Ruckle Provincial Park (see above): Ruckle's seventy-eight campsites are of the walk-in rather than drive-in variety. There is parking for RVs with eight campsites immediately adjacent. Short trails run from a series of parking lots to Beaver Point, where there are individual and group campsites on cleared embankments next to the ocean. The best campsites are located at the west end of Beaver Point. Lie in your tent at night and watch the ferries passing, lit up like floating hotels. A self-registering camping fee is charged.

Salt Springs Spa Resort (1460 North Beach Road; 250-537-4111 or 1-800-665-0039; www.saltspringspa.com): Self-contained Gothic arch chalets overlook Trincomali Channel with Galiano Island in the far distance. Pick up everything you need in Ganges and head here for the rest of your stay, where the staff may have to pry you out of the mineral spring soaker tub to get you to leave.

Hastings House Country Estate (160 Upper Ganges Road; 250-537-2362 or 1-800-661-9255; www.hastingshouse.com): When a memorable time is called for and money is no object, spend a night here between mid-March to mid-November—preferably two. Rooms, suites, and cottages are nestled within a forest canopy and surrounded by gardens and sheep-grazed meadows. Optional dining choices range from breakfast hampers to weekend Dungeness crab trap-and-feast excursions with the chef. There's no better reason to dress up than to dine in the romantic intimacy of this English-style country estate. One caveat: the cozy ambience comes at a premium. *Note*: Book visits to the on-site spa in advance.

> A NOTE ON THE SPELLING OF THE ISLAND'S NAME

ACCORDING TO tradition, the name is two words, Salt Spring, a spelling that dates back to the nineteenth century. In 1905, when the Geographic Board of Canada conducted a study of place names across the country, they decided on simplicity by tidying double-barrelled place names into one-word forms. Long-time residents still spell it with two words to differentiate themselves from more recent arrivals.

> 16

SATURNA ISLAND

. . . . .

> ACCESS: Saturna Island is a 2- to 3-hour ferry ride from BC Ferries'
Tsawwassen terminal, 40 km south of Vancouver, via a transfer at
Galiano or Mayne Island, or Swartz Bay on Vancouver Island. For
detailed sailing times, fares, and reservations, visit www.bcferries.
com or call 1-888-223-3779.

Seair (1-800-447-3247; www.seairseaplanes.com) offers three
scheduled flights per day from Vancouver International Airport at
$82 per person each way. There is no ground transportation for hire
on Saturna, although the Saturna Island Family Estate Winery and
Saturna Island Lodge run shuttles.

> WHY GO: Saturna is the quietest of the southern Gulf Islands, with
spectacular views and walks from Mount Warburton Pike, and it
boasts the largest portion of Gulf Islands National Park Reserve with
extensive access to shoreline.

> KEEP IN MIND: There are generally two departures a day from
Vancouver, except on Sundays when there is only an evening boat.
The weekday morning boat requires a 6:30 AM check-in at Tsawwassen for a three-hour trip via Swartz Bay. Always reserve during peak
periods, and remember that although there is no charge for making
reservations on Gulf Island routes, there is a $25 fee for unclaimed
reservations. *Note:* There are no camping facilities on Saturna.

ALL THE Gulf Islands are different. But among Galiano, Mayne,
two Penders and Saturna, Saturna is more different. If you
take the big Gulf Islands boat out of Tsawwassen to Saturna,
you can only do it once on any given day. And you have to get off at
Mayne or sometimes Galiano, and wait, and often wait some more,

130

Winter Cove, Saturna Island

and then take the wedding cake–like *M.V. Mayne Queen*, possibly to Pender and then back again, and by the time the captain announces the near presence of Saturna's Lyall Harbour you could have driven to Kamloops or flown most of the distance to Toronto. But there's something about this ferry trip that helps to shed the stress of the city so that once you've arrived you're already attuned to the island's slow rhythm.

Some residents want better ferry service. Others know that the unique character of Saturna is defined by its isolation. As one long-time islander has wryly observed, "The quality of your insularity is in inverse proportion to the quality of your transportation system."

As such, Saturna has remained pretty rural, with just 359 official permanent residents and not much in the way of man-made attractions. But it has a well-stocked store next to a great café, a waterfront pub with unbeatable sunsets, and a beautifully located bistro overlooking the Gulf Islands' first winery, all in service of a wealth of quiet beaches and hikes that at their best are astonishingly beautiful.

Feral goats range across the spectacular bluff east of Mount Warburton Pike, and killer whales run close along the rocky shore where the tide rips past East Point. At Winter Cove, a network of trails leads to the site of tidewater cascading through narrow Boat Pass. A ruined stone house and the remnants of a sandstone quarry enliven an afternoon spent on the expansive sand beach at Taylor Point. The island is a kayaker's paradise.

Historically, on a largely undeveloped island where everyone waves at everyone else because everyone knows everyone else, some residents have been averse to parks, imagining them as a magnet for fire-starting, garbage-leaving strangers. Ironically, the lack of development made Saturna a major target when the federal government began acquiring land for Gulf Islands National Park Reserve, which was formally established in 2003. Now, nearly half of Saturna's 3,422 ha is part of the park reserve. Although there are plans to develop some modest camping facilities at Narvaez Bay, conservation remains the overriding concern. For the time-being, however, there are no camping facilities.

On July 1, 2007, Saturna-bound *Robertson II*, the last schooner licensed to fish on the Grand Banks, ran aground near Winter Cove. Its wreck may be seen north of the ferry as it approaches Saturna.

Saturna developed as two communities—a collection of cottages near the East Point lighthouse and homes at Lyall Harbour and nearby Boot Cove. They weren't connected until the so-called missing link road was built north of Lyall Harbour in 1959. The ferry arrives at the entrance to Lyall Harbour where there is a pub, a modest store and gas station, a public dock, and a community hall. These are at the western end of East Point Road, which runs down into the Lyall Harbour valley, across the island and then along Saturna's northern shore to East Point, where it becomes Tumbo Channel Road. It's 16 km from the dock to East Point. About 2 km from the dock, at the site of the Saturna General Store and Café and the expansive new Saturna Recreation and Cultural Centre (also home to the local Parks Canada office and a medical clinic), Naravez Bay Road branches off to the east while Harris Road goes south, up towards Staples Road and Mount

Warburton Pike and then down to the Saturna Family Estate Winery and Thomson Park. A bit more than 5 km along East Point Road, Winter Cove Road branches off to the west.

Saturna Sea Kayaking (121 Boot Cove Road; 250-539-5553; www.saturnaseakayaking.com) offers rentals, lessons, and tours close to the ferry dock. Basic single kayak rentals are $30 for three hours and $100 for three days. Basic two-hour lessons are $40 per person, $20 for children under twelve.

An excellent map and detailed information on Saturna history and businesses is at saturnatourism.com.

> ### SATURNA LAMB BARBECUE

The barbecue has been held each July 1 since 1950, when it began at Saturna Beach on the Campbell farm as a school picnic. Today, at Hunter Field near Winter Cove, two dozen lambs are barbecued Argentine-style, flayed on iron crosses arrayed around an open fire, with the head cook whipping them with swatches of vinegar-drenched mint. There are sack races for the kids, tug-o-wars, and ladies nail-driving, but sadly no more pig-diapering contests for newlyweds. Boaters come from all over the Pacific Northwest, and 1,100 tickets are regularly sold for this community fundraiser.

> ### EAST POINT

ACTIVITIES: *Beachcombing, boating, paddling, swimming*
The site of the East Point Lighthouse is a wonderful place to spend an afternoon, swimming in the bracing water off of Shell Beach opposite Tumbo Island, listening to sea lions bellow out towards

> ## TERROR ON THE COAST

IN THE EARLY 1860s at Murder Point below Brown Ridge, a settler and his daughter who had camped for the night were killed by local Indians. In response, a British vessel shelled the Lamalchi village on Kuper Island. Five men, widely believed to be innocent, were eventually tried and executed.

Boiling Reef, watching ships round the corner from Boundary Passage as they head towards Vancouver, clambering over the rocks to marvel at the force of the tides just offshore, spotting oystercatchers as they look for shellfish, marvelling at the sight of Mount Baker in the distance, and waiting for the sun to set to the north. In summer, orcas are often seen just offshore, and in fall you may occasionally see salmon swimming close along the rock faces that plunge into the ocean on the southern edge of the park.

> MOUNT WARBURTON PIKE

ACTIVITIES: *Nature observation, viewpoints, walking*

The view from across the U.S. San Juan Islands and the southern tip of Vancouver Island to the Olympic Mountains is remarkable. Mount Warburton Pike, at 497 metres, is the second-highest point in the Gulf Islands, and on a clear day, you can see Mount Rainier in the far distance, more than halfway to Oregon. There is no better walk in the Southern Gulf Islands than the 3-km trip east along Brown Ridge. Eagles and hawks soar below you. Cliff swallows dip and dive around you. Feral goats, which have ranged across the bluff for most of a century, are a frequent sight.

The goats have created a lattice of trails across Brown Ridge, and although they are narrow and the bluff is steep, walking is easy along

> PIKE'S PEAK

. . . .

WARBURTON PIKE came to Saturna Island in 1884, at twenty-three, from Dorset, and bought land below the mountain that bears his name, where the Campbell farm and the Saturna vineyard are now located. It was his occasional winter home while he explored the far north. Pike wrote two books (*The Barren Ground of Northern Canada* and *Through the Subarctic Forest*), made modest sums as a placer gold miner near Dease Lake, and returned to England in 1915 to fight in the Great War. Biographies of his life, which is fictionalized in the epic novel *Vancouver*, often conflict, but it's commonly written that upon arriving in England he was rejected as unfit for service, walked into the ocean up to his neck, and plunged a pocket knife into his heart.

the top, where winter gales have bent many first-growth coastal Douglas-firs and Garry oaks into fantastic shapes. Although a right-of-way has been granted to the park reserve across the top of the ridge, visitors should be aware that it crosses private property, and much of the bluff is part of the Campbell farm, which can be seen below.

The Campbell family also sold and donated the foreshore of their farm to the park, expecting that a circle hike might eventually be created, but at present there are no trails and limited access along the shoreline of Plumper Sound. The park reserve's section of the beach at Taylor Point, where the ruined Taylor family's stone house is located, is currently accessed only by water.

On the 5-km drive up in the morning, or down in the evening, deer are abundant along the roadside, and pileated woodpeckers will likely dance ahead of your car and into the trees. To get to the summit, take Harris Road up from the Saturna General Store for half a kilometre, then turn left at the Parks Canada sign onto Staples Road, which ends at the top.

> **WINTER COVE**

ACTIVITIES: *Boating, paddling, picnicking, walking*
Winter Cove is a former provincial marine park that is now part of the Gulf Islands National Park Reserve. There are public toilets and picnic tables, and a lovely network of forested trails provides a short walk out to Boat Pass, where the tides pour through the narrow opening between Saturna and Samuel islands. Although the footing can be dangerous, the tidepools and sandstone formations between Boat Pass and Russell Reef are well worth exploring. There is also an intriguing tidal marsh along the beach near the park entrance.

> **THOMSON PARK**

ACTIVITIES: *Boating, paddling, swimming, walking*
This park, named for the Thomson family, which bought the land in the 1930s and developed a modest resort of cottages along Saturna Beach, was also the site of Saturna's first post office. When the property was developed as a subdivision and winery, the original buildings were moved or demolished. The park has a lovely sand and pebble beach from which to watch the sun go down over North Pender Island.

> OTHER ATTRACTIONS

Narvaez Bay: José María Narváez was the first European known to have explored the Strait of Georgia, in 1791 in the *Santa Saturnina*, for which Saturna itself is named. The southern shore of the bay that bears his name, now part of the park reserve, includes two small coves with pebble beaches, some picnic benches, and pit toilets and is the potential location of Saturna's first campsites. The bay is shady late in the day, and less spectacular than other Saturna points of interest, but a pleasant destination nevertheless.

Harvest Festival: In mid-September, the Saturna Island Family Estate Winery hosts a harvest festival, with excellent food and music, at the site of the vineyard bistro between the general store and Thomson Park.

Lyall Creek: A lovely forest trail runs from the mouth of Lyall Creek in the valley just north of the general store, along the creek and up to Narvaez Bay Road. The creek was recently restored to allow access for spawning salmon, and it's one of the few salmon-bearing creeks in the Gulf Islands.

Artists' studios: There are just a handful of artists' studios on Saturna, including the Jack Campbell Gallery and Studio (240 East Point Road; 250-539-5810), Donna-Fay Digance's Dreamscapes Studio (121 East Point Road; 250-539-5577), and Karen Muntean's Gallery Rosa (111 East Point Road; 250-539-2866). Gallery Rosa, a wee purple shed by the road just above the dock, is usually open on Sundays when the ferry boards; other studios may be visited by calling ahead.

> DINING

Saturna Point Pub (102 East Point Road; 250-539-5725): The food's good at the Saturna Point Pub next to the ferry dock, and the sunset on the waterfront patio is unbeatable.

Saturna Island Family Estate Winery Bistro (8 Quarry Trail; 250-539-5139): This bistro is open daily for lunch, from Easter to Thanksgiving. The winery was the first established in the Gulf Islands and grows a wide range of grapes—mainly pinot gris, pinot noir, and gewürztraminer. There's a tasting bar, of course, and vineyard tours are available by arrangement, but the real pleasure here is to sit on the patio over lunch and drink in the glorious view across the vineyard and Navy Channel to South Pender and Blunden islands.

Saturna Café (101 Naravez Bay Road; 250-539-2936): The Saturna Café offers fabulous, affordable food from Hubertus Surm at this café adjoining the Saturna General Store. It is open for lunch and dinner, and dinner reservations are recommended.

> ## ACCOMMODATION

Breezy Bay Bed and Breakfast (131 Payne Road; 250-539-5957; www.saturnacan.net/breezy): The century-old Payne farmhouse on the site of a former free school is Saturna's most uniquely charming B&B. The beds are less luxurious than they are old, but there's a wonderfully idiosyncratic library, and it costs as little as $70 for a double.

Sandy Bay Bed and Breakfast (449 East Point Road; 250-539-2641; www.sandybaysaturna.com): This B&B offers a great breakfast and island hospitality, with a lovely safe sandy beach on your doorstep. Expect to pay $100 per night based on double occupancy, with $10 per day off for repeat guests, two-room bookings, seven-day stays, and winter visits.

Saturna Lodge (130 Payne Road; 250-539-2254; www.saturna.ca): The small lodge keeps changing hands but has recently reopened under new management, and its dining room, the Dejavu Seafood and Steakhouse, serves dinner seven days a week.

VANCOUVER ISLAND

VICTORIA

SOOKE

COWICHAN VALLEY

NANAIMO

GABRIOLA ISLAND

COMOX VALLEY

> 17

VICTORIA

. . . . .

> ACCESS: BC Ferries' regular service from Tsawwassen terminal, 40 km south of Vancouver, to Swartz Bay, 32 km north of Victoria, runs every hour in summer and every two hours in winter, with some supplemental sailings during busy off-season periods. For details and reservations, visit www.bcferries.com or call 1-888-223-3779.

Pacific Coach Lines (1-800-661-1725) offers downtown-to-downtown service for $37.50 each way including the ferry fare.

Harbour Air (1-800-665-0212; www.harbour-air.com) and West Coast Air (604-606-6888; www.westcoastair.com) offer scheduled flights approximately every 30 minutes during the day to Victoria's Inner Harbour from downtown on Coal Harbour and from Vancouver International Airport's seaplane terminal for about $120 per person each way. HeliJet (1-800-665-4354; www.helijet.com) offers similarly scheduled flights from its Coal Harbour terminal and the airport, with adult one-way fares ranging from $124 to $229. Travel time for all trips is 30 to 35 minutes.

> WHY GO: Head across the strait for Victoria's laid-back downtown rich with Victorian and Edwardian architecture; scenic Inner Harbour and shoreline; pleasant parks, gardens, and neighbourhoods; and historical attractions.

> KEEP IN MIND: Victoria is extremely busy during the summer tourist season, when advance travel and hotel bookings are highly recommended.

VICTORIA IS a very comfortable small city, and, I think, the best place in B.C. to experience the vestiges of the province's early colonial history. It's easy to walk around the downtown core, which has largely maintained its low-rise heritage character. The city hasn't been immune to the province's development boom—mid-rise towers are appearing on the fringes of downtown and on the far side of the Inner Harbour, western suburbs are sprawling, and social dislocation is evident on the streets—but the city hasn't been overwhelmed by the change that has affected Vancouver. Victoria is still a comforting trip back in time.

Whether you're taking afternoon tea at the Fairmont Empress Hotel (see under Accommodation), savouring the sweet possibilities in the 1891 Rogers' Chocolates storefront (913 Government Street), or cruising the Fort Street antique shops on your way out to Craigdarroch Castle, the city remains full of century-old pleasures.

As well, Victoria's more modern amenities are increasing in number. Restaurants have become more diverse and sophisticated. Although some city festivals and cultural institutions have faltered, June's JazzFest International (www.jazzvictoria.ca), August's Fringe Festival of theatre (www.intrepidtheatre.com), and the quintessentially Victorian Classic Boat Festival (www.classicboatfestival.ca) on the Labour Day Weekend are reliably satisfying events. There are also many outlying attractions, easily reached by bus, taxi, or car. In some cases, if you're at all energetic, a bicycle is an attractive way to get around, both on winding seaside roads and on the famed Galloping Goose Trail (www.gallopinggoosetrail.com), particularly the route between Victoria and Sidney.

No Victoria attraction is more internationally famous than Butchart Gardens, which draws more than a million tourists a year to the Brentwood Bay area, but there are other paths less travelled, like those at Fort Rodd Hill and the Fisgard Lighthouse, two adjoining historical sites. The drive out to Mount Douglas Park, through Oak Bay and Cordova Bay, is as lovely as the destination. If you've taken the ferry from Vancouver, on your way home it's well worth wandering the charming rural back roads of Saanich in search of farm-fresh produce or an ice cream by the water.

The main draw, however, remains the city itself. Francis Mawson Rattenbury's Parliament Buildings, the Empress Hotel, and the Inner Harbour provide a grand centrepiece. The residential architecture, best exemplified by Samuel Maclure's craftsman homes, offers a rich background. In the charming Victorian neighbourhood of James Bay, just behind the legislature, you can stop at Emily Carr House (207 Government Street), a modest shrine to the pioneering

Historic Victoria, Inner Harbour

B.C. painter. Beacon Hill Park, just south and east of the Empress, offers Garry oak meadows and manicured duck ponds, and perhaps an impromptu noon-hour summer concert. Windswept Dallas Road is just beyond the park, with rocky beaches below, kite surfers over the water, and the glacier-capped Olympic Peninsula's Hurricane Ridge in the distance, across Juan de Fuca Strait.

To explore the city by bike consider Cycle BC (747 Douglas Street; 1-866-380-2453; www.cyclebc.ca), which rents bikes, scooters, and motorcycles year-round. For information on cycling around Victoria, including a copy of the Vancouver Island Cycle Map and Guide, contact Tourism Victoria at 1-800-663-3883 or visit www.tourismvictoria.com.

The Victoria Harbour Ferry (250-708-0201; www.harbourferry.com) runs daily from March to October and on weekends year-round. Rates are $4 for harbour hops, $20 for tours (contingent on season and weather). Whale tours are ubiquitous in Victoria; dozens of boats frequently crowd the small pods of killer whales that spend their summers among the Gulf Islands. Among the tours, which generally cost about $80, SeaKing Adventures is highly regarded, with Captain Ron operating a small customized motor boat out of Fisherman's Wharf (Pier 4; 250-381-4173; www.seaking.ca).

For general travel information contact Tourism Victoria (812 Wharf Street; 250-953-2033 or 1-800-663-3883; www.tourism victoria.com).

> **B.C. PARLIAMENT BUILDING** *(Belleville Street; 250-387-3046; www.leg.bc.ca)* &
Free visitor tours usually run every 20 minutes from 9 AM to 4:30 PM between the Victoria Day and Labour Day long weekends, hourly in winter, but the public is welcome to wander unaided through portions of the impressive building, where you may still be able to see the controversial murals depicting historically incorrect Aboriginal nudity, which the provincial government intends to remove. When the legislature is in session, the public is welcome in the gallery.

> **BUTCHART GARDENS** *(800 Benvenuto Avenue, Brentwood Bay; 250-652-5256; www.butchartgardens.com)* &
This elaborate century-old 22-ha garden created in an old limestone quarry draws people from all over the world. It's packed with bus tourists and the things they like. However, I go for the summer Saturday fireworks display, an old-fashioned European-style spectacle that wonderfully illuminates the gaudy landscape. Take a picnic and a blanket. Butchart Gardens is a 21-km bus ride from downtown Victoria, but bus tours are ubiquitous, and some are just $10 or $12 more than the basic adult admission, which is about $26.50 in summer.

> **FORT RODD HILL AND FISGARD LIGHTHOUSE NATIONAL HISTORIC SITES** *(Colwood; 250-478-5849; www.fortroddhill.com)*
ACTIVITIES: *Picnicking, viewpoints, walking*
From its establishment in 1878 until it was decommissioned in 1956, Fort Rodd Hill, 14 km west of downtown Victoria, housed three batteries of artillery designed to guard the Victoria and Esquimalt

harbours. The notion of poking around concrete bunkers and walled barracks may not sound compelling, but the site is well preserved and maintained and augmented at every turn by fresh ocean breezes and views of Fisgard Lighthouse, as iconic a sight as anything on Canada's coastlines. A short causeway links the beach with the lighthouse, which once stood in solitary splendour offshore. The beacon atop the two-storey brick house still serves to warn mariners away from the treacherous shoals at the mouth of the Esquimalt harbour.

Late April is one of the best times of the year to visit Fort Rodd Hill, as well as the nearby gardens on the grounds of Royal Roads University (www.royalroads.ca). That's when the meadows bloom thickly with deep-blue common camas flowers, a member of the lily family that thrives in rain-shadow climates. Overhead, the long branches of Garry oak will be bursting with new greenery. Perhaps spring's urge to wander will lead you by the nose downhill from the fort and further west along Ocean Boulevard's open beach from where you can look back at the lighthouse from a conveniently placed concession stand, drink in hand.

> ### GALLOPING GOOSE TRAIL &

ACTIVITIES: *Cycling, nature observation, running, viewpoints, walking*

The Galloping Goose Trail officially begins on the west side of the Johnson Street Bridge in downtown Victoria, and all distance markers on the trail refer to this point. The trail's Saanich Peninsula extension runs between the waterfront intersection of Lochside Drive and Beacon Avenue in Sidney to Quadra Street in Victoria, a comfortable 27-km, two-hour bike ride one-way. Although the Lochside section is rougher and less well marked than other sections of the Galloping Goose, the route is highly enjoyable as it passes through rural Saanich. Watch for where the trail crosses Island View Road south of Sidney. If you are looking for a break, head east to nearby Island View Beach Regional Park for a swim.

The Swan Lake/Christmas Hill Nature Sanctuary near the Quadra Street trailhead provides another pleasant rest stop. Here you'll find an interpretive display, complete with archival photographs of the railcars that once saw service on the route. (*Note:* Bikes are not permitted in the nature sanctuary trails.)

ACTIVITIES: *Cycling, viewpoints, walking*
Walk, cycle or cruise around the Inner Harbour, buzzing with
commercial and tourist traffic. It's well worth riding the charming
passenger boats operated by the Victoria Harbour Ferry Company,
which can take you to tea and croquet at Point Ellice House (2616
Pleasant Street; 250-380-6506; www.pointellicehouse.ca), a restored
1860s home just north of town with an extensive collection of Victorian furniture. The Victoria Harbour Ferry (250-708-0201; www.
harbourferry.com) runs daily from March to October and on weekends year-round. Each morning during summer months the ferries
perform a ballet in the inner harbour at 9:45 AM to the strains of
the "Blue Danube" waltz. Best viewing is from the Upper Causeway in front of the Fairmont Empress Hotel. The ferry's skipper will
helpfully pinpoint the walkways and bike routes to follow for a closer
inspection of downtown once you get back to shore. Conveniently,
passengers can alight at any of the seven stops
en route, spend time exploring, then at no
extra charge catch another ferry to continue   **The Johnson Street**
the tour.   **Bridge, which crosses**
    Victoria's Chinatown, around Fisgard and
Government streets, is distinguished by some   **the Inner Harbour where**
fantastic examples of the traditional Ital-   **it narrows into Gorge**
ian- and Portuguese-influenced Guangdong
architecture recreated in just a few cities along   **Inlet, was designed by**
North America's west coast. The top floor of   **Joseph Strauss—designer**
the Yen Wo Society Building (1713 Govern-
ment Street) contains the Tam Kung Temple,   **of the Golden Gate**
the oldest Chinese shrine in Canada. More   **Bridge—in 1925.**
contemporary pursuits include shopping for
bargain housewares or high-end tea—Silk
Road (1624 Government Street; 250-388-6815) has the tea *and* a stylish spa. Or you can relax in Bastion Square, site of the original Fort
Victoria, after a visit to the Maritime Museum (see below), and imagine you're waiting for your own ship to come in.
    Among Victoria's naturally abundant fish and chipperies are two
fine choices along the Inner Harbour. Barb's Place (250-384-6515),
a floating eatery at Fisherman's Wharf near Erie Street west of the

legislature, has become a legend since it opened in 1984. The Harbour Ferry stops there. Red Fish Blue Fish (1006 Wharf Street; 250-298-6877), operating out of a shipping container near the foot of Broughton Street north of the Empress, has been a sensation since its arrival in 2007.

Much like the transformation of former industrial lands around False Creek, Victoria has seen a makeover of its harbour over the past decade, particularly in the Vic West neighbourhood that buffers the downtown core from neighbouring Esquimalt, home of Canada's Pacific Command naval fleet. Low-rise condominiums line the high ground above a seawall walkway that leads west through Vic West from the Johnson Street Bridge for almost 3 km to the West Bay marina. The seawall hugs an indented rocky shoreline as it leads beneath overhanging boughs of arbutus trees past the Matson Lands, the last remaining Garry oak meadows on the harbour. In the 1850s, colonial governor James Douglas described this open space as "a perfect Eden." Despite the recent developments surrounding the township of Esquimalt's Matson Lands, its meadows— home to nearly a hundred rare or endangered species of plants, such as camas, satin flowers, fawn lilies, shooting stars, and sea blush, as well as birds such as Cooper's hawk and Bewick's wrens, plus butterflies and other delicate creatures—are now protected by the Nature Conservancy of Canada.

Although the seawall is off-limits to cyclists, there are plenty of designated bike routes that lead around the harbour, through street upon street of well-preserved commercial brick buildings that date back over 150 years, and off into surrounding neighbourhoods, such as James Bay and Fairfield that bookend the inner city's Beacon Hill Park. By the time you cycle to Willows Park in the Oak Bay neighbourhood several hours later, you'll come to understand how welcoming the open coastline must have appeared when the first Europeans came ashore here in 1842. A small plaque affixed to a rock in the park conveys a tantalizing piece of information. On May 20, 1901, Captain John Voss and his first mate, Norman Luxton, had departed here on a global circumnavigation in a 7-metre cedar dugout, the *Tilikum*, now on permanent display at the Maritime Museum of B.C. in Victoria's Bastion Square, site of the original Hudson's Bay Company's Fort Victoria.

Abkhazi Garden (1964 Fairfield Road; 250-598-8096; www.con servancy.bc.ca/abkhazi): It's not just Butchart Gardens that earned Victoria the moniker "garden city." This formerly private garden was created by Georgian Prince Nicholas Abkhazi and his wife, Peggy. The garden's protection by The Land Conservancy of B.C. is a fitting tribute to the couple's own epic effort to overcome separation, imprisonment, exile, and loss. Tea is served, and there's a modest shop. The exquisite garden, open March to September, can be reached on the Number 7 bus to the University of Victoria, on your way to another garden or to the Art Gallery of Greater Victoria.

Art Gallery of Greater Victoria (1040 Moss Street; 250-384-4101; www.aggv.bc.ca): An extensive collection of Japanese and Chinese art and artifacts and a permanent Emily Carr exhibit distinguish this gallery, on a quiet street near some of Victoria's most well-appointed homes. If you're visiting the gallery or nearby Craigdarroch Castle, it's also worth wandering a few blocks down to Government House (1401 Rockland Avenue), where expansive volunteer-maintained gardens surround the B.C. Lieutenant-Governor's residence in one of Victoria's wealthiest neighbourhoods.

Craigdarroch Castle (1050 Joan Crescent; 250-572-5323; www. craigdarrochcastle.com): This nineteenth-century castle, built for coal baron James Dunsmuir and completed just after his death, is Victoria's most famous home. It's somehow blandly extravagant inside (the Dunsmuir clan's fraught history and the building's curious usage hold as much interest) but it's worth a look if only from the outside, after cruising Fort Street antique shops or on your way to a nearby gallery or garden.

Great Canadian Beer Festival: Victorians love their microbrews as evidenced by the turn-out at the annual Great Canadian Beer Festival in September (www.gcbf.com), the longest-running beer festival in the country. A showcase of the brewer's craft exclusively features all-natural varieties. Over forty breweries from British Columbia and across Canada as well as the Pacific Northwest are in attendance, and most brewers are on hand to answer questions. The Great Canadian Beer Festival is held outdoors at Royal Athletic Park, and a free shuttle bus runs between downtown Victoria and the venue. At other times of the year, here are my picks around town: The Canoe Brewpub (450 Swift Street; 250-361-1940), Swans Brewpub (506 Pandora Avenue; 250-361-3310), and Spinnakers Gastro Brewpub (308 Catherine Street; 250-386-2739) are excellent and beautifully located restaurant bars. Canoe and Swans are near the Johnston Street Bridge on the northwestern edge of downtown, Spinnakers, the first brew pub in Canada, is across the bridge in Vic West and can also be reached on the Inner Harbour passenger ferries.

Maritime Museum of B.C. (28 Bastion Square; 250-382-2869; www.mmbc.bc.ca): This museum is a showcase of Victoria's rich maritime history, including Esquimalt's naval and shipbuilding traditions, the stories of the explorers who mapped the West Coast, and whaling and fishing traditions on the coast. One showpiece is the *Tilikum*, a vessel adapted from a dugout cedar canoe that sailed from Victoria to London between 1901 and 1904, while its headstrong owner worked his way through twelve mates. There's also a nineteenth-century courtroom on the third floor, a remnant of the building's history as a courthouse. For a ride back in time, hop aboard the museum's ornate elevator. North America's oldest working lift is a gilded cage large enough to hold a grand piano, complete with a velvet-upholstered bench.

> **DINING**

Rebar Modern Food (50 Bastion Square; 250-361-9223; www.rebarmodernfood.com): Set in the heart of downtown, this relaxed resto offers healthy breakfasts, juices, and cardiovascular-friendly

> **CRYSTAL GARDEN**

THE CRYSTAL GARDEN, behind the Empress Hotel, once contained the largest saltwater swimming pool in the British Empire. But the weight of the water eventually caused the building to settle into unstable soil—the roof leaked, the pool was drained, and it's since been home to two failed tourist attractions. When it opened in 1925, however, swimmer and future Tarzan Johnny Weissmuller set the 100-yard world record in the pool.

vegetarian (and pescatarian) lunches and dinners in a suitably stylish room festooned with cake pans.

For a smorgasbord of eating, drinking and entertainment choices, the complex of bars and pubs adjoining the *Strathcona Hotel* (919 Douglas Street) is hard to beat. Big Bad John's is a "hillbilly bar" with fifty years of flotsam and jetsam on its walls. The Sticky Wicket, in contrast, epitomizes the faux British pub. There's beach volleyball on the roof, and popular touring bands frequent the Element in the basement. And the Strath liquor store has an excellent selection of wines and spirits, including some hard-to-find scotch.

Zambri's (110–911 Yates Street; 250-360-1171): The strip mall just north of Fort Street shouldn't discourage you. The pastas, soups, and sandwiches are spectacularly good and reasonably priced. Dinners are deliciously good value—real Italian food at its best.

Café Brio (944 Fort Street; 250-383-0009; www.cafe-brio.com): This café serves fresh, high-end West Coast food with a Tuscan bias in a comfortable Mediterranean-style room on the downtown's eastern edge.

> ### ACCOMMODATION

Brass Bell Floating Bed and Breakfast (475 Hidden Harbour Marine Centre, 4530 Markham Street; 250-480-0958): As well as building the harbour ferries, Paul Miller has restored two heritage boats, the *Dreamboat* and the *Thalia B* (formerly the *Brass Bell*) as floating bed and breakfasts, conveniently moored close to Spinnakers Gastro Brewpub (see above).

Swans Suite Hotel (506 Pandora Avenue; 250-361-3310 or 1-800-668-7926; www.swanshotel.com): Victoria's art hotel is unlike anywhere else I've stayed. An astonishing collection of 1,600 pieces of art are displayed throughout the hotel, the on-site brew pub, and the Wild Saffron Bistro (music and dancing nightly). The boutique suites feature loft bedrooms, fully equipped kitchens, and spacious living rooms overlooking the harbour. For an over-the-top treat, book the penthouse suite, which comes complete with a Roy Henry Vickers floor-to-ceiling sculpture and a rooftop terrace.

Delta Victoria Ocean Pointe Resort and Spa (45 Songhees Road; 250-360-2999 or 1-800-667-4677; www.deltahotels.com): On the west side of the Johnson Street Bridge, the Delta enjoys one of the best views of Inner Harbour, especially with the B.C. Legislature lit up at night. The seawall winds around the Vic West property and invites an extended exploration of the Gorge Inlet waterway. The resort's spa offers a kelp wrap that makes you feel like a nigiri sushi roll. (*Note:* Make spa reservations when you book your stay.)

Fairmont Empress Hotel (721 Government Street; 250-384-8111; www.fairmont.com/empress): Francis Mawson Rattenbury's grand hotel, built by the Canadian Pacific Railway and named for its Empress line of steamships, is a pastiche of Elizabethan, Jacobean, and Gothic styles. Demolition of the increasingly dowdy hotel, which is still supported by Douglas-fir pilings driven into the muddy harbour foreshore, was seriously proposed in the 1960s, but the *belle dame* endured partly because of public outcry. The hotel was extensively renovated in 1988, with a new lobby and the restoration of many heritage features, such as the Palm Court. The hotel's history is partly documented in the basement. The original lobby now attracts as many as eight hundred a day for afternoon tea; at a price of about $50 that's as extravagant as the sandwiches and desserts, but it remains a quintessential Victoria experience, and reservations may be required weeks in advance. The Bengal Room offers a hint of the Raj era with its lunch and dinner curry buffets. The room also features live jazz and a chocolate buffet on Fridays and Saturdays.

SOOKE

. . . . .

> **ACCESS:** Sooke lies 34 km west of Victoria on West Coast Road (Highway 14).

> **WHY GO:** Take in beach upon beach upon beach.

> **KEEP IN MIND:** Although curvaceous Highway 14 is paved, road conditions between Sooke and Port Renfrew can be challenging in rough weather. Take care.

OR SOME, the more remote the location, the more romantic the mood. Most of us probably prefer something that's not too wild, not too tame, spiced with a generous portion of time spent together alone. Sooke serves up this recipe better than most. This oceanside fishing port offers just the right balance of outdoor adventuring and indoor snuggling. The fact that the Sooke Harbour House Inn, one of B.C.'s premier luxury getaways, is located here is testimony enough.

Long before that vaunted *auberge* opened, the world knew of Sooke. In the mid-1800s, the town supplied towering masts to ship builders in San Francisco, Chile, and Australia. Search out the quaint collection of mossy cabins, including a pole cutter's shanty on skids, that house the Sooke Region Museum to learn more of those early years.

To explore the region by bike, check out Sooke Cycle and Surf (6707 West Coast Road; 250-642-3123) for rentals. Paddlers will want to visit Rush Adventures (5449 Sooke Road; 250-642-2159; www.rush-adventures.com) for lessons, rentals, and tours.

For general tourism information, stop by the Sooke Region Museum and Visitor Info Centre (250-642-6351; www.sookeregion museum.com).

ACTIVITIES: *Driving, picnicking, viewpoints, walking*

Indulge yourself in a bit of beaching as soon as you get to Sooke. This is what you came for, so don't waste time getting down to it. After all, the southwestern corner of Vancouver Island is a West Coast dream scene: beach upon beach raked by wave trains of surf that swash the foreshore with effervescent foam. Spend a weekend here at various points along West Side Road between Sooke and Port Renfrew, and you'll come away knowing each beach by name, as if they were new-found friends. Choose from Gordon's, Muir, French, Sandcut, Jordan River, China, Mystic, Sombrio, and Botanical. Each displays its own unique characteristics and rhythms. Some are carpeted with compacted sand; a stroll on these is easy. Others are more challenging; mounds of cobblestones and pea gravel make these an ankle-twisting challenge to explore. Driftwood lies jackstrawed above the high-tide lines, flung by the violence of winter storms. Fortunately the fallout from this kind of explosive surf is largely non-life-threatening.

Beware the rare but ever-present threat of a rogue wave. Also known as snap waves, these terrifyingly large single swells can suddenly appear out of nowhere.

Reaching the many beaches that line Highway 14 between Sooke and Port Renfrew can be as easy as pulling off the road and stepping out of your vehicle or as challenging as strapping on a backpack and hiking the 50-km Juan de Fuca Marine Trail past remote Bear and Chin beaches, plus many a nameless cove. Given a choice, I would recommend opting for a blend of the two experiences. It also helps if you focus on what you wish to see or do at the beach. Wildlife abounds around French Beach and Botanical Beach. Caves reveal themselves at low tide on the western perimeter of Mystic's and Sombrio's eastern reaches. Surfers drop in at Jordan, China, and Sombrio. Waterfalls spill onto Sandcut and China beaches.

As Highway 14 heads north from Sooke it begins to live up to its posted name, West Coast Road. The challenge is how many beaches to visit in the course of an odyssey here. There are ten major ones in all. Allot at least a half-day each to explore the two big stretches at Sombrio and Botanical; don't attempt more than three per day or you'll short-change yourself. Patience is the key to uncovering the identity of each. Some are possessed of a regal presence and command a thoughtful, measured approach. Others come veiled by a mist that enthrals one's sensibilities and banishes time.

Relaxation is the byword along this coast, particularly where you can find a broad driftwood behemoth on which to perch or behind which to shelter from the wind. At China Beach, waves twice as tall as surfers curl onshore with the colour and shape of oyster shells. Sea shells aplenty are scattered along the crescent-shaped, mile-long sandy beach, the backshore of which is stacked with driftwood and above which rise old-growth Sitka spruce and western red cedar. A wide, gently inclined trail leads to the beach. Posted as a 15-minute walk from the parking lot, in fact it's more like a 10-minute walk, less if you don't pause to ogle the big trees. As you near China Beach, the sound of the surf intermingles with the soughing of wind high in the boughs above. Across Juan de Fuca Strait to the west, Cape Flattery begins to define itself as the northwestern tip of Washington state. Beyond there, open water stretches all the way to Asia.

China Beach shares a common parking area with the Juan de Fuca Marine Trail's eastern terminus. Hike the first 3 km of the trail to Mystic Beach aided by boardwalks and a suspension bridge. You'll quickly grasp why the mucky route that eventually leads to Botanical Beach has a reputation for difficulty. Chalice-shaped Mystic Beach contains all the mysteries of the West Coast. Like its longer neighbour, China Beach, it presents a quintessential coastal image: a gauzy coastline fronted by stately trees, the tallest of which displays skinny, wind-thinned spires. Mist from a waterfall weaves itself into the spindrift from the surf. Stand on a shelf inside the falls. Sunlight transforms the tumbling drops into fat glass beads. The history of the earth is revealed in the layers of sandstone and conglomerate rock rippled by thin strata of lava on the exposed cliff face. The waves go ballistic, hurling themselves onto the beach, then withdrawing with an exhalation like the hiss from an artfully opened champagne bottle.

Farther west along the coast are the two finest examples of beaches in the region; Sombrio and Botanical (see below). Separated by almost 20 km of coastline, the two could hardly be more dissimilar. Sombrio's impressive gravel beach is hemmed with walls of cobblestone piled yards high. It looks as if someone has tried to erect a formidable breakwater with no thought for expense. Each pounding wave plays percussive notes, drawing handfuls of pea gravel towards the ocean with a thousand glottal clicks. When struck by the wash, the gravel pops up like sand fleas. Small karst formations close to shore provide limestone perches for gulls and cormorants.

Sombrio is three scallop-shaped indentations. There's a sense of this being an anything-goes party beach where surfers rule. In fact, by day, most surfers are too busy attending the wave party offshore. Stretched out across their boards, completely clad in black wetsuits, they resemble a flock of cormorants or a group of seals.

> **BOTANICAL BEACH**

ACTIVITIES: *Nature observation, viewpoints, walking*

At the north end of Highway 14 BC Parks signs point the way to the day parking lot at Botanical Beach, a further 3 km west. From there, an old logging road scraped from the bedrock and overhung by salal and alder leads walkers in a wide loop for 2.5 km. Bear left at the trail's first divide for the shortest approach to the beach. A longer, more rugged, and arguably more picturesque route via Botany Bay leads 1.5 km to the shore.

Imagine a treasure chest that makes Tiffany's or Cartier's look like also-rans. One of the world's premier jewel boxes is on open display at Juan de Fuca Park's Botanical Beach, a one-hour drive northwest of Sooke. But there's a catch: viewing hours vary with the tides. In the beach's case, the lower the better. Only then can you venture into the heart of the vault.

Sandstone and basalt shelves skirt out from thickly forested ridges. High above the gravelled beach's foreshore, every inch of soil erupts with life. Greenery dominates the skyline and overflows from ridges onto sheer, bare walls of shale and quartz, a conglomerate of the West Coast's geological history built up over the past 100 million years or so.

Life is displayed on a dazzling scale. All this before even stepping out onto flat runways grassy with green growth and stippled in places with hummocks of black granite. If you timed it right, you'll be staring bug-eyed into jewel boxes carved into the shelves by the spinning

Botanical Beach, Juan de Fuca Park

of rocks loosened within the sandstone and rounded by the swirling motion of the tides. Colonies of blue and California mussel shells appear to have been stuffed into the pockmarked rock face like snails in escargot shells. Starbursts of purple sea urchins and wreathes of giant green anemones necklace the sides of the tide pools.

Pull out a guide to seashore marine life from your pack and do some sleuthing into the more delicate, though no less resplendent, creatures, such as chitons, whose backs are plated like tortoise shells and whose undersides are as nacrescent as mother-of-pearl.

Whatever you do, look but don't touch. Pretend the surface of the clear sea water is glass plating on these extraordinary showcases. Botanical Beach, which became a protected area in 1985, has been an area of keen scientific study since the early 1900s. There are other tide pools on the coast, but because of its easy accessibility, Botanical Beach has become a world-renowned focus point. The area is naturally protected by the elements. Over the winter, plankton and organisms return to places where people have worn trails and the beach repairs itself. However, what people consider low impact is not always so. There are three things visitors should know: turning over rocks disturbs habitat; sea shells, such as dogwinkles and whelks, need to stay where they are as shelter for hermit crabs; and plunging your hands into the tide pools, especially if you're wearing sunscreen, may contaminate them with oils.

The best way to prepare for a visit to Botanical Beach is to bring rain gear or at least windproof clothing and waterproof footwear before striking out for some of the beach's more rugged places, such as a point dubbed the Amphitheatre.

For more information on Juan de Fuca Park, visit www.bcparks. ca. To make the most of your visit, pack along *The Beachcomber's Guide to Seashore Life in the Pacific Northwest* by J. Duane Sept or *Seashore of British Columbia* by Ian Sheldon. Monthly tide charts are posted at www.waterlevels.gc.ca; link to "Port Renfrew" under the site's index. During Daylight Savings add an hour to the listed times. A low tide of 1.2 metres or less is best for viewing tidal pools. Some of the lowest tides of the year occur in the days leading up to the summer solstice around June 21.

> **EAST SOOKE REGIONAL PARK** &

ACTIVITIES: *Hiking, nature observation, picnicking, walking*

To reach East Sooke Park, drive south off Highway 14 on Gillespie Road (just west of the historical 17-Mile House Pub) to East Sooke Road. Follow the signs from this point east to Becher Bay Road or west to Pike Road.

Over the course of several visits to East Sooke Regional Park it has occurred to me that the 10-km Coast Trail that runs beside Juan de Fuca Strait would be the ideal testing ground for a longer journey.

It takes seven hours to cover the trail, which runs through the thickly forested rolling hills of East Sooke that rise above the strait between Becher and Iron Mine bays. The shoreline, as rugged here as anywhere farther up the coast, forced the trailbuilders to deal with everything from windswept bluffs to rainforest ravines. Occasionally the trail descends to sea level, allowing a hiker's eyes the chance to range across the strait to the peaks of Washington State's Olympic Mountains that dominate the southern horizon.

Of course you don't have to traverse the entire length of the Coast Trail in order to enjoy a visit to this large 1,422-ha park. On one foray I went specifically to see a large petroglyph that is carved into the rock face at Aldridge Point, a mere 20-minute ramble from the east entrance at Becher Bay. Although it's helpful to have an incentive such as an ancient rock carving to draw you out along the trail, the natural beauty of the environment is enticement enough. Wild rose blossoms perfume the breezes that blow among the gnarled smooth-skinned limbs of arbutus trees. Some of the park's best beaches are located in several small coves around the bay at Creyke Point.

Once you reach Aldridge Point the large sea-lion petroglyph is easy to locate. An interpretive marker is fixed on the hillside directly above the rockface on which it is inscribed. According to legend, the petroglyph represents a supernatural animal like a sea-lion who was responsible for the deaths of many of the Becher Bay Indians when they ventured out in their canoes. The tribe became nearly extinct; the remaining members were afraid to go on the water until one day a mythical man caught the sea-lion and turned him into the stone representation as seen on Aldridge Point.

As you admire the 3-metre-long outline you also begin to notice rune-like inscriptions on the nearby rockface. As well, the natural colouring of the rocks, complemented by patches of lichen, lend an artistic aspect to the overall scene that will leave you wondering if you are really seeing distinctly recognizable shapes or just imagining patterns.

Find a sheltered spot nearby to look out at Hurricane Ridge's snowy crest to the south, or east across Becher Bay towards the lighthouse at Race Rock. Follow the well-marked Coast Trail west of here to Beechy Point where the ocean swells beat up against the craggy shoreline. The old-growth forest is marvellously shaped by years of spindrift driven on the wind by winter storms. Far off in the west you can make out where the trail ends at Iron Mine Bay. Shoulder your pack and head that way if you wish, or simply retrace your steps back to Becher Bay and drive 12 km along East Sooke Road to reach it.

> ## GALLOPING GOOSE TRAIL &

ACTIVITIES: *Cycling, picnicking, swimming, walking*

One of the more rural—and rewarding—sections of the multi-use Galloping Goose Trail runs for 20 km from Roche Cove Regional Park in East Sooke to Sooke Potholes Provincial Park and Leechtown. Soon after you set out from my suggested start point, just west of the intersection of Rocky Point and Malloch roads, trails lead down a steep hillside to Matheson Lake. (*Note:* No bikes are permitted on the Matheson Lake trails.) Although the Galloping Goose trail is mostly level, it covers bumpy but solid ground with the exception of short patches of gravel near several bridges. The parking area beside Roche Cove Regional Park, another good starting point, appears at K35 as the trail emerges onto the east side of Sooke basin. From here, ocean vistas begin to open to the west, and the temptation is to pause beside the clear blue-green water to enjoy the view. Just as the Lions dominate the Vancouver skyline, so too do the peaks of Hurricane Ridge, which lord over the Olympic Peninsula to the south across Juan de Fuca Strait.

A variety of rough but idyllic picnic spots sit along the trail between Roche Cove and Sooke and only require a short scramble downhill to reach. The forested environment features deep greens of broadleaf maples and rich auburn tones of arbutus. Snowbrush scents the air, and its large clusters of white flowers provide a rich contrast to the evergreen forest. And if you ramble along this trail during the week you'll encounter few other visitors; in summer, butterflies outnumber bikers along this stretch of trail that is referred to by local Salish people as Saseenos, "sunny land sloping gently up from the sea." Nearby is Sooke Potholes Park, where a refreshing dip in the clear, fresh water of the Sooke River is sure to either revive you for the last push to Leechtown or provide enough satisfaction that you'll end your ramble along the Galloping Goose Trail with a long soak here. On this trail, there's always another section waiting to be explored.

> **WHIFFEN SPIT PARK**

ACTIVITIES: *Viewpoints, walking*
Kick up some sand out at Whiffen Spit, south from Highway 14 to the end of Whiffen Spit Road, the natural barrier that not only protects Sooke Harbour but also fronts the Sooke Harbour House Inn. Let the ocean sneak up on your unsuspecting city mind as you walk the 2 km to a light station at land's end. Waves reach higher up the shore than you first expect. Lift your eyes to take in the enormity of the horizon and the combers will be lapping at your ankles.

> **DINING**

The Fish Trap (6688 Sooke Road; 250-642-3474): Come here for excellent fish and chips with a "plain Jane" ambience.

Mom's Café (2036 Shields Road; 250-642-3314): Mom's is a genuine delight and is not to be missed. If you're in a mood to leave the cooking to someone else, homestyle is always on the menu. Fresh Dungeness crab is one of their specialties.

Sooke Harbour House Inn (see also under Accommodation): In the vanguard of the local-eating trend for decades, the inn's restaurant is as cutting-edge now as ever.

> **ACCOMMODATION**

Camping &: Surf and stars make a potent camping combo at *French Beach Provincial Park's* sixty-nine vehicle-access sites. *Juan de Fuca Provincial Marine Park* also offers camping at seventy-eight drive-in sites at wheelchair-accessible China Beach. Reservations may be made at both; call 604-689-9025 or visit www.discovercamping.ca. Those keen on backpacking a section of the 47-km Juan de Fuca Marine Trail, as muddy and rugged in places as the better-known West Coast Trail whose southern terminus lies in Port Renfrew, would do well to hike 6 km south from Botanical Beach to the pleasant Payzant Creek campground. For details, visit www.bcparks.ca.

Point-no-Point Resort (10829 West Coast Road, 25 km west of Sooke; 250-646-2020; www.pointnopointresort.com): A warren of cabins shelter beneath a Douglas-fir grove. Even if you don't spend the night, you're welcome to walk the trail leading down to the point itself. (Yes, there is one.) Stop for afternoon tea and check out the restaurant's decor, which depicts the history of the point, including the origins of its name.

Fossil Bay Resort (11033 West Coast Road; 250-646-2073; www. fossilbay.com): Although not as well known as its neighbour, Point-no-Point Resort, Fossil Bay Resort radiates comfort for the amorously inclined. Six fully equipped cabins (maximum two persons per cabin) with fireplaces boast sweeping views of Juan de Fuca Strait. The best place to take it all in is from a hot tub on a cabin's outside deck. Sounds of surf beating on the rocks below rise in the air, offering all the enticement you'll need to explore anew in the morning. Tonight, rock to its rhythmic beat. And if you've been hitting it hard in the city, the resort offers massage treatments by prior arrangement.

Sooke Harbour House Inn, Restaurant and Spa (1528 Whiffen Spit Road; 250-642-3421; www.sookeharbourhouse.com). At least once in a lifetime, stay here as training for when you die and go to heaven.

> 19

COWICHAN VALLEY

. . . . .

> ACCESS: The Cowichan Valley stretches between Mill Bay, 40 km north of Victoria, and Chemainus, 20 km south of Nanaimo. From Vancouver, BC Ferries links with Nanaimo via Horseshoe Bay or the Tsawwassen terminal in Delta, and with Victoria from Tsawwassen via Swartz Bay. For schedules, fares, and reservation information, call 1-888-223-3779 or visit www.bcferries.com.

Harbour Air offers flights from Vancouver to Duncan (Maple Bay). For fares and departure times, call 1-800-665-0212 or visit www.harbourair.com

> WHY GO: A World Heritage river flows through "Canada's Provence."

> KEEP IN MIND: The Brentwood Bay–Mill Bay ferry offers a time-saving connection between Brentwood Bay in North Saanich (a 30-minute drive southwest of Swartz Bay) and the Cowichan Valley. *Note:* This small ferry accepts cash only, about $22 one-way for a vehicle and two passengers; discounted tickets are available at Thrifty Foods and Pay Less Gas locations near each ferry.

IN COAST SALISH, the name Cowichan translates as the "warm land." This valley boasts the longest growing season in Canada, a fact that may come as a surprise to residents of the Okanagan Valley. Long renowned as *the* place to pick magic mushrooms on southern Vancouver Island, this largely rural region is quietly developing a reputation for high-quality produce and locally produced wines and ciders. It also has its poetic side. Robert W. Service lived in Cowichan Bay before striking out for the Klondike. Although the oceanside towns of Chemainus and Ladysmith attract their fair share of visitors to the valley, I prefer Duncan and Cowichan Bay. This big valley stretches from one side of Vancouver Island to the other. Those of you in search of a magnificent primal rain forest experience would do well to head for Carmanah Walbran Provincial Park (www.bcparks.ca) to the west of Lake Cowichan, a long, bumpy journey. For the purposes of a weekend getaway, I've opted to stick to the east side of the valley this time around and leave the wild and woolly logging roads for another place and time. For now, there's plenty to do right here to keep you focused closer to home, including fishing and kayaking on the river.

For fishing licences, tackle, and advice, visit Bucky's Sports Shop (171 Craig Street, Duncan; 250-746-4923 or 1-800-667-7270; www.buckys-sports.com). Paddlers will want to check out Cowichan Bay Kayak and Paddlesports (1765 Cowichan Bay Road, Cowichan Bay; 250-748-2333 or 1-888-749-2333; www.cowichanbaykayak.com), Gumboot Guiding (5155 Samuel Road, Duncan; 1-866-748-7430; www.gumboot.ca or www.affinityguesthouse.ca) for canoe tours, lessons, picnics, as well as lodging at the Affinity Guesthouse on Cowichan Bay, Kindred Spirit Kayak (250-701-1888; www.kindred spiritkayak.com) for river tours, Sealegs Kayaking Adventures (Transfer Beach Boulevard, Ladysmith; 250-245-4096 or 1-877-529-2522; www.sealegskayaking.com) for rentals, lessons, and tours, and Wilderness Kayaking (Maple Bay; 250-746-0151; www.wilderness-kayaking. com) for tours and rentals.

For the free *Official Cowichan Travel Planner* as well as detailed online listings, contact visit.cowichan.net. Other informative sources include the Cowichan Bay Improvement Association (www. cowichanbay.com), the Duncan-Cowichan Visitor Info Centre (Highway 1, Duncan; 250-746-4636; www.duncancc.bc.ca), and the South Cowichan Visitor Booth (Highway 1, Mill Bay; 250-743-3566; www.southcowichanchamber.org).

> **COWICHAN BAY**
ACTIVITIES: *Cycling, paddling, picnicking, shopping, viewpoints, walking*
Located on Cowichan Bay Road east off of the Island Highway, Vancouver Island's second-oldest European settlement next to Victoria features a block-long row of shops, boat sheds, a kayak centre, several

Trail of the Totems, Duncan

restaurants, a resort, a dozen private homes suspended on pilings and fronted by a series of wharves, and a public boat launch. This little town shines with authenticity. Although it caters to tourists, it does so with a refreshing lack of pretentiousness. Shop for ceramics at the Mud Shop, baked goodies at True Grain Bread (www.true grain.ca), picnic ingredients at Hilary's Cheese and Deli, and happy-hour supplies at the local liquor store and seafood market. If you appreciate wooden boats, visit the Cowichan Bay Maritime Centre (1761 Cowichan Bay Road, Cowichan Bay; 250-746-4955; www.classicboats.org), one of the finest free exhibits on the West Coast. Walk out along the centre's wharf to explore four display pods. Each has a theme, from First Nations dugouts to an impressive display of model boats by members of the Cowichan Bay Wooden Boat Society, which operates the facility. Walk down on the centre's wharf to truly appreciate the beauty of a restored charmer.

You could easily spend a weekend relaxing here without the need to venture any farther. If you get antsy, explore the inviting 17-km stretch of the Rotary Route Trail (www.rotaryroute.org) that winds its way beside farm fields between here and Maple Bay, where you can pause for refreshment at one of two oceanside watering holes. Cyclists will enjoy the ride, since the trail features generous paved shoulders and the amount of vehicle traffic is limited. Highlights to watch for include a rock cairn beside the Koksilah River Bridge just north of the village, which honours the arrival of the first boatload of European settlers in 1862. Stone benches flank the cairn, one dedicated to pioneer women and the other to poet Robert W. Service. Northeast of the cairn, follow Tzouhalem Road as it leads past Providence Farm (www.providence.bc.ca), a unique endeavour that styles itself as a therapeutic community. Tucked behind the Sisters of St. Ann's impressive wooden residence, now unoccupied, is the Farm Store where fresh produce, bedding plants, and a variety of crafts are for sale.

> **COWICHAN RIVER PROVINCIAL PARK** &

ACTIVITIES: *Camping, cycling, fishing, hiking, picnicking, swimming, viewpoints, walking*

To get to Cowichan River Park, head west off Highway 1 on Highway 18, then follow BC Parks signs that lead to various trailheads, including Skutz Falls Road.

There are many places to explore and things to do in this string-bean-shaped park. It hardly matters where you begin; just choose a site between Skutz Falls and Stoltz Pool and start walking the 20-km Cowichan River Footpath, which accompanies the Cowichan River west of Duncan, or cycling a section of Trans Canada Trail, which follows a former CNR railway line that once linked Shawnigan Lake with Lake Cowichan.

The Cowichan River is a powerful fish magnet, attracting anglers with its fall and winter salmon runs as well as its year-round schools of trout. Many of the best locations for casting or viewing are easily reached along the World Heritage River's banks. Budget a half-day to puddle-jump along the Cowichan River between Skutz Falls and Stoltz Pool. Two of my favourite sites are 66 Mile Trestle and Stoltz Pool.

66 Mile Trestle is a choice place to connect with the Cowichan River by either heading up- or downriver on foot or bike. Even if you only walk from the parking lot to the bridge high above the river, pause here. The North Side Trail is an inviting stretch of single-track that leads upstream for 5 km to Skutz Falls. This section of the footpath is far more aesthetically pleasing than the level, hard-packed Trans Canada Trail hemmed in by the dense forest nearby. No matter which approach you take, enjoy the sound of the river as it flashes past. By late October, the trestle at Marie Canyon, 6 km south of the bridge, is one of the best places to watch salmon spawn.

By the time the Cowichan reaches Stoltz Pool, most of its whitewater ways lie upstream. A beach, picnic tables, a boat launch, and a gentle walking path welcome swimmers and paddlers. Tucked off in the woods is the Burma Star Memorial Cairn, a quiet reminder to savour these peaceful surroundings.

> **DUNCAN** &

ACTIVITIES: *Sightseeing, walking*

Although you might be mistaken for thinking that nothing stops but time in railway towns like Duncan these days, the Cowichan Valley proves it's possible to combine both Old and New World sensibilities. Although the naturally water-repellent woollen sweaters, which generations of Cowichan tribeswomen have knitted for generations, are the best-known local handicraft, other lesser-known aspects of the valley, including seven wineries and a cidery, await discovery. A good place to begin is Duncan, the valley's commercial hub. To get to the heart of town, turn west off Highway 1 from Duncan's Visitor Information Centre (Tourism Information Office; 250-746-4636 or 1-888-303-3337; www.duncan.ca) on Coronation Street and drive several blocks west to Canada Avenue.

A weekly Saturday Farmers' Market is held from 9 AM to 2 PM, April to Christmas in Market Square beside Duncan's red-brick City Hall. (A summer produce market is also held on the west side of Highway 1 just south of the Cowichan River Bridge.) Stalls feature baked goods, preserves, locally raised lamb, knit wear, and hand-crafted furniture, among other items. In the weeks leading up to Christmas, the square is packed with goodies much like a European Advent market. If your visit doesn't coincide with the market, budget several hours to stroll the downtown streets. The more you ramble, the more you'll discover.

Duncan's historical town centre is spread out over a four-square-block radius. At every turn you'll come upon toy stores, coffee shops, antique dealers, book sellers, restaurants, and art galleries, including the E.J. Hughes Gallery on Station Street. Hughes, who died in Duncan in 2007, was a longtime valley resident. Two doors down is the Judy Hill Gallery, which represents over a hundred First Nations artists. Stop in to admire the owner's collection of Northwest Coast woven reed baskets on display but not for sale.

Whereas another Cowichan Valley town, Chemainus, is renowned for its collection of murals depicting historically themed local scenes, Duncan's century-old streets are dotted with ceremonial poles, including one labelled the world's largest-diameter totem, *Cedarman*. Set in front of the provincial law courts buildings, whose round tower is reminiscent of Los Angeles's Decca Building, the pole is one of twenty-six installed in laneways and on street corners. Simply follow the yellow footprints painted on the sidewalks for a self-guided tour, or pick up a guide from the Cowichan Valley Museum housed in the 1912 train station on Canada Avenue. A particularly impressive group of four stands beside the platform where the E&N Railway pauses twice daily on its run between Victoria and Courtenay.

> **OTHER ATTRACTIONS**

Cowichan Wine and Culinary Festival (www.wines.cowichan.net): This festival, held in late September, is a three-day celebration of Vancouver Island wines, culinary excellence, and original music and art. Growers and producers invite wine and food aficionados to their doorsteps to experience the best of the region firsthand. Pre-arranged tickets are not required; however, there may be nominal fees at each of the participating properties.

Divino Estate Winery (1500 Freeman Road; 250-743-2311): When it comes to one-liners, Cowichan Valley winemaker Joe Busnardo is the local king of quips. At least that's the impression visitors get when they drop by his Divino Estate Winery, open Friday and Saturday afternoons, on southern Vancouver Island. Joe's motto is simple: there are only two kinds of wine—the ones you like and the ones you don't like. Vintners don't come much more down to earth than Busnardo, who established a reputation for himself as a maverick in 1967. After arriving in Canada from his family home near Venice, the construction contractor began to plant Old World vinifera in his fledgling vineyard in Oliver. In those bad old days of plonk, Canada was bound by an archaic international trade agreement that only allowed wines made from hybrid varietals to be sold. Although a few hybrids still persist today in B.C., such as Marechal Foch, for the most part they've long since been uprooted and replaced by the now-familiar likes of merlot and pinot gris.

Joe Busnardo was one of the first growers to experiment with imported grape stock to see which ones might flourish in the Okanagan's dry climate. His efforts with chardonnays and pinot noirs were dismissed as pipe dreams by many observers. Try telling that to imbibers of B.C. wine today, and they would think you were talking about the dark ages. Given the burgeoning state of vinifera currently cultivated in the Okanagan, Cowichan and Fraser valleys, in the space of one generation production has evolved at warp speed. And since Divino opened in 1982, Busnardo has seen it all.

When Divino relocated to the Cowichan Valley in 1996, Joe once again raised a few eyebrows. Even though Vancouver Island was home to Growers, B.C.'s first winery, which used loganberries as its base, the climate hadn't been considered adequate for grape growing. Since the Cowichan Valley enjoys the warmest year-round temperature in the country, Joe knew better. In addition to a host of grape varietals, he also cultivates apples, another crop that fuels his passion for cultivation. Cox's Orange Pippens and Royal Galas are just two of a half-dozen or more apple varieties mounded up in bins beside his compact wine-tasting room. Busnardo sources root stock originally imported from Wales, the Netherlands, Germany, and New Zealand. It's clear that he relishes the panoply of apple flavours just as much as he does his trebbiano,

A good place to source Cowichan sweaters is Hills Native Art (5209 Trans-Canada Highway; 250-746-6731; www.hillsnativeart.com) a short distance south of Duncan in Koksilah.

castel, and a host of other varietals that make up the grape content of his Cobble Hill estate. Joe's wry advice is that the best way to learn about apples is to try them all, just like sex.

Pacific NorthWest Raptors (1877 Herd Road, Duncan; 250-746-0372; www.pnwraptors.com): Stop by Pacific NorthWest Raptors just west of Maple Bay for an up-close look at falcons, eagles, owls—some of which are bred in captivity while others, such as a sweet little pygmy owl recovering from a collision with a logging truck, are being nursed back to health. Informative "Hawk Walks" and flying demonstrations are on offer daily between April and October. A variety of courses and programs are offered year-round.

Vancouver Island Feast of Fields (www.feastoffields.com): Wander the picturesque farmland with a wine glass and napkin in hand, sampling the gourmet offerings of over fifty of the island's top chefs, wineries and microbreweries while enjoying a delightful day in the country. Feast of Fields is an annual fundraiser held in September for FarmFolk/CityFolk (www.ffcf.bc.ca), a B.C. organization that works to promote ethical and sustainable food systems and develop relationships between local chefs and farmers. Partial funding also goes to a chosen community project.

Whippletree Junction: Whippletree Junction, 3 km south of Duncan on the east side of Highway 1, is the creation of the late Randy Streit, a local entrepreneur who in 1968 began taking local buildings that were about to be demolished and moving them to this makeshift village. The Wickertree was the first building and came from Duncan's old Chinatown. Wagon Wheel Antiques was once a fish cannery in Sooke. Black Coffee and Other Delights was a post office and bank in Cobble Hill. Unique handmade Canadian arts and crafts are featured behind a façade of salvaged storefronts and historical buildings. Whippletree Junction's name derives from the horse-and-buggy era when a whippletree was an important harness part to hitch up a wagon.

> **DINING**

The Community Farm Store (330 Duncan Street, Duncan; 250-748-6227): Housed in the heritage 1912 Duncan Garage, this store, a fine coffee shop and bakery, and Ten Old Books (one of a quartet of bookstores in this overachievingly literate town) that has an Old

World feel to its display. Photos and memorabilia from the garage's heyday are mounted inside as well. If you enjoy Granville Island, this place will suit you just fine.

Nha Trang-Maki Sushi (62 Kenneth Street, Duncan; 250-746-8999): Peace and tranquility reign in the centre of what is an already mellow environment. Park yourself at the small sushi bar to catch the maki-rolling action, or surrender to the eye-catching Vietnamese-influenced decor that reflects the cross-cultural interplay.

The Masthead Restaurant (1705 Cowichan Bay Road, Cowichan Bay; 250-748-3714; www.themastheadrestaurant.com): Make a reservation, but still be prepared to line up for a table in this intimate room in the former Columbia Hotel built in 1862. A jazz duo spins Johnny Mercer tunes on Saturday nights. A three-course table d'hote offering is a great help in making quick decisions, leaving you to linger over the wine list. Give the house label a try, sourced from the nearby Alderlea Vineyards.

> ## ACCOMMODATION

The Quamichan Inn (1478 Maple Bay Road, Duncan; 250-746-7028; www.thequamichaninn.com): This country estate offers both bed-and-breakfast rooms and a suite as well as a fine-dining restaurant.

Oceanfront Grand Resort and Marina (1681 Cowichan Bay Road, Cowichan Bay; 250-701-0166 or 1-800-663-7898; www.thegrandresort.com): Spread beside the bay at the south end of town, the resort is Cowichan Bay's sole concession to modernity. Sunday brunch is not to be missed, nor are the day spa, swimming pool and fitness centre.

The Blue Heron and The Huntress flotels (1765 Cowichan Bay Road, Cowichan Bay; 250-748-2222; www.bluenosemarina.com): Take your pick of two houseboats moored side by side on the Bluenose Marina, which also shares space with Cowichan Bay Kayak and some fine pleasurecraft. The Blue Heron features high-end spaciousness while its companion, the Huntress, is much more like a cozy ship's cabin. The manager's mother runs Anchors Guesthouse (1793 Cowichan Bay Road; 250-748-7206 or 1-877-991-1199; www.anchorsguesthouse.com) several houses north, which features a private dock, a rowboat to explore the harbour (or perhaps paddle to dinner at the Masthead), and a crab trap for DIY-inclined guests.

> 20

NANAIMO

. . . . .

> ACCESS: Take a two-hour ferry ride from Horseshoe Bay in West Vancouver to Departure Bay, or from Tsawwassen in Delta to Duke Point. For detailed sailing times, fares, and reservations, contact www.bcferries.com or call 1-888-223-3779. Harbour Air Seaplanes (604-274-1277 or 1-800-665-0212; www.harbour-air.com) operates multiple daily float plane flights from both Vancouver and Richmond to Nanaimo Harbour. Travel time is 20 minutes at a cost of $69 one way.

> WHY GO: Go for the bars, as in Nanaimo, and a host of related goodies.

> KEEP IN MIND: Ferry reservations are a must on long weekends from April to October and during summer months when there may be as much as a sailing or more wait without one.

NANAIMO, OR SNE-NY-MO, is said to be an Island Halkomelem word meaning "people of many names." Before the arrival of the first Europeans, several Indian communities in the Sne-ny-mo region formed a confederation to provide better protection against raids by northern tribes. Nanaimo bills itself as the Harbour City because of its naturally sheltered, deep-water port beside a narrow coastal plain, surrounded by rich agricultural land and dense forests. The port is lightly industrialized compared with Vancouver's inner harbour, and much of the downtown waterway is the domain of marinas and parks. For a century between the 1850s and the 1950s, Nanaimo was the centre of a large coal-mining operation. Fortunately the scent of coal dust no longer hangs in the air. The smell of money these days comes more from colleges, research stations, high-tech firms, government offices, and the like than lumber mills. That change is nowhere more visible than Nanaimo's revitalized inner city, anchored by a new cultural centre, the eight hundred-seat Port Theatre and the Vancouver Island Conference Centre. Pair these with over one hundred parks and trails, and prepare for well-rounded indoor-outdoor experience.

For information on attractions, activities, accommodation, and dining in Nanaimo, as well as trail maps, call 1-800-663-7337 or visit www.tourismnanaimo.com, or www.nanaimodowntown.com.

To get out on the water Alberni Outpost (1-866-760-0011; www.albernioutpost.com) offers guided kayak tours, as well as bike tours. Sailors should consider Gilligan Sailing Charters (250-753-9245; www.gilligansailingcharters.com) or Jadeo (1250 Stewart Avenue; 250-668-2501).

If, however, you're looking to relax the cream of local pamper parlours are Breze Aveda Concept Salon and Day Spa (10–3200 North Island Highway; 250-758-6822), Regis Salon and Spa (Woodgrove Centre; 250-390-0545; www.woodgrove.shopping.ca), and Shades Aesthetic and Wellness Spa (101–335 Wesley Street; 250-754-6414).

> **INNER HARBOUR AND THE BASTION** &

ACTIVITIES: *Cycling, viewpoints, walking*
If you've never been to Nanaimo before, or at least not in the past few years, you'll want to look around the harbour to get your bearings. No mountains rear above. Instead, rolling hillsides guide your eyes to the waterfront to a seawall route, the 4-km Harbourside Walkway, which leads from the BC Ferries terminal in Departure Bay to Cameron Island, a snout of land seamlessly attached to the city's downtown core and the jumping off point for Gabriola, 20 minutes away.

Soon enough you'll be slowing down to read interpretive signs and take in sculpture installations along the pathway. An imposing statue that at first glance might be mistaken for a British naval commander in a tri-corner hat turns out instead to be a likeness of former mayor Frank Ney, who inaugurated the city's annual bathtub race in 1967. (Ney also spawned the sprawl of shopping malls along the Island Highway that unwittingly drained the life out of Nanaimo's historical downtown core, now in the throes of a spirited revival.)

Time to get a move on. Don't dawdle as you cross the Lions Great Bridge that spans the intertidal Millstone River in Maffeo Sutton Park. A jetty juts out towards Newcastle Island. If you're up for an extended walk or bike ride, passenger ferries run daily from May to mid-October to the provincial marine park there, all of five minutes away.

Nanaimo is home to the oldest preserved Hudson's Bay Company bastion in Canada. This two-storey wooden tower, completed in 1853, dominated the inner harbour as a paramilitary installation until it was turned into a museum in 1910. During summer months it now functions as a tourist information centre. A gun ceremony is performed each day at 11:45 AM from May to Labour Day.

The city's inner streets are laid out in a radial pattern popular in England a century ago, quite distinct from the usual grid. The streets around the inner harbour may remind visitors of Vancouver's Gastown, with its cobblestone surfaces and block upon block of heritage buildings. In Nanaimo's case, the graceful curve of many of the streets lends an air of intimacy to the inner city.

Of course the best way to appreciate the big picture is from the water. Take a tour aboard the Nanaimo Harbour Ferry, which operates a fleet of "pickle boats" similar to those in False Creek. Stops along Harbourside Walkway include Fisherman's Market Pier and Maffeo Sutton Park.

> ## NEWCASTLE ISLAND
ACTIVITIES: *Birding, camping, cycling, paddling, picnicking, swimming, viewpoints, walking*

Newcastle Island and aptly named Protection Island perfectly shelter Nanaimo's inner harbour. The whole of Newcastle, formerly the site of coal and sandstone quarries as well as a fish-salting plant, was turned into a provincial park in 1961. Visitors can still see many signs of the former commercial activity on the island. The old sandstone quarry is fascinating for the remnants of partly completed pillars. (Pillars quarried here support the roof of the original U.S. Federal Mint in San Francisco.)

Newcastle Island is a hub of activity in summer months, when the foot-passenger ferry sails to it from downtown Nanaimo, but the

Neck Point Park, Nanaimo

rest of the year it's a much more subdued environment. Off-season visitors make their way to the island via private water taxi service or by dint of their own efforts. For those who cross by ferry from Vancouver with a boat on top of their car, there is a launch next to the ferry terminal in Departure Bay. You can paddle from there to the government wharf on Newcastle's south end.

Newcastle Island is a birdwatcher's paradise, especially for shorebirds such as the red-billed black oystercatcher. The island is also intermeshed with trails leading off in many directions. From a variety of viewpoints you can take in the sight of the Coast Mountains in the distance across the Strait of Georgia or of the Vancouver Island Ranges rising to the north of Nanaimo. If you'd like to spend the night there are eighteen walk-in campsites with wood, water, and toilet facilities. The island even has room for Mallard Lake, complete with a beaver colony.

For information on Newcastle Island Provincial Marine Park, including ferry schedules, visit www.bcparks.ca or www.newcastle island.ca.

> ### PETROGLYPH PROVINCIAL PARK &

ACTIVITIES: *Walking*

Petroglyph Park lies a short distance south of Nanaimo on the east side of the Island Highway (Highway 1). *Note:* Don't drive too quickly or you'll miss the roadside pullout that marks the entrance to the park. A short, wheelchair-accessible walkway leads from the parking lot to the viewing site.

The park's petroglyphs are estimated to be at least a thousand years old. Mythological creatures—sea wolves in particular—and a variety of other symbolic designs with creatures resembling birds, humans, and fish have skilfully been carved into the sandstone. Examples of this art form exists elsewhere in the region, such as on Gabriola Island, but rarely in such concentration as viewed here.

An interpretive display of concrete castings taken from the nearby petroglyphs welcomes visitors to make rubbings of the coffee table–size replicas. The originals are just a short distance farther along the walkway on a hill that overlooks the Nanaimo harbour. From here it's easy to fantasize that sea wolves once mingled with the California and Stellers sea lions that haul up on the logs boomed offshore. Tie in a visit to the Nanaimo District Museum (100 Cameron Road) to view a large boulder that once stood at Jack Point in the harbour.

> ## STONED CARVER

S EA WOLFS were supernatural beings, and archaeologists conjecture that the petroglyphs may be associated with Kun-nook, the guardian spirit of fresh water, who occasionally assumed the guise of a wolf. Members of the Nanaimo Snuneymuxw First Nation community believe that the petroglyphs were carved by Thochwan, who is present among the petroglyph carvings, having himself been transformed into stone by a supernatural visitor.

Stylized representations of fish are carved on one side of the boulder, which today is displayed in front of the museum.

> ## PIPERS LAGOON AND NECK POINT PARKS

ACTIVITIES: *Beachcombing, cycling, picnicking, swimming, viewpoints, walking*

Chances are that if you've landed at the BC Ferries docks in Nanaimo's Departure Bay before you've seen Pipers Lagoon and Neck Point parks in the distance, 5 km to the northeast, perhaps without knowing how easily accessible they are and what an interesting perspective a visit there gives on the harbour and adjacent strait. As is often the case, when you get to the park it is nothing like you have imagined.

To begin, perhaps you thought of the coastline north from Nanaimo to Nanoose Bay as rather flat and uninteresting. This misapprehension might have been fostered by your travels along the stretch of the Island Highway immediately beyond Nanaimo, truly one long strip mall that is more to be endured than enjoyed.

Instead of following the flow of traffic from the ferry to the highway, escape on Departure Bay Road, which follows the natural arch around the north arm of Departure Bay and runs past a broad stretch of public beach and the Pacific Biological Research Station, up and down and around a few curves and through an oceanfront neighbourhood where you might like to live if you were to move to Nanaimo. Turn right onto Hammond Bay Road, which will take you to Pipers Lagoon Park at the end of Place Road.

At first glance, Pipers Lagoon appears uncomplicated, a simple stretch of beach with a trail running off to a treed headland. Several hours later you'll realize how wrong first impressions can often be! Set out from the parking lot along a rough trail to explore the headland, with the open waters of Horswell Channel to the east and the sheltered calm sea of the lagoon on the leeward side. One of the first things that becomes apparent is the difference in the flora from one side to the other. Eelgrass thrives on the shore of the lagoon, while kelp beds bob in the gulf, with a profusion of wildflowers everywhere. Columbian blacktail deer frequently come out from the nearby forest to walk the curve of the lagoon, nibbling on new growth as they cast a wary eye at visitors scrambling over a rocky knoll on their way to the far reaches of the headland. Now, suddenly, you have access to the series of small coves that indent this point of land. A forest made up almost exclusively of Garry oak spreads its limbs high above. In warm months the closer you look for wildflowers, the more you'll see—bring an identification guide with you. As you round a corner, a mounting wind from the gulf may blow in hard, sending you searching for shelter after a few minutes' observation of the boats being tossed around in the swells. In the distance to the south you can see ferries making their way in and out of Departure Bay. Suddenly, you seem a world away.

Cosseted in the lagoon are two small islets almost entirely taken up by old fishing shanties built cheek by jowl. At low tide it's possible to wade over to them from the public boat launch located just north of the parking lot. A summer swim in the warm waters of the lagoon is ideal, just the right tonic if you've cycled from the ferry.

At Neck Point Park, 4 km north of Departure Bay on Hammond Bay Road, you'll find longer trails better suited to cycling in places, wider beaches, with a similar forest of Garry oaks and arbutus spreading their gangly limbs high above rocky headlands. Trails and boardwalks lead out to beaches with views east across the Strait of Georgia to the Lower Mainland and north towards Texada Island and south to Gabriola.

> **OTHER ATTRACTIONS**

Wildplay Elements Parks (1-888-668-7874; www.wildplayparks. com): The Nanaimo River presents a tranquil sight as it rolls down to the Salish Sea. Just before the river fans out into an estuary on the southern harbour, it passes through a short stretch of narrow canyon. An iron bridge arches above, on which petrified thrill-seekers perch, screwing up their courage before hurling themselves off. Fortunately, bungee cords are well tethered to their ankles. Judging from the screams, it's hard to tell if participants find this reassuring or not. Just watching is reason enough to visit. There's no better free entertainment in the Harbour City. Suspended in the nearby forest, an adventure challenge course leads visitors on a self-guided journey that may well take several hours to complete. Along the way, seventy ziplines, swings, nets, and suspension bridges lead from limb to limb. Such element parks are already a big hit in Europe, where there are three hundred element parks in France alone, but Nanaimo hosts the only one in Canada. Now *that's* cachet.

> ## DINING

If you're looking to pick up some goodies, good choices include the *Nanaimo Downtown Farmer's Market*, held in Pioneer Plaza beside the Bastion (from 10 AM to 2 PM on Fridays from May until mid-October), *Maclean's Specialty Foods* (426 Fitzwilliam Street uphill from the harbour), and *Fisherman's Market Pier*, where you'll find a selection of fresh seafood.

Penny's Palapa/Troller's (Pioneer Waterfront Wharf): Two of Nanaimo's best bets float steps away from each other: Penny's for delicious margaritas and Troller's for fish and chips.

Modern Café (221 Commercial Street; 250-754-5022): Killer Nanaimo Bar martinis set the tone. Atmosphere, service, food—it all works here.

> ## ACCOMMODATION

The Buccaneer Inn (1577 Stewart Avenue; 250-753-1246 or 1-877-282-6337; www.buccaneerinn.com): The Buccaneer is a cozy, clean, affordable motel, several blocks from the Departure Bay ferry terminal in the heart of the dive-shop district. Diving is one of owners Dave and Marlene's specialties. With three sunken wrecks to explore in some of the most marine life–rich waters on the Pacific, scuba is understandably huge.

MGM Seashore Bed and Breakfast (4950 Fillinger Crescent; 250-729-7249; members.shaw.ca/mgmbandb/index2.html): Glenn McKnight engineered this cliff-hanging marvel, and his figure-skating partner, Marilyn, put the icing on their home's airy interior. Swim off the rocks or relax in the hot tub while taking in the panoramic views of the strait near Neck Point Park. The B&B features a private kitchen for guest cooking.

Coast Bastion Inn (11 Bastion Street; 250-753-6601; www.coasthotels.com): Go for a junior suite, located on the seventh, fourteenth, and fifteenth floors, complete with Jacuzzi tubs and amazing views.

> 21

GABRIOLA ISLAND

. . . . .

> ACCESS: Connecting with ferries to Gabriola Island from Nanaimo via Vancouver is best accomplished from Horseshoe Bay rather than the Tsawwassen terminal. You'll arrive at the BC Ferries terminal in Nanaimo's Departure Bay in under two hours. Watch for Gabriola's white sandstone cliffs on the southern horizon as you approach Departure Bay. There is regularly scheduled bus service to downtown Nanaimo for foot passengers. Once there, it's a short walk from the Hudson's Bay Company Bastion beside the inner harbour to the Gabriola ferry dock. Gabriola is easily identified offshore to the east; closer at hand, Newcastle and Protection islands shelter Nanaimo's inner harbour.

Ferries to Gabriola leave every hour from 6:15 AM to 10:55 PM (departure times vary). Sailing time to Descanso Bay on Gabriola is 20 minutes. Pick up a complimentary island map when you purchase your ferry ticket. It will orient you upon arrival and will also help you decide which location to visit. Gabriola is a narrow island about 20 km long, and how much of it you can explore over the course of a day's visit will be determined by whether you've come on foot, with a bicycle or by car.

For a more direct journey to Gabriola consult Tofino Air (250-247-9992 or 1-800-665-2359; www.tofinoair.ca), which has multiple float plane flights scheduled daily between Vancouver and Gabriola.

> WHY GO: See the finest naturally sculpted sandstone on the West Coast.

> KEEP IN MIND: Cell phone service is spotty on the island. Also, use water sparingly, as it's in short supply.

Cottage Garden, Orlebar Point

NOT QUITE nestled in Nanaimo's embrace, yet close enough to feel as though it's a partner of the Harbour City, Gabriola Island is another piece in the Gulf Island jigsaw puzzle worth adding to your collection of travel memories. Although it's third largest in size and second in population of all the southern Gulf Islands, you won't be overwhelmed by a choice of destinations for your trip as you might be on Salt Spring.

Gabriola invites you to explore on foot along the island's weathered coastline, where sandstone formations dazzle the imagination. Visit any of its three provincial parks to become instantly enchanted by the island's unique natural identity. Come with your car and boat if you wish to explore the calm waters in the shelter of the Flat Top

Islands, or walk or ride your bicycle to reach the picnic grounds and beaches. Don't leave the island without first having seen the ancient rock carvings that populate an open field near Gabriola's south end.

For hiking and cycling routes consult the *Guide to Trails on Gabriola Island,* posted at the Mid Island Co-op (548 North Road; 250-247-8450) and the Gabriola Land and Trails Trust map (www.galtt.ca). Cliff Cottage B&B (1235 South Road; 250-247-0247; www.cliffcottage.ca) rents and repairs mountain bikes. *Note:* North Road lends itself to cycling far more than South Road, replete with thigh-testing hills.

For kayak rentals and tours, contact Jim's Kayaking (250-247-8335 or 250-751-5887; www.jimskayaking.com).

For general information consult the Gabriola Island Info Centre (3–575 North Road; 250-247-9332 or 1-888-284-9332; www.gabriola island.org) or the *Gulf Islander* visitors' guide (Driftwood Publishing; www.gulfislands.net).

> ## GABRIOLA SANDS PROVINCIAL PARK/ MALASPINA GALLERIES

ACTIVITIES: *Picnicking, swimming, viewpoints, walking*
The park lies 2 km north on Taylor Bay Road from Descanso Bay. For the Malaspina Galleries, follow Malaspina Drive west off Taylor Bay Road to its end. A trail leads out to the point from where you can scramble back along the rocks to the southern side where the galleries lie.

Grass fields surround Taylor and Pilot bays, lending a breezy feeling to Gabriola Sands Park. Walk out along the beach on Taylor Bay past eroded sandstone formations characteristic of many Gulf Island coastlines. The Malaspina Galleries, the best-known of these sandstone formations, are a short distance south of the park. In archival photographs, the galleries appear as a smooth curl of rock in the shape of a cresting wave. Today that form is showing signs of erosion, which lends it the appearance of a chipped-tooth smile. Graffiti has been carved and painted on the walls. Because of concern about deteriorating rock, visitors are not allowed to stand on top of or inside the smooth, semicavernous galleries. *Note:* Beware slipping on smooth rock shelves, especially as the nearest emergency medical aid is in Nanaimo.

> **PETROGLYPH MEADOWS**

ACTIVITIES: *Walking*

During investigations of the shorelines around present-day Nanaimo and Gabriola Island in the 1790s Spanish and British navy survey crews marvelled at various zoomorphic images—petroglyphs— carved in the bedrock. No one among the large resident population of Coast Salish Indians could explain the petroglyphs' origins. Since the Salish have a strong tradition of oral history, this would seem to date the petroglyphs back a considerable distance in time. Visiting Gabriola today, you can share in the sense of wonder, both at forms carved in sandstone by relentlessly repeated rhythms of nature— tides, winds, waves—and those etched by human hands.

The best example of pecked rockwork is on the southern half of Gabriola on the island's west side. Some petroglyph designs found elsewhere on Gabriola have an X-ray quality, showing off their interior bone structure, whereas others depict faces peering outward like friendly gargoyles. Much harder to decode is the menagerie of images in the field a short distance behind Gabriola United Church, 10 km south of Descanso Bay along South Road. Shielded from sight by a thick coat of moss for many years, these carvings were originally unearthed by Mary and Ted Bentley and their family in 1976, and they documented the carvings in the book *Gabriola: Petroglyph Island*. If you visit when the church is open, take time to view the Tree of Life–themed windows created by local artist Delores Brace.

A trail leads through the forest from the church to a flat rock outcropping the size of several city lots. Moss carpets much of the rock face, framing a host of petroglyphs that lie revealed in faint outline.

> **PETROGLYPHS ELSEWHERE**

• • • • • • • • • •

SOLITARY EXAMPLES of petroglyphs in Sandwell Provincial Park and near the government wharf at Degnen Bay on the southeastern end feature dorsal fins and flukes, which make these designs easily identifiable as marine life—perhaps killer whales or porpoises. They're located near the tide line, and it's quite possible they were carved as an act of invocation or propitiation.

Their fluid forms have been shaped by imaginations given full rein. This field is a storybook, and a creation myth or two would seem to be behind its deeply resonant theme. Human figures are interspersed among the animal menagerie as the petroglyphs spiral gently uphill towards the forest. As you kneel beside the rocks, peering back through the frosted windowpane of time, you'll find yourself flying kite after kite of hypotheses in the breeze sweeping across the creation-filled field. *Note:* The petroglyphs are best viewed during dry weather.

> ### SANDWELL PROVINCIAL PARK
ACTIVITIES: *Picnicking, swimming, walking*
After the Malaspina Galleries, visitors well-enough equipped to do a little scrambling around in search of a secluded beach should make the effort to find Sandwell Provincial Park. Follow South Road a short distance from the ferry dock at Descanso Bay to its intersection with North Road, the commercial centre of the island. Take North Road for 3 km to Barrett Road, where you make the first of a series of left turns, followed by lefts at Bluewater, Bond, and finally Strand, which you trace to its end. There is public parking here.

The short, steep trail to the sand and pebble beach is challenging; sturdy footwear will help. If your appetite for sandstone formations has been whetted by what you've already seen, you'll love what's in store here at Lock Bay, where it appears that a baker has been shaping dough, now miraculously transformed into rock.

> ### OTHER ATTRACTIONS
Drumbeg Provincial Park: Eagles circle above an old-growth forest of Douglas-fir, thick-trunked Garry oak, and arbutus, which shade a trail that traces the shoreline of this intimate park, found 2.5 km south of Silva Bay off South Road on Stalker Road. Look closely for signs of an extensive First Nations midden that runs along the shoreline, evidence of past feasting by the Snuneymuxw and Lyackson First Nations. At low tide, explore the rock shelves that plane out into the passage between land's end and a jigsaw puzzle of nearby islands. All the standard ingredients of a Gulf Island ecosystem are on display here within easy range of the parking lot. Check www.bcparks.

ca for details, including a warning note about giant hogweed, an introduced plant that, if touched, can burn your skin or eyes.

Orlebar Point: One of the best views anywhere in the Gulf Islands is on offer at the northeastern corner of the island 7 km east of Descanso Bay on Berry Point Road. There are benches to recline on if the scene overwhelms you, as it well might. Although Clark Bay's sandstone shoreline may not be as extravagantly sculpted as the Malaspina Galleries the location can't be topped. For starters, there is always a ferry coming and going in Fairway Channel at the mouth of Nanaimo's Departure Bay. Closer to shore, narrow Forwood Channel separates the point from Entrance Island with it's cluster of red and white buildings surrounding its lighthouse. Stake out a picnic table or driftwood perch and marvel as ferry wakes break on the beach like surf.

Silva Bay: You can easily see why Silva Bay, at the junction of South and North roads, 13 km south of Descanso Bay, was one of the first pieces of land on Gabriola to be settled by Europeans in the 1880s. The bay is a popular stopover for marine traffic in summer. Nearby is a log church, St. Martin's, built in 1912. No matter what time of year you may be visiting, Silva Bay is always a welcome point of rest, especially for bicycle riders. It's also a good place to launch a boat to explore the nearby Flat Top Islands. Check out the Silva Bay Shipyard School (www.boatschool.com), one of only two such training facilities left in Canada, then walk down to the marina to see splendid wooden examples afloat, such as my personal favourite, a nutshell pram row boat.

Annual Studio and Gallery Tour: Gabriola, the self-styled Isles of the Arts, is home to 150 artists. The annual celebration of all things artistic takes place over three days on the Thanksgiving long weekend in October. Maps for the tour are available from Gabriola Artworks (575 North Road; 250-247-7412; www.gabriolaartworks. com) where, at other times, many of these same artist's works are on exhibition.

> **DINING**

Harvest Thyme Vegetarian Café (580 North Road; 250-247-8824): Although there are other good coffee shops and bakeries on the island, Harvest Thyme, open for breakfast and lunch, is renowned for consistently good quality. Wraps are a specialty.

MFP Seafoods (3155 Coast Road; 250-247-8093): Wild salmon and a variety of smoked products are featured at the island's main seafood store.

Silva Bay Resort and Marina (3383 South Road; 250-247-8662; www.silvabay.com): One of Gabriola's most picturesque dining location belongs to this "resort" with its oceanfront view of the Flat Top Islands crowding in on all sides of narrow Silva Bay. This casual bistro puts proof to the fact that above-average is the new average when it comes to pub grub on the coast. Treat yourself to a Boat School Ale from Vancouver-based Shaftebury Brewing, and the resort will donate $0.50 to the Silva Bay Shipyard School. The walk-the-talk 100-Mile Diet–inspired menu features a host of locally sourced items, such as steamed Salt Spring mussels and clams, island-reared beef, chicken, and lamb, and Gabriola veggies galore. Pull up a chair beside the fire and enjoy some live music in the evening. If you've spent any time at a pub on the Gulf Islands, the welcome extended visitors here will feel all too familiar. As a letter posted at the marina attests, "Gabriola Islanders are slow to anger, slow to criticize, and very quick to help out."

Surf Lodge (885 Berry Point Road; 250-247-9231; www.surflodge. com): Peeled log walls, full-length windows, and a fieldstone fireplace set the tone at this Gabriola landmark. New owner Michael Brown has instigated extensive renovations while adhering to the

> WHAT'S IN A NAME?

THE NAME GABRIOLA is a twisted, third-hand interpretation of the Spanish word gaviota (seagull), which metamorphosed into Gabriola by the mid-1850s. There's still evidence of this transition in the form of small Gaviola Island, a member of the Flat Top Islands chain, located just offshore at Gabriola's east end. Gaviola and eight other islands in the Flat Top chain shelter Silva Bay, site of one of the island's earliest European settlements.

Spanish credo "With bread and wine you can walk your road." All I need say is "wow." The same goes for the view as ferry traffic glides past. The wine list offers astonishingly varied and affordable choices, a reflection of Brown's other island venture, the Village Liquor Store (250-247-7616).

> ## ACCOMMODATION
Descanso Bay Regional Park (595 Taylor Bay Road; 250-247-8255): A short distance from the Descanso Bay ferry terminal lie thirty-two oceanfront camping sites. Two oyster-filled bays attract sea kayakers, picnickers, and campers alike. Landlubbers can explore a network of forested trails in the adjacent 45-ha Cox Community Park. *Note:* Drinking water is not available.

Casa Blanca by the Sea B&B (1707 El Verano Drive; 250-247-9824; members.shaw.ca/casa_blanca): Several room selections, including a large two-bedroom downstairs suite, plus a waterfront location on False Narrows opposite the De Courcy Group of islands, make this an inviting place to stay. Kayak rentals and guided tours are offered April to October.

Cliff Cottage B&B (1235 South Road; 250-247-0247; www.cliff cottage.ca): Perched on a west-facing bluff, Cliff Cottage has two bedroom suites on offer, one with wheelchair access, including an extra-large shower with sitting area. The owners also rent mountain bikes, cars, scooters, and a vintage Yamaha motorcycle. Given the steepness of west side roads, mechanized exploration is the recommended way to see this half of Gabriola.

The Haven Resort (240 Davis Road; 250-247-9211; www.haven. ca &): Many visitors journey to here to participate in personal development courses offered at the Haven since it opened in the 1970s. The resort must be doing something right, since a large majority of guests are repeat customers. Others simply check in for a night or two to relax and enjoy the extensive waterfront grounds and a variety of facilities, including outdoor hot tub, indoor swimming pool, fitness centre, and body work rooms. The resort's buffet restaurant serves three healthful meals daily, although serving times are limited to an hour for each sitting. Check the website for current menu listings. Reservations are recommended.

> ## 22

COMOX VALLEY

. . . . .

> ACCESS: The Comox Valley lies 105 km north of Nanaimo on either Highway 19 (Inland Island Highway) or 19A (Oceanside Route). Pacific Coast Airlines (1-800-663-2872; www.pacific coastal.com) offers daily service from Vancouver International Airport, and the Comox Valley Airport Ambassador Shuttle Service (250-339-5252 or 1-877-339-5252; www.ambassadorshuttleservice) provides pickups or dropoffs, complete with ski and bike racks; also see Sky High Shuttle Service (1-866-331-4737) and United Cabs (250-339-7955).

In winter, Smith Transportation (1-877-756-2544) runs daily bus service between downtown Courtenay and Mount Washington Alpine Resort.

> WHY GO: Check out the abundant ocean to alpine attractions.

> KEEP IN MIND: You have the option of returning to Vancouver via Powell River and the Sunshine Coast.

OVER THE past decade I've seen numerous people flee Vancouver for greener pastures in the Comox Valley. Affordable housing heads the list of attractions, but so too do outdoor pursuits. Like to ski or snowboard? Mountain bike? Golf? Sail? All on the same day? 'Nuff said.

Together, the valley's three principal towns—Courtenay, Comox, and Cumberland—go back to the days of first contact between Europeans and First Nations in colonial New Caledonia, as B.C. was known in the mid-1800s. Attractions for new arrivals are as evident now as then. From abundant seafood to lush farmland, this valley provides all the necessities of life, including wireless high-speed Internet. Yes, the times are changing in the valley, although what I enjoy as much as anything is the journey itself. Driving the Ocean-side Route (Highway 19A) offers a glance back in time to an era before the Inland Island Highway (Highway 19) was completed. Since then, the welcomed difference is the pace of traffic, much more sedate now as speed-driven travellers head for the express route. Take your time getting to the Comox Valley. Trust me. Something serene will happen in the process.

The Comox Valley is well served by extensive networks of both roads and off-road trails. There are bike shops to serve each specialty, including Mountain City Cycle (120–5th Street, Courtenay; 250-334-0084), Simon's Cycles (3–1841 Comox Avenue, Comox; 250-339-6683; www.simoncycle.com), and Trail Bicycles (1999 Lake Trail Road, Courtenay; 250-334-2456) for sales, service, rentals, gear, and trail info.

For a variety of outdoor gear, including climbing and camping equipment, check out Valhalla Pure Outfitters (219–5th Street, Courtenay; 250-334-3963; www.vpo.ca).

With both ocean and freshwater routes aplenty, paddlers should check with Comox Valley Kayaks (2020 Cliffe Avenue, Courtenay; 250-334-2628 or 1-888-545-5595; www.comoxvalleykayaks.com) and Tree Island Kayaking (3025 Comox Road, Courtenay; 250-339-0580 or 1-866-339-1733; www.treeislandkayaking.com) for lessons, rentals, and tours.

Water sport fans will find all-in-one shopping at Pacific Pro Dive (101–2270 Cliffe Avenue, Courtenay; 250-338-6829 or 1-877-800-3483; www.scubashark.com) including scuba and snorkelling gear, as well as kite, surf, boogie, and skim boards.

As well as the on-hill ski and snowboard shop at Mount Washington, winter sports enthusiasts should check out Ski Tak Hut (267–6th Street, Courtenay; 250-334-2537; www.skitakhut.com) or Ski and Surf Shop (335–5th Street, Courtenay; 250-338-8844; www.skiandsurfshop.ca) for retail, rentals, and repairs.

All the travel info you need to know can be found at the Comox Valley Visitor Info Centre (2040 Cliffe Avenue, Courtenay; 250-334-3234 or 1-888-357-4471; www.discovercomoxvalley). Guide books are available at Blue Heron Books (1775 Comox Road, Comox; 250-339-6111) and Laughing Oyster Book Shop (286–5th Street, Courtenay; 250-334-2511).

> **MOUNT WASHINGTON ALPINE RESORT** &
(1-888-231-1499; www.mountwashington.ca)
ACTIVITIES: *Mountain biking, running, snow sports*

Imagine having more snow than any other winter resort in the country, maybe the world. That's Mount Washington's claim to fame. B.C.'s third-most popular snow sport resort (after Whistler and Big White), located 25 km west of Courtenay, has long had a reputation for good snow conditions that arrive early and last well into spring, despite the fact that the top of the mountain is 400 metres shorter than the peaks of Blackcomb or Whistler Mountain. What distinguishes the alpine runs here from other B.C. resorts are the natural glades of old-growth subalpine fir and mountain hemlock through which skiers and snowboarders twist and shout in winter, and mountain bikers and hikers pedal and pant in summer.

A great deal of Mount Washington's charm comes from its stellar location. On a clear day visitors look out across the Strait of Georgia to see a panorama of the Sunshine Coast, from Powell River to Sechelt, with the peaks of the Coast Mountains rising in a long march behind. Closer at hand, the many peaks adorning Strathcona Provincial Park's Forbidden Plateau region look suitably magnificent.

One of my favourite options when visiting Mount Washington is exploring the cross-country ski trails that extend from the private ski area out into 245,807-ha Strathcona Provincial Park, Vancouver Island's largest protected area. Snowshoers, skiers, and those intent on winter camping use these trails as starting points for exploring the Battleship Lake and Lake Helen Mackenzie region, and beyond. Closer at hand is the gentle terrain of Paradise Meadows where a series of loop trails offer 3- to 12-km-long workouts. All told, there are 55 km of groomed cross-country trails with another 25 km for snowshoeing. One feature unique to this mountain is that intermediate and advanced Nordic skiers can take advantage of a specially priced lift ticket for the Red Chair that rises to an elevation from which you can descend into the upper West Meadows along 10 km of tracked trails.

Built in 2001, with timber felled and milled on-site from yellow cedar, Douglas-fir, and mountain hemlock, blond-hued Raven

Comox Valley Farmer's Market, Courtenay

Lodge serves as the Nordic ski centre. There's an unhurried nature to cross-country skiing here coupled with the convenience of having the downhill facilities a short distance away. The rewards of exercising in the quiet of the backcountry are some of the best views of Mount Washington's alpine terrain from out in Paradise Meadows. In summer, Paradise Meadows offers a wheelchair-accessible trail that is also suitable for battery-powered scooters. On foot, a network of boardwalks leads out over sensitive wetlands for wildflower viewing.

Snowshoes and tow sleds are also available from the cross-country rental shop. For runners inclined to do some winter cross-training, snowshoe sprint racing has become a fixture at Mount Washington, including the challenging Yeti Snowshoe Series (www.theyeti.ca).

In the run-up to the 2010 Olympic and Paralympic Winter Games, the Raven Lodge will buzz with activity as the hub of the Vancouver Island Mountain Sports Centre. The elevation, climate, and snow conditions here match those in the Callaghan Valley near Whistler where the Nordic events will be staged. Similar to Sun Peaks Resort and Silver Star Resort, Mount Washington has established itself as the training centre for national ski teams, which in this case includes Canada and Sweden.

> **SEAL BAY FOREST AND NATURE PARK** &

ACTIVITIES: *Cycling, nature observation, picnicking, running, swimming, walking*

Follow signs to Seal Bay east from the Island Highway to the Powell River Ferry on Ryan Road, then head north on a blend of Anderton, Waveland, and Bates roads. Alternatively, head east from Island Highway on Coleman and south on Bates Road to the main parking; trails can also be accessed from Hardy, Huband, and Mitchell roads, among others.

This park is an official BC Wildlife Watch viewing site, so be prepared to whoop like a loon on the 15-km multi-use, single-track trail that loops around the western portion of this park's diverse landscape. By bike, the soft, undulating pathway breeds confidence in your ability to go fast and feel safe at the same time as you roll through the forest. The high-pitched sound of your approach will also help alert others who in all probability will be in the same exalted head space. Start anywhere along the loop and follow the yellow markers. As well, a 1.8-km wheelchair loop leads through the woods from Bates or Seabank roads.

If you're not feeling quite so pumped, numerous trails are marked solely for those on foot, such as the Don Apps Trail, which leads hikers down through fern-clad ravines to a wide bay, a special place worth seeking out in its own right. In spring, California and Steller sea lions appear along this coast, particularly around Seal Bay, as they pursue the eulachon migration.

> OCEANSIDE ROUTE (ISLAND HIGHWAY 19)

ACTIVITIES: *Driving, sightseeing, viewpoints, walking*

Oyster Bay. Fanny Bay. Clam Bay. Shelter Bay. Get the picture?

If you're in no hurry coming or going, this route, beginning 25 km north of Nanaimo at Craig's Crossing and leading 80 km to Courtenay, is the more scenic bayside approach to the Comox Valley that travellers on the Inland Island Highway never experience. Don't resist the temptation to stop when the feeling grips you, particularly north of Parksville where an expanse of sandflats and oyster beds fan out into the Strait of Georgia. Slow down as you pass through Union Bay, whose historical brick post office gives mute testimony to the little village's past as an important port a century ago. A steady breeze blows across cobblestone beaches, which give way at low tide to hardpacked beaches where herons stalk, seals bark, ravens caw, and bald eagles intermingle with skimboarders. Pull in at the rest area at Oyster Bay Shoreline Park where the coastline suddenly opens up with sweeping vistas north to Quadra Island and Campbell River. A monster midden of shells packing a powerfully salty aroma surrounds Mac's Oysters on Fanny Bay just south of the Denman Island ferry dock. Quaint restaurants and guest lodges dot the coast and beckon you to stop. And so you should, especially since towns like Qualicum Beach go to such admirable effort to put their best faces forward with showy floral displays.

> OTHER ATTRACTIONS

Nymph Falls Regional Park: From downtown Courtenay, follow Condensory Road north. Bear left on Piercy Road and left again on Forbidden Plateau Road. The Nymph Falls trailhead appears on the left. Never have waterfalls lent themselves to such enjoyment. You don't need a barrel to go over these cataracts. Simply sit down in the shallow water, lie back, and let the Puntledge River do the rest as its current whisks you over smooth rock shelves before depositing you in one of many clear swimming holes. It's a sensation unlike any I've ever experienced. In addition to the natural water slides, a network of trails interlace the forest on each side of the river, some designated as multi-use for cyclists while others are solely for those on foot.

Trumpeter Swans: Trumpeter swan numbers on North America's western seaboard have rebounded from a dismal low of several hundred in the 1960s to well over ten thousand today. More than a thousand of them winter in the Comox Valley and form the largest colony on the West Coast. Viewing sites abound in the valley, including along the well-marked scenic route on Comox Road between Courtenay and Comox, equally well suited to driving and cycling. Best time to see the swans in flight is towards sunset when they return from farm fields to nearby lakes and ponds. With a 2.5-m wingspan, the world's largest waterfowl exemplifies aerodynamic magnificence. To find your way around, two helpful companions are *Nature Viewing Sites in the Comox Valley and Environs* (Comox Valley Naturalists Society) and Comox Valley Tourism's detailed recreation map (www.comox-valley-tourism.ca).

Goose Spit Regional Park: Comox Harbour is as good a place for storm watching in winter as beachcombing in summer. In winter, as a tempest buffets your vehicle, flinging sand across the road, it may be all you can do to open the car door. Seafoam dances across the driftwood and gathers in spongy clumps at the tideline. In summer the sheltered lagoon behind the spit welcomes wetsuited windsurfers who fly back and forth. A visit here provides a good perspective on Comox's inner harbour at any time of year, either before or after some mainstreeting through downtown.

> DINING

Comox Valley Farmers' Market (At various locations depending on the day of the week and time of the year; www.comoxvalleyfarmers market.com): The farmers' market is one of the best ways to connect with locals as well as sample valley crafts and produce, from berry pies to venison sausage, handwoven baskets to gold-medal cheese.

Natural Pastures Cheese Company (635 McPhee Avenue, Courtenay; 250-334-4422 or 1-866-244-4422; www.naturalpastures. com): The Smith family is just as proud of their Certified Heritage Farm status as they are about their award-winning Camembert-style cheese, as well as a seven other soft and semi-soft varieties, including Wasabi Verdelai, where Japan meets Switzerland.

Atlas Café and Bar (250–6th Street, Courtenay; 250-338-9838; www.comoxvalleyrestaurants.ca/atlas.htm): As one of the longest-running success stories of any restaurant north of Victoria, the team of head chef Trent McIntyre and manager Sandra Viney perform the almost impossible task of keeping everyone happily fed morning, noon, and night. Must be the large portions, reasonable prices, and a variety of surf, turf, or vegan options. Since reservations are not accepted, be prepared to spend some time in line or the café's martini lounge, or simply head across the river to the Atlas's culinary companion, the Avenue Bistro (2064 Comox Road; 250-890-9200), which McIntyre and Viney opened in 2007.

Tomato Tomato (The Old House, 1760 Riverside Lane, Courtenay; 250-338-5406; www.tomatotomato.ca): Courtenay was one of the first towns settled by Europeans in the early history of the province, and the wood-beamed architecture of the Old House's Restaurant showcases both the valley's heritage and locally grown produce in its bright riverside location.

> ## ACCOMMODATION

Although there is plenty of on-hill accommodation at Mount Washington, by staying down in the Comox Valley you'll get a better look at a part of the province that continues to attract newcomers from the Lower Mainland. It won't take long to discover why. The valley's temperate climate, similar to Squamish's, makes it possible to cycle on local trails year-round, yet be up in the snowfields within a half-hour drive. Here are a selection of places I've enjoyed resting my head.

Kitty Coleman Provincial Park: Kitty Coleman Park is located 6 km northwest of Courtenay via Coleman Road off Highway 19A. Turn left on Left Road, then right on Whittaker Road. This hidden gem features sixty-five drive-in oceanfront campsites, picnic tables, fire rings, walking trails, a boat launch, and a pebble beach.

Foskett House Bed and Breakfast (484 Lazo Road, Comox; 250-339-4272 or 1-800-797-9252; www.fosketthouse.ca): Dove and Michael Hendren's lovingly maintained wooden bungalow was built in the 1920s in the style of a South African colonial ranch house. They take just as active an interest in the well-being of trumpeter swans (see above) and will gladly screen a locally produced video that explains the historical connection between the Comox Valley and the birds.

Kingfisher Oceanside Resort and Spa (4330 Island Highway South, Courtenay; 250-338-1323 or 1-800-663-7929; www.kingfisherspa.com): Set at the mouth of Comox Harbour 5 km south of

Courtenay, the Kingfisher benefits from a panoramic vantage point. Treat yourself to a beachfront suite (with kitchenettes), dine at the resort's top-ranked restaurant, where guest chefs include John Bishop, take a couples massage class, ride a mountain bike into town, and walk the trails around Gartley Point. The resort's spa is consistently popular with locals and Lower Mainlanders alike, particularly for its unique Pacific Mist Hydropath, which, over the course 90 minutes, offers an array of water-themed features in a faux sandstone-and-driftwood rainforest environment. What particularly endears this place to me is the whimsical, maritime-themed, hand-carved decor displayed throughout, the creation of local folk artist David Boorah.

Old House Village Suites and Hotel (1800 Riverside Lane, Courtenay; 1-888-703-0202; www.oldhousevillage.com): On the banks of the Puntledge River in the heart of town, the Old House features fully equipped suites with warmly designed wood decor. You'll sleep well here. That's my bottom line wherever I stay. And it's only steps from Tomato Tomato (see above) and the Courtenay River Walk greenway.

THOMPSON OKANAGAN

KAMLOOPS

SUN PEAKS RESORT

VERNON

KELOWNA

PENTICTON

OSOYOOS AND OLIVER

KAMLOOPS

. . . . .

> ACCESS: To reach Kamloops drive 355 km on Highways 1, 3, 5, and 1 again via Hope and Merritt or 423 km on Highway 1 via Hope.

> WHY GO: This sagebrush river city is the tournament capital of B.C.

> KEEP IN MIND: Weather at the Coquihalla Summit can be extreme at any time of year. Plan ahead if this is your route of choice.

FOR WELL over three millennia, travellers have journeyed along the sandy banks and watery surfaces of the North and South Thompson rivers, which merge in Kamloops. Even the town's name is taken from this important geographical intersection; it translates from the local Secwepemc language as "where the rivers meet." These days, Kamloops is more than just a place of natural convergence. It's also where golf, baseball, hockey, curling, and cycling aficionados gather. Inspired by the success of hosting the 1993 Canada Summer games, city officials set out in 2001 to transform Kamloops, the largest city on the Trans-Canada Highway between Vancouver and Calgary, into the tournament capital of Canada. Each year, a growing roster of sports events, including the BC Summer Games in 2006, draws crowds to an array of indoor and outdoor facilities. At the same time, Rocky Mountaineer Vacations, a Vancouver-based rail excursion company, chose Kamloops as the hub for its passengers to overnight. Their multinational presence on the downtown streets, coupled with the youthful energy brought by students at the city's Thompson Rivers University, has sparked a renaissance centred on the heritage downtown area along Victoria Street. That's why I suggest visiting with no grander desire than simply enjoying all the city has to offer. There's a timelessness in the surrounding weathered cliff faces that stare down on the rolling rivers. When the rich scent of sagebrush wafts off the hillsides and grabs you by the nose, magic happens.

If you wish to explore Kamloops by bicycle, you may want to visit the Bicycle Café (1648 Valleyview Drive; 250-828-2453; www.bicyclecafe.com/kamloops), Full Boar Bike Store (310 Victoria Street; 250-314-1888; www.fullboarbikes.com), Fun Stuff Recreational Equipment (3–2160 Flamingo Road; 250-374-8400; www.funstuffbikeshop.com) or Spoke 'N Motion (194 W Victoria Street; 250-372-3001 or 1-888-372-2044; www.spokenmotion.net). Each caters to specific styles of cycling.

With a critical mass of five courses, including McArthur Park (see below), Kamloops offers golfers plenty of reason to keep swinging. For information, visit www.golfkamloops.com.

River paddling, whether in a canoe, kayak, or raft, doesn't get much better than on the North or South Thompson. A good place to begin is Ocean Pacific (238 Lansdowne Street; 250-828-0188; www.opwatersports.com).

For general sporting and camping goods visit Valhalla Pure (749B Notre Dame Drive; 250-377-0157 or 1-877-360-6600; www.valhallapurechallenge.com).

For general information, contact Tourism Kamloops (1290 Trans-Canada Highway West, Exit 368; 250-372-8000 or 1-866-372-8081; www.tourismkamloops.com or www.adventurekamloops.com). The City of Kamloops website is a good source of maps (www.kamloops.ca).

> **MCARTHUR ISLAND PARK** &

ACTIVITIES: *Cycling, in-line skating, nature observation, picnicking, running, tennis, walking*

To find this park travel north across the Overlander Bridge onto Tranquille Road, then west on Mackenzie to a bridge that links with the island. On foot or by bike, follow the Rivers Trail greenway.

A 3-km greenway circles McArthur Island's perimeter on the north side of the Thompson River, site of a recreational complex of playing fields, indoor rinks, a public golf course, a massive skateboard park—which also appeals to local in-line skaters who carve amazing lines of their own in the park's deep bowl—and the Xeriscape

Demonstration Garden, which promotes the benefits of landscaping with the minimum amount of water required to sustain an attractive and functional garden. The park's resident mascots would seem to be yellow-bellied marmots, which shamelessly panhandle visitors for handouts. These members of the squirrel family are as harmless as they are cute, but be cautious of making contact in any case.

My favourite place is the Gregson Butterfly Garden, created in honour of a lifelong local naturalist and his family. Have a seat and watch the flickers and hummingbirds at work, not to mention a dozen or so varieties of butterflies. In summer, the garden is a riot of bright shades. If you're cycling, the adjacent BMX park offers a rollicking ride no matter what type of bike you're on. No need to act your age—just float like a butterfly.

> **THE RIVERS TRAIL AND RIVERSIDE PARK** &

ACTIVITIES: *Cycling, in-line skating, picnicking, running, swimming, viewpoints, walking*

Fans of multi-use urban greenways will instantly fall in love with this linear trail, which runs for over 40 km along the banks of both Thompson Rivers. Riverside Park marks the starting point, with kilometre 0 at its hub on Highwater Plaza, where a detailed trail outline is posted. From there the paved trail branches out in both directions beside the river. Along the way it passes through Overlander Beach Park, Westside Centennial Park, and McArthur Island Park (see above).

In July and August, one of the pleasures on a warm evening is enjoying live music in Riverside Park's bandshell at 7 PM. If you're on foot, bring your lawn chair or beach blanket and stake out some space beneath the graceful weeping willows that line the riverbank above a sandy swimming beach.

I value cycling the greenway as much for the cooling breeze it creates as for the enjoyment of stretching my legs after a car ride. Once you get started, it's hard to say where you'll wind up. Head to the Overlander Bridge for an elevated view of downtown. Along the way formal gardens, art installations, historical plaques, interpretive displays, and a restored steam locomotive are just some of the unexpected attractions that will expand your enjoyment. Once across the

Kamloops Bike Ranch

bridge, the trail branches north to Schubert Park Lookout and west to McArthur Island, both easily reached but little more than a start on the way to the Rivers Trail's eventual conclusions.

> ### SECWEPEMC NATIVE HERITAGE PARK

ACTIVITIES: *Walking*

The Secwepemc Museum and Native Heritage Park is located on the east side of Highway 5 (Yellowhead Highway). From downtown Kamloops, head north across the Yellowhead Bridge, then turn right onto East Shuswap Road, which quickly leads to the park entrance. For information, call 250-828-9801.

Kitty-corner across the South Thompson River from Riverside Park stands an imposing red brick building on the slopes of Mount Paul. This is the former Kamloops Indian Band residential school. It sits in isolation from the downtown core. Like many such schools, this one carries its own sorry history of cultural oppression and child abuse. Rather than tear it down, the Kamloops Indian Band maintains it as a symbol of the Secwepemc people's struggle to retain their identity. Band offices and a daycare centre now occupy the former classrooms.

Beginning in the early 1990s, the Kamloops Indian Band began to make its presence felt here with an architectural project intended to overshadow the recent past. The Secwepemc Native Heritage Park harkens back to a time when this was a gathering place where people sang and danced. To this end, in an open field adjacent to the school and within sight of almost all who pass through town, the largest wooden structure in Canada was erected. Dubbed the powwow arbour, its design mimics a traditional pit house dwelling, just as cool in summer as it is warm in winter. Tall timbers thrust up above the circle-shaped arbour's square-shingled roof, which at its centre opens to the sky.

The Kamloopa Pow Wow is held here (see below). Although no one should pass up the opportunity to attend if given the chance, I far prefer a stop here without having to jostle with the 15,000 or so spectators who converge on the site for the powwow. And although the powwow arbour is the park's centrepiece, I find a visit to the more recently developed Secwepemc Ethnobotanical Gardens on the banks of the South Thompson River equally attractive.

Spring is one of the most colourful times to stop here. For starters, that's when an old orchard of gnarled crabapple trees, a holdover from the residential school's days, comes into blossom. The pink and white petals stand out in sharp relief to the region's weathered, sun-bleached landscape.

The ethnobotanical garden is laid out in five separate garden sites, all of which are linked by a network of loop trails. Each site features indigenous plants that range from ground-hugging berry bushes to fledgling groves of trees. All of the species found here have a historical association with the Secwepemc people's cultural and economic traditions. These plants were used for both medicine and food, as well as in the manufacturing of tools and implements, for building materials, and for fuel. For example, in the Moist Forest Garden you'll find red huckleberry and oval-leaved blueberry bushes whose fruit, along with the cooked bulbs of tiger lilies, was

Quilchena Hotel, Nicola Lake

a kitchen staple. Trunks and limbs of trembling aspen were use-
ful as tent poles and drying racks, and paper birch trees provided
bark for baskets, canoes, and cradles. As well, a shampoo and soap
was made from birch leaves. Other garden environments include a
wetland marsh (developed in co-operation with Ducks Unlimited
as part of the Interior wetlands program), a moist open meadow, a
flood plain, and a drought-tolerant section featuring the widest plant
selection of all. Species are clearly labelled for easy identification; as
well, the park offers a detailed brochure for those who enjoy taking a
self-guided visit. Vancouverites who've witnessed the steady growth
of VanDusen Botanical Garden since it first opened in 1975 will not
only appreciate the thoughtful planning that imbues the layout here
but will also be able to visualize how the Secwepemc garden will
continue to fill out in the years ahead.

If time allows, I recommend taking a tour led by one of the
knowledgeable hosts. Their perspective comes in particularly handy

when exploring the reconstructed winter village that stands beside the garden. Four pit homes have been built, each representative of a different architectural time phase. Evidence indicates that settlement occurred here as far back as 8,200 years ago, primarily during winter months. Dwellings not only include the cozy pit homes but also teepees, covered with mats woven from thule stalks, a type of bulrush. Unlike the powwow arbour, the pit homes blend in so perfectly with the landscape that they are all but invisible until you stand beside them. A stone's throw away is the gently flowing river, a welcome place to stretch out in the shade with a picnic, particularly if the park's snack shack has freshly baked bannock buns for sale.

> ## OTHER ATTRACTIONS

Bike Ranch: Follow Valleyview Drive east of the Yellowhead Bridge to Highland Drive, then uphill to its intersection with Qu'Appelle Boulevard. Even if you don't journey here to ride a mountain bike walk out on the bluff beside the BMX track to appreciate the extraordinariness of the sagebrush and grass–covered hillside. Naturally shaped tabletops, rollers, and berms mimic a BMX park on an enormous scale. The eroded landscape possesses a unique beauty and scale unlike anywhere else I've seen. Hard-packed trails make for smoother riding than the rocks and roots found at many mountain resorts.

Fraser Canyon and Nicola Lake Loop: One of the joys of journeying to and from Kamloops, particularly if you're not in a rush, is to make a circle tour through the imposing Fraser Canyon and rolling ranch land around Nicola Lake. The added time and distance required is balanced off by the fact that you will avoid paying the $10

> # COMMUNITIES IN BLOOM
· · · · · · · · · · · · ·

KAMLOOPS BLOSSOMS more than your average B.C. town. In 2004 the twin river city won the national Communities in Bloom championship. In 2006 Kamloops won the International Champions Edition in the Very Large Municipality category.

toll on the Coquihalla Highway, the more direct, though less visually stimulating, approach. Prior to the opening of the Coquihalla Highway in 1986, Highway 5A was the principal route. The 90-km section between Kamloops and Merritt touches on a series of lakes, the largest of which is Nicola. A rest stop at the lake's southeastern corner provides not only picnic tables but also the best place to enjoy a refreshing dip. A must-see is the historic Quilchena Hotel located at the halfway point along the lake, complete with its bullet hole–punctured bar. During spring and fall migration, the lakes attract as many as five thousand birds a day. Watch for the wildlife-viewing signs that indicate good pullouts from which to observe some twenty species of waterfowl. In addition to Nicola, Stump and Shumway, as well as four lesser roadside lakes, provide ample opportunity for anglers. Weather-beaten barns and bleached hay fields of both the Quilchena and Douglas Lake cattle companies, as well as smaller spreads, offer mute testimony that this is cowboy country. Then again, there's nothing remotely subtle about the four-day Merritt Mountain Music Festival held each year in early July, the largest outdoor country music festival in Canada.

Kamloopa Pow Wow: Held the third weekend in August on the east side of Highway 5 just north of the Yellowhead Bridge, this event features over a thousand performers, competitors, artists, and craftspeople drawn from thirty First Nations across Western Canada and the U.S. For details, call 250-828-9700 or visit www.kib.ca/powwow.htm.

> **DINING**

Hello Toast (428 Victoria Street; 250-372-9322): This busy eatery, open for breakfast and lunch, is as casually urban as it gets downtown anywhere.

Storms Restaurant (1502 River Street; 250-372-1522 &): You can have a lot of fun here even if it isn't your birthday. If it is, so much the better: dinner is free. Tasty fresh-fruit margaritas complement full lunch and dinner menus of creative pastas, seafood, ribs, and racks, best enjoyed on the sheltered patio overlooking the river.

The Brownstone Restaurant (118 Victoria Street; 250-851-9939; www.brownstonerestaurant.com): Possibly the most upscale restaurant in town is housed in a 1904 brick building with tall glass windows. The emphasis here is on local produce done up Pacific Coast style. I like this place because the menu offers an entire meal of small dishes before getting to the entrees. If you're here on the last Sunday of the month, stop by for a wine-tasting event.

This Old Steak and Fish House (172 Battle Street; 250-374-3227): New Mexican–inspired cuisine, including authentic southwest chili and hot and crispy *sopaipilla* bread, suits a sagebrush town. Locals rate this intimate restaurant, set in a 1911 heritage home, and the Brownstone as the two best in town. Everything on the menu is fresh, including "boozy" margaritas, a must-try.

> ## ACCOMMODATION

Riverland Inn (1530 River Street; 250-374-1530 or 1-800-663-1530; www.riverlandmotel.kamloops.com): Indoor pool, in-room kitchenettes, Storm's Restaurant just next door: travel stops don't get much more convenient than that. The Thompson River flows past the gracious lawn that backs onto the inn, compensation for the bland interior decor. Be sure to request a river-facing room.

Thompson Hotel and Conference Centre (650 Victoria Street; 250-374-1999 or 1-888-374-8999; www.thompsonhotel.ca): I like the fact that this hotel provides complimentary cruiser bikes for guests, especially with the Rivers Trail greenway several blocks away.

Plaza Heritage Hotel (405 Victoria Street; 250-377-8075 or 1-877-977-5292; www.plazaheritagehotel.com): One of the best views of the city is from a north-facing, sixth-floor suite at this lovingly restored 1920s-era hotel. Floral prints abound from the wood-panelled lobby and restaurant on up the stairs, down the hallways, and into the rooms. Air conditioning is a modern touch that makes sleeping possible on hot summer nights.

> 24

SUN PEAKS RESORT

· · · · ·

> ACCESS: Reach Sun Peaks Resort by driving 405 km on High-
ways 1, 3, 5, 1, 5 and Tod Mountain Road via Hope, Merritt, Kamloops, and Heffley Creek. To check weather and road conditions
in advance, including at the Coquihalla Summit, visit www.th.gov.
bc.ca/weather/Index.asp.

> WHY GO: Sun Peaks is a model resort in more ways than one.

> KEEP IN MIND: Allow 45 minutes to reach Sun Peaks from Kam-
loops. The first 30 minutes feature a scenic drive beside the North
Thompson River.

As TEENAGERS, most of us endured an ugly-duckling phase.
Despite the reassurances of our parents, we despaired of ever
being considered attractive. Sooner or later, most of us mer-
cifully blossomed into maturity. A similar analogy could be applied
to ski areas in B.C.'s Interior. In the 1970s, most were small, locally
operated, and as plain as a peanut-butter sandwich. On-hill digs
were rare. When I first visited Sun Peaks in the mid-1980s (then
called Tod Mountain), the closest lodgings to the lifts were cabins
at a nearby ice-fishing "lodge." If I didn't stay there the only other
option was to crash in downtown Kamloops.

Today, such ugly ducklings have grown almost beyond recogni-
tion, financed by domestic and foreign investments. In 1995, Sun
Peaks Resort assumed its new identity courtesy of Japanese investor
Masayoshi Ohkubo, although the name most often associated with
the resort is Canada's female athlete of the twentieth century, Nancy
Greene Raine, director of skiing at Sun Peaks and the resort's biggest booster. Sun Peaks officially arrived as a four-season mountain
resort when it received its own postal code in 1998, thus emerging

from the shadow of Heffley Creek, where ranching has defined the local identity for the past century.

Despite a steady influx of visitors, the spirit at B.C. resorts is still defined by locals. Sun Peaks has long held a reputation as the home of extreme telemark skiing. As you make your way through the village, don't be surprised to see telemarkers riding a few kinks and rails in the terrain park beside the Sundance Express chairlift, just as you will mountain bikers doing flips in summer.

If you think that the problem with winter sports is that they generally take place in winter, beginning and ending with skiing and snowboarding, one glance at the range of activities offered at Sun Peaks will quickly cure the most cynical humbugger of that notion. The resort features an abundance of outdoor options to pursue, including perennial favourites like snowshoeing, skating, and dogsledding. To get geared up, pay a visit to Village Day Lodge, which has it all: alpine, Nordic, telemark, snow bikes, snow blades, outerwear, and accessories. For those game to try something off the grid, ride shotgun in a Pisten Bully snow groomer and witness firsthand how groomers work their magic on the slopes. Tours last 45 to 60 minutes and take place on winter evenings at 5 PM, 6 PM, and 7 PM. Tours must be booked by 3 PM.

Lest the impression be that everything grinds to a halt in summer, I can testify that the mountain bike park is every bit as rock-and-rooty as at Whistler. Hop in the saddle of a bike or a horse, paddle a canoe or kayak on one of many surrounding lakes, swing a club at the eighteen-hole golf course, swim at the sports centre's outdoor pool (heated in winter), walk the village loop, or hike your buns off on Mount Tod to catch the wildflowers in bloom in late July and early August.

If there's one group that knows a good thing when they see it, it's the Austrian alpine ski team that trains here in November in advance of the start of the World Cup race season. In the lead-up to 2010, this is an excellent month to keep tabs on these podium-bound athletes. Get out your cowbells.

Cyclists should visit Time to Ride (Village Day Lodge; 250-578-5430) for parts, service, rentals, and apparel. If you'd rather explore the resort on horseback, Sun Peaks Trail Rides (250-318-1835;

Nordic Skiing, Sun Peaks resort

www.sunpeakstrailrides.ca) operates during winter and summer, including a popular three-day cattle drive in June.

> ## MOUNT MORRISEY

ACTIVITIES: *Skiing (Alpine and Nordic), snowboarding*

Most skiers and snowboarders at Sun Peaks prefer to ride the lifts on 2,152-m Mount Tod and 1,730-m Sundance, where multiple Olympic medallist Nancy Greene Raine can be found giving mountain tours that typically evolve into free ski lessons. Although you can pursue a passion for powder in a variety of ways here, even cat skiing in the backcountry around Mount Tod, I'm more inclined to ride the Morrisey Express to the top of 1,675-m Mount Morrisey where a dozen or so intermediate-level routes lead through the most creatively designed trail network of any ski resort in Canada. Once you've discovered these runs, your conversation that evening may sound remarkably like the classic Bud Abbott and Lou Costello "Who's on First?" routine. Where'd you ski today? "I dunno." Your favourite run? Ditto: "I dunno." Play this line of patter out until the point sinks in that I Dunno is the name of one of Morrisey's smoothest runs.

Mount Morrisey's reputation rests on the way its trails intermingle, often leading to meadows of untracked powder artfully concealed behind islands of conifers. In the 1970s and 1980s, local skiers and off-duty first-aid patrollers would hike the slopes of Mount Morrisey to explore hidden stashes of powder. As Mount Morrisey was being developed as Sun Peaks' third peak, some of them revisited their old haunts and helped brush out these overgrown pistes. When you're schussing along, watch for narrow approaches that lead off to covert corners with knee-deep pockets of powder. And since there are remarkably few other skiers on underappreciated Morrisey, relax and flow around and through the trees and across open meadows without fear of being bushwhacked.

> ## NORDIC SKIING

All told, there are 28 km of track-set trails around the resort with another 12 km ungroomed. In a unique twist not found at resorts elsewhere, cross-country ski passes allow you to ride the Morrisey Express to the top of that mountain. From there, an 8-km circuit of backcountry and track-set trails leads downhill through the solitude of the forest and past frozen McGillivray Lake, on whose opposite shore are clear visible scars from one of the forest fires that ravaged the region in the summer of 2003. If the bottom drops out of the thermometer as sometimes happens on the Thompson Plateau, pause at the warming hut.

> ## OKANAGAN ICEWINE FESTIVAL *(www.thewinefestivals.com)*

A breath of fresh winter air is a surefire appetite stimulant. Snowsports enthusiasts enjoy their outdoor activities even more when there's food involved. This stems from a long tradition known as "après," where everyone gathers to share food and drink in celebration of the day's accomplishments. The operators of Sun Peaks Resort took the après concept to new heights when they hosted the inaugural Icewine Festival. Today, no less an authority than writer-broadcaster Jurgen Gothe considers the event "about the best wine festival there is on five continents."

Given the impressive market that B.C. winemakers have carved out over the past decade, launching an icewine festival was a smart move back in 1997. You could also make the case that Sun Peaks' blossoming as an Interior playground through the 1990s paralleled the success of the viticulture industry in the nearby Okanagan Valley. As testament, you'd be hard-pressed to find a more open-minded audience these days to the notion of combining a day on snow with a night on ice than in B.C. (Icewine, that is.)

The third week in January finds Sun Peaks buzzing with Okanagan winemakers eager to display the fruits of last year's harvest. Icewine tasting is the festival's highlight. A little of its intensely sweet, silken essence goes a long way. Several courses before the icewine, you'll sample plenty of laudable Okanagan table wines. But of all the matchmaking that goes on during the Icewine Festival, the best kind is still pairing your skis or snowboard with the champagne powder snow.

> **SPAS**

Like all true resorts, Sun Peaks makes a great spa destination in itself. Within the village there are two spas, while another lies a short distance away. The high demand for spa treatments for tired bodies is strong, so book well in advance.

The Pinnacle Lodge and Spa (2503 Eagle Court; 1-866-986-2222 or 250-371-7376; www.pinnaclelodgesunpeaks.com) offers a variety of treatments that stretch from an hour to an entire day, some with lunch included. I've come to treasure side-by-side sessions so that I can share my enjoyment with my sweetie.

At *Sun Peaks Spa* (3180 Creekside Way, Sun Peaks Lodge; 250-578-0086; www.sunpeaksspa.com) a dynamic group of B.C. Registered and Certified Practioners have combined their experience and knowledge to create a variety of rejuvenating treatments, including massage therapy, aesthetics, and a salon in one of my favourite hotels (see below).

If you can't leave to mountain for a massage, the massage will come to the mountain, or at least your room. German-trained physiotherapist Uli Johnson, of *Uli's Mountain Massage* (250-319-8933; ulismountainretreat.com), specializes in holistic personalized massages, sports massages, reiki, the Bowen technique, and a new one on me, Touch for Health (Hypoton-X). Uli and her husband also operate a spa and retreat from their home located 10 minutes from the resort in Heffley Creek. Registered with the Association of Massage Therapists and a certified Holistic Practitioner, Uli caters to special needs based on physiotherapeutic work in hospitals and as well through her work as a rehabilitation/injury prevention coach.

> **OTHER ATTRACTIONS**

Nancy Greene Raine's Trophies: If you've ever wanted to try on an Olympic gold medal or feel the heft of a crystal world championship trophy, here's your chance. Nancy Green Raine's impressive collection is on display in the lobby of her Cahilty Lodge. Ask her for a close-up look and see what happens next. Nancy's not one to be shy about showing off the hardware.

Snowshoeing: Snowshoeing continues to maintain its reputation as the fastest growing winter sport in North America. Not surprisingly, this form of snow trekking is featured at Sun Peaks Resort. The resort's moonlight outings include marshmallow roasting around a blazing campfire, a sure way to keep the winter cold at bay. On snowshoes, the wintery quiet is broken only by the sound of your own breathing, coupled with the soft swishing of the snow beneath your feet. Almost entirely composed of air, snow seems possessed by a magic that elevates the minds of all who come in contact with it. This is one elixir that can't be bottled.

> **DINING**

Sunburst Restaurant (at the top of the Sunburst Express Chairlift; 250-578-7222): When it comes to rating resorts, the quality of their cinnamon buns is one of my personal barometers. Those baked at the Sunburst are every bit as good as my all-time fave from the Bugaboos Bakery Café in Silver Star (see chapter 25). Scenic views are served up along with a pasta bar, sandwiches, and baked goods. On Thursday evenings, the Sunburst hosts the International Fondue and Torchlight Descent, complete with live music. The menu includes a variety of meats, seafood, breads, and vegetables to accompany the oil and cheese fondues as well as chocolate fondue dessert with a selection of fresh fruits. Afterwards, cruise down the torchlit slopes of the 5 Mile Trail. Reservations are a must (250-578-5542).

Masa's Bar and Grill (Village Day Lodge; 250-578-5434): Pub fare with flair. That's Masa's, hands down the best bistro (and dance club) of any resort with the possible exception of Blackcomb's Merlin's Bistro but on a much more intimate scale. High ceilings, a fireplace, decent acoustics, and an above-average kitchen combine to create the ideal laid-back environment. When the dining's done, the tables are pushed back to enlarge the dance floor where you practise your smooth moves without fear of doing a face plant the way you might on the slopes.

Mantles Restaurant and Bar (Delta Sun Peaks Resort; 250-578-6000): For breakfast, lunch, or dinner, my favourite table for two sits beside the fireplace from where I can admire the open kitchen as well as revel in the brightly coloured tiling, which sets a festive mood. Pacific Northwest culinary influences abound on the menus.

> **ACCOMMODATION**

Sun Peaks Townhomes (1-800-807-3257; www.sunpeaksresort.com): Scattered throughout the resort are a series of fourteen townhomes featuring fully equipped suites, perfect if you're staying longer than a night or two. For DIYers, whatever you don't bring in the cooler can be supplemented at the resort's grocery and liquor store.

Sun Peaks Lodge (3180 Creekside Way; 250-578-7878 or 1-800-333-9112; www.sunpeakslodge.com &): I've always felt as right at home here as I have anywhere in Europe, especially after checking in. Leave the road behind, sink into a comfy couch, and revel in your good fortune. Many of the forty-four rooms feature window nooks that overlook the chairlifts that ascend Mounts Tod and Sundance, the ideal place to enjoy your first cup of coffee for the day while assessing the non-existent lift lines. Tucked into the ground floor is the Sun Peaks Spa (see above).

Delta Sun Peaks Resort (3240 Village Way; 250-578-6000 or 1-866-552-5516): It took a while for the heart of Sun Peaks to be complete, but the Delta finally wrapped things up neatly with a big bow on top. The hotel's spacious, wood-panelled lobby imparts a welcoming sense of what to expect in your room. Coziness abounds. Slip into a robe and check out the full health club, heated outdoor pool, hot tubs, steam room, and fully equipped exercise room. That's what you're here for, right?

>25

VERNON

. . . . .

> ACCESS: 442 km northeast of Vancouver on Highways 1, 5, 5C and 97C via Hope, Merritt, and Kelowna; 472 km on Highways 1 and 97 via Kamloops.

> WHY GO: Snow sports, the best mountain bike park in the Okanagan, plus golf and more golf.

> KEEP IN MIND: To fully appreciate the North Okanagan and surrounding regions, make a loop tour, particularly as the added distance via Kamloops is a mere 30 km.

VERNON, AND the North Okanagan in general, is noticeably different from its sister cities to the south. Its environment, which can be wetter and cooler than elsewhere in the valley, intangibly implies that this is a place where people live to work rather than work to live. Not that its 35,000-plus residents don't know how to have fun—far from it. Surrounded on all sides by sandy beaches on Okanagan, Kalamalka, and Swan lakes, who wouldn't be enticed to knock off early on occasion and down a cold one? It's not just coincidence that Vernon is the home of Okanagan Spring Brewery, now a nationally recognized, micro-beer brand. In the 1980s, OSB's two brewmasters led the charge to reclaim the golden amber's pure roots just as the vintners at nearby Grey Monk Estate Winery began raising the bar for their elixir of choice. Just the thought makes me want to put my feet up and toast the taste revolution every time I journey here.

Vernon boasts a population with the youngest median age in the Okanagan; these folks are active, a characteristic that comes with the turf. Vernon's long history of working family farms and orchards is still very much in evidence in the surrounding landscape. If

Vernon suffers from an inferiority complex, that's because, despite the wealth of nearby lakes, its downtown lacks a waterfront to match Kelowna, Penticton, or Osoyoos. This feature may account for the temptation to simply drive through the somewhat non-descript downtown on the way to somewhere more picturesque. Thus the accommodations suggested in this chapter all lie beyond sidewalk's end. One thing evident no matter where you explore around Vernon is a genuineness to the residents that reflects a love of the life here.

To explore the area by bike, first pay a visit to Olympic Cycle and Ski (3102–31st Avenue; 250-542-9684), Sun Country Cycle (102–1340 Kalamalka Lake Road; 250-545-8775) or Vernon Bike World (3106–32nd Street; 250-545-0140). Paddlers will want to check out Heavy D's Kayak Rentals (250-309-0877), which will deliver to Swan, Okanagan, and Kalamalka lakes.

For general information consult Tourism Greater Vernon (701 Highway 97 South; 1-800-665-0795 or 250-542-1415; www.tourism vernon.ca). At tourism information displays throughout the Okanagan you can pick up a discount coupon to the Far West Factory Outlet Store (2463 Highway 97; 250-545-9098; www.farwest canada.com), a well-known local company that offers good-quality outdoor gear and snowboard equipment. Other sources of gear for snow sports include Olympia Cycle and Ski (2211–48th Avenue; 250-542-9684) and Vernon Outdoor Store (2709A–43rd Avenue; 250-558-1523).

> ## ELLISON PROVINCIAL PARK &

ACTIVITIES: *Boating, camping, fishing, paddling, picnicking, swimming, walking*

To get to the park drive 20 km south of Vernon on the east side of Okanagan Lake, just north of Carr's Landing; from Highway 97, turn west on 25th Avenue, which becomes Okanagan Landing Road.

Visit Ellison to experience the northern end of Okanagan Lake's rocky, forested headlands and sheltered, sandy bays. When you get restless between swims, explore the 6 km of trails leading around two beautiful bays, magnets for boaters. The rock faces offer boulder-climbing excitement and wildflower viewing for those bold enough to do a little scrambling.

> **FINTRY PROVINCIAL PARK**

ACTIVITIES: *Boating, camping, hiking, paddling, picnicking, swimming, walking*

Fintry Park lies 49 km southwest of Vernon on Okanagan Lake. Follow Highway 97 south to Westside Road, then drive downhill on Fintry Delta Road. Access is also possible by boat: travel 6 km across Okanagan Lake from Ellison Provincial Park (see above).

In its early years, Vernon attracted its share of American and European entrepreneurs who were quick to appreciate its vast agricultural potential set in the midst of captivating natural beauty. None was more gifted in this respect than British army captain James Dun-Waters whose Fintry Estate is impeccably preserved in this park set on the northwest side of Okanagan Lake, just enough off the beaten path to preserve a sense of the isolation that inspired Dun-Waters to creative feats of self-sustainability. The setting, complete with stretches of sandy beach, is a mirror of tranquility. If you're looking for a stair climb–style workout, try the stairway, complete with suspension bridge, that leads through steep canyons to the top of Fintry Falls from where you can experience the twin joys of catching your breath while drinking in the panoramic view of the lake and the Manor House below.

> **KALOYA REGIONAL PARK**

ACTIVITIES: *Boating, paddling, picnicking, swimming, walking*

To get to Kaloya Park drive 21 km south of Vernon off Highway 97 on the southern shore of Kalamalka Lake in the village of Oyama. Turn east on Oyama Road, then left on Trask Road.

A locals' favourite, Kaloya Beach anchors this Lake Country park, complete with a sandy swim area, covered picnic grounds, walking trails, lily pond, playground, and boat launch. The fact that this is a favourite spot for wedding photographs pretty much sums up Kaloya's magical setting. *Note:* Dogs are not allowed in this park.

> **SILVER STAR MOUNTAIN RESORT** *(1-800-663-4431; skisilverstar.com)*

ACTIVITIES: *Hiking, mountain biking, snow sports, walking*

North Okanagan skiers are a spoiled lot. So habituated are they to silently gliding through fluffy powder that when they hear their skis

Silver Star Resort

chattering on packed snow, they call it a day. Fortunately, Silver Star, 22 km northeast of Vernon on well-maintained Silver Star Mountain Road, gets plenty of champagne powder. Even when that's in short supply, the resort's impeccably groomed runs are as wide and smooth as the rolling mountain meadows through which they lead.

Unlike elsewhere in the Okanagan, not much has changed outwardly here since Silver Star's village core took shape in the mid-1980s. No matter where you stay, the ski-in/ski-out concept has just become more refined, with all trails leading to the resort's block-long, car-free main street, possibly the only thoroughfare in Canada that receives a nightly snow-cat grooming.

Skiers and snowboarders have a choice of the front (Vance Creek) or back (Putnam Creek) sides of the forested mountain from whose summit you can clearly glimpse Apex, Big White, and Sun Peaks resorts. Silver Star's Comet Six-Pack Express lift is a highly efficient people-mover. To get the big picture of the skiing here, cruise the resort's 8-km Eldorado Trail that winds from the summit to the base of Putnam Creek's Powder Gulch Express lift. Along the way it passes most of the resort's most challenging runs. If you're the kind of skier or snowboarder who likes to get air—big air—or simply watch as others launch complex tricks like 900 Cab Corkscrews, head for the three on-hill snow kickers built on the Christmas Bowl. From there you'll be looking down on skaters circling Brewer's Pond and kids bouncing around in the Tube Town adventure park.

Nowhere else in B.C. are downhill and cross-country trails as integrated as at Silver Star. Trails link the resort with adjacent Sovereign Lake Ski Area in Silver Star Provincial Park whose ski club has its own Nordic lodge (250-558-3036; sovereignlake.com).

Silver Star has focused on reintroducing skiing to those who may not have tried the sport in a while. And this strategy—long advocated by ski apostle Warren Miller as a way to revive interest in the millennia-old sport—seems to be working. On Friday evenings, over a thousand locals show up. The cool thing about it is the atmosphere. Some folks show up in their hunting gear. It's that grassroots. Of course, it helps that lift tickets are priced at $5 and equipment rentals at $10.

Out on the slopes, there's more to Silver Star's evergreen-forested ambience than simply long, smooth trails. The terrain park is as full of berms and boxes, tabletops and rails as a toy box whose contents spill across the open face of the wide, intermediate Big Dipper run. One of the most under-reported aspects of terrain parks in general is that skiers and snowboarders will discover some of the most untouched terrain off to the sides of the main features. These are ideal places not only to catch the action out of harm's way but also to carve a turn where few others venture. The park's open slopestyle features entice you to drop in for a looky-loo, even if you never plan to huck off a tabletop. And if you do, watch out for those folks in hunting gear.

Silver Star benefits from having Brewer's Pond, a 1-ha expanse with plenty of room for both classic blading to the rhythmical strains of Emil Waldteufel's "The Skater's Waltz" and shinnying with a puck and stick to Tom Cochrane's "Big League." Both camps agree on one thing: if your toes get cold, nothing beats standing around a bonfire with a hot cup of cocoa.

Of all three major Okanagan mountain resorts, Silver Star does the best job of reinventing itself from winter to summer. Not only does the village host the Okanagan Summer Wine Festival in mid-August, one of the high points of the year, it welcomes mountain-bike riders onto its chairlifts as soon as trails dry out in June. Ask bike enthusiasts in the region for their opinion and the uniform response will be that Silver Star's bike park rocks. That goes equally for both easy riders and hard-core bombers alike.

If you haven't been here before on a bike, I recommend a quick reconnaissance along a mostly level paved trail that leads from the village across Vance Creek and intersects with numerous single-track trails that lace through the forest and across open slopes. One of the rewards of exploring the paved route is the cooling shade provided on hot days. Given that this is a wooded environment, come prepared with insect repellent until later in the summer.

Once you've gotten a feel for the bike park, pick a trail that suits your ability and energy level and start ripping. Trails are well marked, and all lead to the bottom of the Comet Six-Pack Express chairlift where you can start all over again. One of my favourite mellow routes is Cabin Trail, a blend of paved and hardpacked dirt that rises and falls as it loops its way around mid-mountain. An unexpected reward is the sight of alpine wildflowers, which bloom profusely from mid-July to mid-August. If there's a downside to witnessing the cavalcade of colour from blue lupine and red paintbrush, it's that biting insects are just as much drawn to the blossoms as they are to those on two wheels. Mountain wildflower tours are offered in the afternoons from Monday to Saturday, July to September (250-545-7446; www.out doordiscoveries.com); and the same company offers bears and berries tours in the mornings from Thursday to Saturday. For those hikers who prefer to ride up and hike down, the Summit Chair runs with you in mind. *Note:* The best places to stay here are the condominiums in the Knoll neighbourhood, where Victorian Gaslight replica homes are decorated in four or five exterior hues and trimmed with cookie-cutter moulding. For reservations, visit www.staraccom.com.

> **OTHER ATTRACTIONS**

Golf: A total of eight courses lie spread throughout the North Okanagan, in Vernon as well as the nearby communities of Armstrong and Enderby. By far the most prestigious is the twenty-seven-hole (soon to be thirty-six) Predator Ridge (1-888-578-6688; www.predator ridge.com). Even if you don't golf, Predator Ridge is a quiet and welcoming place to stay, complete with an Aveda spa, tennis courts, restaurant, and small convenience store—handy, since rooms come equipped with full kitchens. Established in 1913, the Vernon Golf and Country Club (800 Kalamalka Lake Road; 250-542-0151) is one of the most venerable courses in B.C.

Davison Orchards (3111 Davison Road; 250-549-3266; www. davisonorchards.com): For starters, sample some twenty varieties of apples. Small wonder that this North Okanagan family farm, open to the public early May through October, has been famous for its ciders and pies since 1933. Did I mention the fudge?

Gray Monk Estate Winery (1055 Camp Road, Okanagan Centre; 250-766-3168 or 1-800-663-4205; www.graymonk.com): The Heiss family has laboured since the early days of the estate wineries in the 1970s to establish a reputation as a grower of Old World varietals such as pinot gris. Gray Monk was the first winery to serve food as well in their Grapevines Restaurant. Despite government intransigence in the 1980s, the Heiss family fought to pioneer this "revolutionary" concept. These days there's no better place to taste food than at a local winery. Vive la différence. Grapevines is open seven days for lunch from March 1 to October 30 and for dinner from June 15 to September 15.

Murals: Vernon is unique in the Okanagan as the only city to have embraced public art displayed on such a grand scale. As you move from block to block, twenty-seven heritage murals, some as large as 100 x 13 metres, vie for attention depicting cowboys and Indians, bicycles and motorcycles, geishas and fire captains. If it happened in Vernon over the past century, you're going to see it depicted on city walls. Lead artist Michelle Loughery, assisted by nine local artists, has created a dreamy feel downtown. To sample their creations, simply slow down to a crawl. A good place to begin is the Old Train Station (3101–29th Street; 250-542-5851; www.down townvernon.com or www.vernonmurals.ca).

O'Keefe Ranch (9380 Highway 97; 250-542-7868; www.okeefe ranch.ca): Fintry Estate (see above) and this nineteenth-century ranch stand as cornerstones of the North Okanagan. These days the working O'Keefe Ranch specializes in raising endangered species of livestock. As much a little village as a ranch, O'Keefe also features a few contemporary touches, including arts and crafts displays, the Cattleman's Club Restaurant, and the Hunting Hawk Winery. I lean towards a tour of the family home with its echoes of earlier times.

> DINING

Bugaboos Bakery Café (Silver Star Mountain Resort): Affable Dutch baker Frank Berkers rolls a combo of cinnamon and sugar in croissant dough. The ambrosial results are a masterful achievement. Daily soups and espressos rank right up there with the best as well.

The Eclectic Med Restaurant (2915–30th Avenue; 250-558-4646): Andrew and Dawn Fradley have lived and breathed life into the local dining scene for a dozen years. I first sought them out for their shaken-not-blended margaritas served in sturdy tumblers, and I've made a point of stopping every time I pass through since. The food's good, too, with influences that stretch from the couple's roots in the Mediterranean and North Africa, to the Caribbean and Asia. The wine list features a deep selection of Okanagan estate reserve wines.

The Swiss Hotel Silver Lode Inn (Silver Star Mountain Resort; 250-549-5105 or 1-800-554-4881; www.silverlode.com): Heidi and Isidore Borgeaud-Mueller are two of the originals who first opened up Silver Star in the 1980s. They've put their well-honed Swiss touch to good use ever since. I recommend the four-course fixed-price special that comes with one caveat: you must be seated before 7 PM. After a long day on the slopes, this requirement is never an issue with me. If you like wild mushrooms, Isidore's your man.

> ACCOMMODATION

Fintry and Ellison provincial parks: Fintry and Ellison parks, on the northwestern and northeastern sides, respectively, of Okanagan Lake offer plenty of inducements for camping. Check www.bcparks. ca for details on reservations.

Castle on the Mountain B&B (8227 Silver Star Road; 250-542-4593 or 1-800-667-2229; www.castleonthemountain.com): Treat yourself to the Copper Moon Cottage for an elevated view of the valley halfway between downtown and Silver Star Resort that you won't get elsewhere.

Lakeside Illahee Inn (15010 Tamarack Drive; 250-260-7896 or 1-888-260-7896; www.illahee.com): I liked this waterfront retreat on first sight and think you will, too.

> 26

KELOWNA

. . . . .

> ACCESS: Kelowna lies 395 km from Vancouver via Highways 1, 5, 97C, and 97 through Hope and Merritt. Air Canada and West-jet offer direct daily flights to Kelowna International Airport (www.kelownairport.com).

> WHY GO: Explore the cultural hub of the Okanagan.

> KEEP IN MIND: Allow extra time to cross the bridge between Kelowna and Westbank, even with the new five-lane span in 2008.

YOU CAN never get enough beach, but over the course of a day or two in Kelowna you can give it your best shot. Garlanded along the sandy shores of Okanagan Lake's hourglass waist, Kelowna ("grizzly bear" in the Interior Salish dialect) is by far the largest—and liveliest—city in the Okanagan. Despite the fact that one in five of its 168,000 residents is over the age of sixty five, making this the Canadian city with the oldest median age, a renaissance fuelled by an influx of young professionals has heralded an explosion of new restaurants, art galleries, artisan specialty food producers, and wineries. Kelowna is a beehive of expanded opportunities for outdoor recreation as well, whether it's cycling the Mission Creek Greenway or the Kettle Valley Railway/Trans Canada Trail, enjoying water sports at lakeside beaches, or partaking in snow sports in the surrounding Monashee Mountains and the gently rolling Okanagan Highlands.

Kelowna is a city of neighbourhoods: the Pandosy and Mission districts along Lakeshore Drive are particularly lively. Then there's the downtown core, one of my favourite places to stretch my legs on arrival, especially if I'm coming in May for Life and Arts, the city's signature festival, or for the Spring and Fall Okanagan Wine

CedarCreek Estate Winery, Kelowna

Festivals in May and again in late September through early October (www.thewinefestivals.com). In 2004 Kelowna was named the cultural capital of Canada, and it shows. A self-guided walking tour of the downtown cultural district leads past seventeen different locations, including the Art Ark, the Kelowna Art Gallery, and Waterfront Park. Pick up a walking tour map at the Kelowna Visitor Info Centre (544 Harvey Ave; 250-861-1515 or 1-800-663-4345; www.tourismkelowna.com) at the corner of Harvey Avenue (Highway 97) and Ellis Street, two blocks south of the cultural district.

No matter when I'm here, the BC Wine Museum and Wine Shop (1304 Ellis Street; 250-868-0441; www.kelownamuseums.ca) in the historic Laurel Packinghouse, is a must-see. Browse through over sixty VQA wineries as you mull which of over four hundred wines to choose from. Nearby, the Okanagan's oldest winery, Calona Wines (1125 Richter Street; 250-762-3332 or 1-888-246-4472; www.calona vineyards.ca), makes a good starting point for a wine country tour.

If you're exploring Kelowna by bike, check out Outbound Cycle and Sport (2417 Main Street, Westbank; 250-768-0799) for service and rentals, gear, bike tours, and a bike shuttle service, or Monashee Adventure Tours (1591 Highland drive; 250-762-9253 or 1-888-762-9253; www.monasheeadventuretours.com) for bike rentals and guided cycle tours of nearby orchards and city greenways, as well as snowshoe tours in winter. For other equipment rentals visit Sports Rent (3000 Pandosy Street; 250-861-5699; www.sportsrent kelowna.com) for Rollerblades, bikes, skis, and water toys or Mountain Surf (2936 Pandosy Street; 250-763-1504) for skis, snowboards, waterskis, kiteboards, wakeboards, clothing, parts, service, and accessories.

Paddlers will want to check out Winds and Rivers Escapes (250-545-4280 or 1-888-545-4280; www.windsrivers.bc.ca). Reg and Heather Scott's Vernon-based paddle adventure company offers canoe and winery tours, both in Kelowna on Okanagan Lake and beyond. And through Selah Outdoor Explorations (2000 Bennett Road; 250-768-4961) you'll meet Jordie Bowen who leads canoe and hiking trips on Okanagan Lake and in Okanagan Mountain Provincial Park. For kayak and canoe rentals, as well as guided land and water tours, drop by Lakefront Sports Centre (1310 Water Street; 250-862-2469; www.lakefrontsports.com) on the lagoon at the Grand Okanagan Resort.

> SUSAN ALISON

MATRIARCH SUSAN ALISON left a stirring account of her life in what is now Westbank. In the 1850s she gave birth to the first non-Native child in a fire-charred homestead. I think she would heartily approve of the Stewart family, scions of Quails' Gate, who now steward the land. Flower beds overflow with colour around the cabin, shaded by two towering beech trees.

For guided tours of the region consider Distinctly Kelowna Tours (250-979-1211 or 1-866-979-1211; www.wildflowersandwine. com) for winery, hiking, and agri-tours or the Adventure Okanagan Co-operative (1-800-549-1114; www.adventureokanagan.com), which represents twenty five guided outdoor adventure companies in the Okanagan, Shuswap, and Monashee regions. You're sure to find one to accommodate your ability and fitness level, whether you're looking for a hiking, biking, walking, paddling, or eco-tour.

> **BIG WHITE SKI RESORT** *(1-800-663-2772; bigwhite.com)*
ACTIVITIES: *Snow sports*
To reach Big White drive 56 km southeast of Kelowna, follow Highway 33 for 32 km to Big White Road, then head 24 km to the mountain village. Big White operates a shuttle service from Kelowna International Airport.

Everything about Big White is big, and getting bigger in a hurry. For starters, the base of the mountain spreads 10 km from the Gem Lake Lodge (a convenient place to park if you're just here for the day) to the heart of the village, where most activities and accommodations (including three hotels and a hostel) are concentrated. Much as you would at its Okanagan counterparts at Apex and Silver Star, forget your car upon arrival. Although a wagon pulled by a team of vapour-snorting Percherons once sufficed to transport visitors around the streets of the steep-sided village, an eight-person pedestrian gondola now connects the Happy Valley neighbourhood with the village centre. Happy Valley, with extensive ice-skating ponds and canals, Canada's largest tube park, a mini snowmobile track, and dog sledding and cross-country trails, epitomizes the trend away from an exclusive focus on skiing and snowboarding.

If there's a fly in the ointment at Big White, it's Monashee Mountain itself, whose south-facing peak's broad dome is exposed to sun and wind. More snow is required to cover its rocky surface than at most other B.C. resorts. By mid-winter, when the snow base surpasses 200 cm, the chance of gouging the bottom off your equipment drops as fast as the resort's package prices, which put to shame filmmaker Warren Miller's old adage that the family that skis together goes broke together. And just to make sure you get your money's worth, Big White also offers night skiing on western Canada's longest lit run.

For my money, the best meal deal at Big White is the soup-and-sandwich combo served at the Ridge Rocket Café, and the White Crystal Inn (1-800-663-2772) is *the* place to stay.

> KETTLE VALLEY RAILWAY/TRANS CANADA TRAIL
ACTIVITIES: *Cycling, viewpoints, walking*
One of the KVR/TCT's most scenic sections can be found on a hillside above Kelowna. Much of the 12-km stretch between the whistle stops of Myra and Ruth lie in shade, a boon on hot summer days. This stretch of the former railway bed hugs the cliffsides of the Okanagan Highlands that rise above Kelowna's orcharded eastern benchlands. Six trestles span the steepest sections of horseshoe-shaped Myra Canyon around whose walls the railbed winds southward for 2 km. From this elevated prospect, the views of the Okanagan Valley in the distance, with its orchards, vineyards, golf courses, and lakes, are superb, the kind most travellers rarely experience if they stick solely to the main roads. If you're hungry for a grand finale ride down the steep, twisty 8-km access road that leads from East Kelowna to the Myra Canyon trailhead, and head for the nearby Mission neighbourhood for well-deserved refreshment.

> MISSION CREEK GREENWAY
ACTIVITIES: *Cycling, horseback riding, nature observation, running, viewpoints, walking*
The City of Kelowna's bicycle route map is the essential guide to exploring the Mission Creek Greenway, a multi-use trail for those on foot, horseback, or bike. Contact Tourism Kelowna (1-800-663-4345; www.tourismkelowna.org) for a copy. Also, visit the Central Okanagan Regional District's Parks website for details (www.cord.bc.ca/departments/parks/regional/reg_parks_mission creek.aspx). Numerous approaches lead into the Greenway. I suggest starting from either Gordon Drive just east of Lakeshore Drive, the parking lots on KLO Road or East Kelowna Road, or the parking lot off Field Road in Scenic Canyon Regional Park.

Mission Creek Greenway bubbles along through a treed corridor of stately cottonwood and ponderosa pines, which act as a buffer

Gellatly Nut Farm Park, Westbank

between the greenway and nearby agricultural land. The 16.5-km greenway provides visitors with both a recreational and a historical perspective on Kelowna's past, as well as a detailed environmental overview at EECO Centre. Interpretive signs line the forested route that winds for 7.5 km between Scenic Canyon Regional Park and Okanagan Lake's sandy shoreline. Although this section of the greenway lacks the drama of the KVR/TCT, it provides visitors with both a recreational and a historical perspective on Kelowna's past. A more rugged stretch winds its way 9 km south through Scenic Canyon Park and through Gallagher's Canyon over boardwalks, bridges, and staircases to a viewpoint of Layer Cake Mountain.

By May an array of wild blossoms—mountain lady's slipper, tiger and chocolate lilies, striped coralroot—sprout in an open meadow, formerly the site of a pioneer homestead. Sweet scents from the sunny yellow blossoms on drifts of Oregon-grape shrubs perfume the air. These represent just a few of the hundred species of flowering plants visible here throughout spring and summer. In fall, the creek runs red with kokanee salmon. One of the best places to catch the action is from the viewing platform adjacent to the Father Pandosy Mission on Benvoulin Road.

> **BEACHES**

Visitors from the West Coast accustomed to ocean rhythms will be excused if during a visit to the Okanagan lakes they keep checking to see if they've left their towels high enough on the beach to escape a rising tide.

Gellatly Bay Aquatic Park on Boucherie Road offers one of the best beaches on the west side of Okanagan Lake. A CPR wharf was built here in the 1930s and remained in use until 1972, one of over twenty such docks and landings around the lake that were gradually closed as roads improved to Kelowna and Penticton. Restored by the efforts of community volunteers, the wharf is partnered with a diving tower just offshore.

On the Kelowna side, Bertram Creek Park and Cedar Creek Park are located within a short distance of each other on Lakeshore Drive south of the Mission district. Sheltered by a point of land, Bertram is the larger and more popular of the two and features an eye-pleasing amphitheatre beneath a stand of ponderosa pines. Its sandy lake bottom is also easier on the feet. However, more exposed Cedar Creek is a true locals beach, complete with a boat launch ramp. Picnic tables line the pea-gravel shore from where concrete steps lead into the lake. You may wish to wear water shoes when entering the lake in order to avoid sharp rocks. This is a good place to storm watch when winds whip up the lake, as well as to marvel at the pace of development consuming the west side of the lake between Westbank and Peachland, where the long lake doglegs south out of sight.

The entrances to both beaches are well marked, although Cedar Creek's requires a sharp turn off Lakeshore Drive directly below the St. Hubertus Winery.

Mission Hill Family Estate's Wine and Food Interpretation Centre (1730 Mission Hill Road, Westbank; 250-768-7611 or 1-888-999-1713; www.missionhillwinery.com) lies perched high atop a ridge on the west side of Okanagan Lake, and it offers one of the best viewpoint-and-sipping experiences in the Okanagan. Its towering arches, keystone, bell tower, and loggia walkway project a domineering image like no other winery in the valley.

Nearby lies Quails' Gate Estate Winery (3303 Boucherie Road, Westbank; 1-800-420-9463 or 250-769-2501; www.quailsgate.com). There isn't a more poignant contrast to how far estate wineries in the Okanagan have evolved than at Quails' Gate whose vineyards cascade downhill towards Okanagan Lake within sight of Mission Creek's bell tower. When the winery opened in 1987, its tasting room was housed in the quaint log cabin, once home to one of B.C.'s best-known pioneer families, the Alisons. It served the winery well for two decades before being upstaged by a panoramic new facility opened in 2007, which now houses the tasting room as well as the Old Vines Restaurant. Tie in a visit here with a cycle tour of Westbank's waterfront whose backroads are far less travelled than Kelowna's eastern lakeshore.

> KOK'D OUT

. . . .

MISSION CREEK was once an important gathering spot for Okanagan Natives. After settlers arrived, however, water from Mission Creek was diverted for orchard irrigation and domestic use. By the 1950s most of the historic spawning habitat had been lost. Sadly, this had a dreadful impact on the source of more than half of all trout and kokanee in Okanagan Lake. The number of spawning kokanee in Mission Creek was reduced from more than one million per year in the 1960s to only thirty thousand today, a steep price to pay for the growth of this otherwise charming community. At least Kelowna has the courage to acknowledge the cost of urbanization and has begun to seek some solutions.

Knox Mountain: Knox Mountain at the north end of Ellis Street in downtown Kelowna is the city's favourite park and preserves an area of environmentally sensitive ponderosa pine forest and grassland roughly half the size of Vancouver's Stanley Park. It is home to a variety of animal and plant life, some of which are endangered species. Come fall watch as kokanee salmon spawn along the lakeshore adjacent to the park. Trails of various ability levels ring the slopes below Mount Knox (623 m) and offer great views of Okanagan Lake from several lookout kiosks, including Pioneers' Pavilion. The park is open to vehicle traffic from mid-March to mid-November. Otherwise just walk or cycle in.

Okanagan Trail (Westbank): This shoreline trail runs along the west side of Okanagan Lake between its trailhead on Boucherie Road at Gellatly Bay Aquatic Park and Gellatly Nut Farm Park beside the Cove Resort on Gellatly Road, a distance of about 4 km. Along the way, it passes a variety of beaches offering perspectives on Kelowna's eastern shoreline and Okanagan Mountain Provincial Park.

Across the lake near the entrance to Okanagan Mountain Provincial Park sits *CedarCreek Estate Winery* (5445 Lakeshore Road; 250-764-8866; www.cedarcreek.bc.ca). One of B.C.'s original estate wineries, CedarCreek debuted in 1987 and is renowned as one of the most consistent producers in the valley. Sit on the terrace and enjoy a leisurely lunch. Why fly to Europe when an equally rich ambience lies so close to home?

Gellatly Nut Farm Regional Park: This park is home to a working heritage farm originally established in 1904 by Jack Gellatly who planted walnut, hazelnut, and butternut trees as well as the first fruit trees in the Okanagan. Today rows of mature trees dominate the park, offering shade to picnickers. As well, the park has a beach for swimming. Historically, the farm sold nuts and seedling trees. By late summer, the ground beneath the trees becomes covered with mature nuts for the gathering. As well, seedling trees are for sale year-round for about $20 each. Old wooden buildings dot the property, including a nut-drying shed shaded by a giant oak. To get here follow Gellatly Road east from Highway 97 to Whitworth Road just south of the Cove Lakeside Resort in Westbank.

Father Pandosy Mission (3685 Benvoulin Road; 250-860-8369): Kelowna's original settlement in the Mission neighbourhood is well preserved, complete with a (likely unintentionally) scary mannequin dressed up as the good priest.

> ## DINING

Kelowna is experiencing a restaurant boom unlike anything the city has ever seen before. The likes of *De Montreuil* (368 Bernard Avenue; 250-860-5508), which also runs the Old Vines Patio at Quails' Gate Estate Winery, and more recent arrivals such as *Fresco* (1560 Water Street; 250-868-8805) have set a benchmark for excellence.

Minstrel Café and Bar (4638 Lakeshore Road; 250-764-2301; www.minstrelcafe.com): Rather unpretentious from the outside, this place rocks, whether live music is on the menu or not.

Hotel Eldorado (500 Cook Road; 250-763-7500; www.eldorado kelowna.com): Although the classic lakeside hotel rooms and spa are the main attractions here, I prefer the restaurant and bar's historic woodsy ambience to just about any place else in town.

Carmelis Artisan Goat Cheese (170 Timberline Road; 250-764-9033; www.carmelisgoatcheese.com): On the doorstep of Okanagan Mountain lies a remarkable family-run cheese factory with goat milk gelato also on offer. Pair the cheese with some local fruit, a jug of wine, and a trusted companion and you have all the makings for one fine time.

> ## ACCOMMODATION

A View of the Lake B&B (1877 Horizon Drive, Westbank; 250-769-7854; www.aviewofthelake.com): Executive chef Steve Marston splits his time between running the Old Vines Restaurant at

> # OGOPOGO
· · · · · ·

KELOWNA HAS its own version of the Loch Ness Monster: Ogopogo. No one has yet claimed the $2 million reward offered for providing proof of its existence, but enough sightings over the past one hundred years have kept cryptologists searching and locals selling T-shirts.

Quails' Gate Estate Winery and the three-suite B&B with his wife, Chrissy, where they host three-course breakfasts and four-course dinners, complete with cooking demonstrations in the Marstons' open kitchen.

Cove Lakeside Resort and Spa/Bonfire Restaurant (4205 Gellatly Road, Westbank; 250-707-1800 or 1-877-762-2683; www.covelakeside.com): The Cove's suites offer an entirely self-contained experience, complete with full kitchens, including wine fridges. A sculpture by Bill Reid in the lobby sets the west-beyond-the-west tone, as does the native plant garden, which surrounds a large pool and barbecue complex. It's close to Westbank wineries, parks, and greenways, and you could spend days here without ever feeling the need to cross the bridge into downtown Kelowna.

Manteo Resort (3766 Lakeshore Drive; 250-860-1031 or 1-800-445-5255; www.manteo.com): Bowls of fresh apples everywhere set the healthful tone at this bright waterfront hotel and villa. Clean, quiet, artsy, and boasting an armful of amenities including the Wild Apple Grill—in 2005 named the Okanagan's finest place to dine by the BC Restaurant and Foodservices Association—this is my preferred place to stay, especially since the Mission Greenway lies within a short distance when you tire of the beach.

PENTICTON

. . . . .

> ACCESS: To get to Penticton travel 391 km east of Vancouver on
> Highways 1 and 3 via Hope and Keremeos, then on Highways 3A
> and 97. Alternatively drive 422 km on Highways 1 and 5 via Hope
> and Merritt, then along Highways 97C and 97.

> WHY GO: Not too big. Not too small. The right size for just about
> everything you need.

> KEEP IN MIND: The town fills up fast when events like the Iron-
> man Triathlon come to town in August or during the spring and fall
> wine festivals. Reserve well in advance or be prepared to take pot
> luck.

WEDGED BETWEEN Skaha Lake on the south and Okanagan Lake on the north, Penticton advertises itself as "the
place to live forever," which is surely the fervent hope of its
retirement-age citizenry who constitute the majority of the region's
41,500 residents. Penticton, the "Peach City," might just as easily
be called the Festival City for the numerous events it hosts each
year. The annual festive season gets underway with the Fest-of-Ale
in April, followed by the Meadowlark and Okanagan Spring wine
festivals in May, the Pacific Northwest Elvis Festival in June, the
campy Beach Blanket Film Festival in July, the Peach Festival and
Ironman Canada Triathlon in August, and the Okanagan Fall Wine
Festival spread over late September and early October. And that's
just skimming the surface. You can count on catching music, dance,
highland games, and farmers' and artisan markets throughout the
year. By far the biggest reason that draws me back to Penticton time
and again is the wide range of outdoor activities, such as skiing at

Apex Mountain Resort or biking the stretch of Kettle Valley Railway Trail. There's something about breathing in the fresh Okanagan air that stokes my appetite for local food and wine and guarantees a good night's sleep. That and the journey itself, especially given the improvements to Highway 3 that make driving the southern route through Manning Provincial Park and the Okanagan-Similkameen region such a pleasure.

For general information on the region, contact the Penticton and Wine Country Visitor Centre (553 Railway Street; 250-493-4055 or 1-800-663-5052; www.vacationshappenhere.com). For guided tours of the region, contact Ambrosia Tours (250-492-1095), which provides shuttle service to KVR trail destinations from downtown Penticton.

Cyclists will want to check out the Bike Barn (300 Westminster Avenue West; 250-492-4140; www.bikebarn.ca). Roadies, triathletes, and off-roaders all gather here at the oldest shop in town. Alternatively, make a visit to Freedom Bike Shop (533 Main Street; 250-493-0686; www.freedombikeshop.com) for sales, repairs, rentals, and maps.

Horseback riding: novice or expert, English or western, trail ride with Wild Horse Mountain Ranch (www.wildhorsemountainranch.com).

In winter visit Apex Ski Shop (1055 W Westminster Avenue; 250-492-8315) or Skaha Outdoor Sport (399 Main Street; 250-493-1216; www.westernfrontboardshop.com).

> **APEX MOUNTAIN RESORT** *(1-877-777-2739; apexresort.com)*
ACTIVITIES: *Snow sports*
Imagine meeting the co-owner of a winter resort, such as Apex's Louise Burgart, while standing in a lift line. At Apex Mountain Resort, 33 km west of Penticton on Green Mountain Road, you might do just that. But don't tarry. Follow the affable Louise aboard a chairlift if you hope to exchange more than a few words. Given the speed with which skiers and snowboarders finish their runs and hop about either the Quicksilver detachable quad chair for a quick trip to the top of Beaconsfield Mountain, or the Stock's triple chairlift to mid-mountain, Apex's almost non-existent lift lines are no place

Kettle Valley Railway trail, Naramata

to dawdle. If you want to talk to the locals, such as a Penticton doctor who prescribes seasons ski passes for those who suffer seasonal affective disorder, chat while catching your breath on the chair.

Burgart brims with pride over her resort's newest five runs on the sunny south side of the mountain. Dubbed the Wildside, these runs complement two dozen expert-rated pistes that for decades have channelled downhill through the pine forests below Beaconsfield's alpine zone. Although the mountain also offers plenty of less intimidating cruising runs—for example, the 5-km Grandfather's Trail that leads from the top of Beaconsfield to the village is one of the gentlest runs on which to hone mountain riding skills—these gunbarrel chutes define Apex. Hero powder—light, puffy snow—that pillows up in the chutes puts up just enough resistance to naturally slow one's speed to that of a controlled free-fall. Those whose knees can't handle such stress search out the Motherlode, the best cruising run at any Okanagan resort. Superbly groomed, its rolling contour is guaranteed to elicit whoops of joy from even the most jaded skiers.

Three culinary must-sees while at Apex are the Fresh Tracks Café and Catering, renowned for chili and ooey-gooey cinnamon buns; the Gunbarrel Saloon, where the walls are bedecked in memorabilia from Apex's early years; and Betty's Billy Goat Hut at the top of the Quicksilver chair. At 2,180 m elevation, Betty Wiedeman runs one of the more exclusive kitchens in Canada. No matter the weather conditions, the mile-high altitude always stokes an appetite. As spring temperatures rise, the hut's deck swell with visitors attracted not only by the cooking but also by panoramic views of Big White and Silver Star Mountains to the north, and Mount Baldy and Copper Butte on the B.C.–Washington State border to the south.

Apex lies a half-hour drive from Penticton. Although many hotels offer shuttle bus service to the mountain, there are an increasing number of places to stay in the resort's boutique village with its restaurants, bars, and a well-stocked grocery, bakery, and liquor store. Almost all accommodations (including a hotel and a hostel) lie within several minutes' walk of the lifts and shops. The resort's ice-skating rink is as active at night as the hills are by day. There's also extensive cross-country skiing at the nearby Nickel Plate Nordic Centre (250-292-8110; nickelplatenordic.org).

> ## KETTLE VALLEY RAILWAY/TRANS CANADA TRAIL
ACTIVITIES: *Cycling, viewpoints, walking*
To reach Naramata via the KVR/TCT from downtown Penticton, follow Westminster Avenue east to Vancouver Avenue, then turn left onto Vancouver Place. To begin from Naramata, park at the junction of Smethurst Road and the KVR/TCT off Naramata Road.

The KVR/TCT winds its way for 477 km through the southern interior of B.C. One of its prettiest stretches runs between Kelowna and Penticton, a distance of about 80 km. You could spend the better part of a day making the journey one way. Although this trip may appeal to seat-hardened members of the cycle set, the majority of us will be happy to cover the same amount of ground—or even half that distance—along a scenic 45 km stretch between downtown Penticton and Chute Lake, where several KVR structures have been preserved at the funky, time machine–themed Chute Lake Resort. Along the way, the KVR passes through the Naramata benchlands, site of intensive viticulture activity and home to over a dozen wineries whose patios provide ample opportunity for cyclists to rest and imbibe. Although one of the KVR/TCT's more appealing features is its gentle grade, you'll find that the trail north of Penticton is nonetheless a steady uphill climb with plenty of opportunities to catch your breath as you read interpretive signs strategically placed along the route. Allow four hours to cover the entire distance one way, half that for the return downhill journey.

For a more moderate approach, join a guided, van-assisted tour, or arrange for a shuttle service to take you to Chute Lake or one of the trail access point along the way, such as the well-marked Glenfir Station whistle stop adjacent to Chute Lake Road. Downhill from Glenfir, the KVR/TCT drops 10 km to the Arawana Station in Naramata. Along the way it passes through Little Tunnel and provides many opportunities to simply revel in the spectacular scenery as Okanagan Lake spreads below Naramata's intensely planted headlands, with the town of Summerland on the west side of the lake and Penticton and Skaha Lake to the south. The appeal of this section of the KVR is difficult to overstate, particularly when you detour into one of the wineries, like Red Rooster or Hillside (the handiest). Others, including Joie Wines and Farm Cooking School and Lake Breeze, require a short detour off the KVR/TCT onto Naramata Road. All connector roads, such as Sutherland, are well marked. Naramata Road is winding with limited shoulder space for cyclists. That said, traffic is usually of moderate volume and speed.

KVR chief engineer Andrew McCulloch is buried in the Lakeview Cemetery overlooking the trail. His grave is located in section D to the right of the main entrance and below the fire hydrant.

Okanagan Lake, Penticton

> **NARAMATA**

ACTIVITIES: *Cycling, swimming, walking*

This picturesque village, 16 km north of Penticton on Naramata Road, is surrounded by wineries, orchards, and beaches. Sage-covered slopes and intensely planted headlands jut out into Okanagan Lake. Just getting there is half the enjoyment as the road winds and dips its way before depositing you at the Village Grounds waterfront, anchored by the classic Naramata Heritage Inn (see under Accommodation) and the golden-hued Sandy Beach Lodge and Resort (250-496-5765; www.sandybeachresort.com). I recommend you pick up the *Discover Naramata* visitors' guide, which is chock full of maps, walking tour directions, and local lore, such as the far-fetched origins of the town's name. Visit www.discovernaramata. com to request a free copy. For information about the wineries on the Naramata Bench, visit www.naramatabench.com.

> SKAHA BLUFFS

ACTIVITIES: *Climbing, hiking, viewpoints*
In the inner circles of the rock-climbing community, this classic rock playground's reputation proceeds itself. There's simply nothing else like it in the Okanagan Valley, particularly for instant access. Only 19 km southwest of Penticton, it can just as easily be explored on foot as spread-eagled across the face of one of the bluff's cliffs. A short, steep staircase leads to the base of the first bluff, dubbed Doctor's Wall, seemingly designed to test a climber's commitment. A lengthy loop trail leads past a series of bluffs from the summits of which are views of extraordinary proportions. Allow 30 to 60 minutes to explore this route. One of the best times of year to visit is in June and early July when wildflowers, such as the exotic Mariposa lily, are in bloom. On hot days, a moderating breeze blows across the bluffs. To gear up for climbing visit Skaha Rock Adventure (250-493-1765; www.skaharockclimbing.com).

> SKAHA LAKE PARK AND MARINA WAY PARK

ACTIVITIES: *Swimming*
Depending on which way the wind is blowing, head for either Skaha Lake Park on the south side of town or Okanagan Beach on Lakeshore Drive in Penticton's downtown neighbourhood. One of the best and least well-known beaches is at Marina Way Park just east of Okanagan Beach at the foot of Front Street.

> MEADOWLARK FESTIVAL

One of Penticton's most successful gatherings is the Meadowlark Festival, which features events throughout the South Okanagan and neighbouring Similkameen Valley in May. The festival is staged by the Okanagan Similkameen Conservation Alliance, a group dedicated to promoting environmental awareness of one of Canada's most endangered ecosystems. Although that hardly sounds as exciting as rolling out a barrel or casting a blanket on sun-baked sand, the festival, which attracts more than three thousand knowledge-hungry visitors, couldn't be more engaging, particularly with those who enjoy celebrating the return of the western meadowlark, one of the most golden-throated denizens of the bird world. As ornithologists say, meadowlark songs are like cups full of music being poured from a pitcher. Once heard, they are not forgotten.

Although this member of the blackbird group may be the festival's poster child, a host of other life forms, such as rattlesnakes, bats, bluebirds, and mountain goats, share top billing, at least when it comes to field trips that focus on these creatures' respective habitats and that are regularly among the first to sell out. Such events are part of a showcase that highlights the hourglass-shaped portion of the Okanagan Valley that lies between Summerland and Osoyoos (with Penticton at its hub) and serves as a concentrated area for bird and animal migration between the Cariboo and the Great Basin Desert to the south. With less than 10 per cent of the Okanagan's original habitat intact (a third of which lies undisturbed on Native lands), it's small wonder that this area is under increasing threat, especially as each year more land is developed into vineyards, golf courses, and residential property. For more information on events and field trip reservations, contact the Meadowlark Festival (1-866-699-9453; www.meadowlarkfestival.bc.ca).

> ### THREE BLIND MICE TRAILS
When exploring the KVR Trail between Naramata and Chute Lake, the Three Blind Mice network of mountain biking and hiking trails offers added excitement. The one caveat is that there are many trails within this area, so pick up a trail map at one of the local bike shops before winding your way among the ponderosa pines, rock bluffs, and grasslands. These trails offer downhill runs that flow through the forest with beautiful views of the orchards and vineyards that border Okanagan Lake. Routes suited to all levels of ability include the Rusty Muffler Trail, the 10-km Reservoir Route Trail, and the White Tail Trail.

> ### DINING
The Bench Artisan Food Market (368 Vancouver Avenue; 250-492-2222; www.thebenchmarket.com): Whether you're coming or going along the route to Naramata, stop here for a shot of rocket fuel. It's also an excellent source for picnic goodies, with all the ingredients you need, from fresh bread to cheeses, plus prepared meals to eat

in or take out. In summer, the patio is a great place to get inside advice from locals on everything from bike and hiking trails to the best beaches.

Theo's (687 Main Street; 250-492-4019; www.eatsquid.com): Enjoy calamari? There's no place better to savour this classic Greek dish—deep-fried or baked—than the cornerstone of Penticton's dining scene. That's just for starters. Did I mention the fresh-fruit margaritas? Life doesn't get much sweeter than this, except perhaps when viewed from the table on Theo's Romeo-and-Juliet balcony reserved for couples. Homey in a grand villa kind of way, this former private residence is so thoroughly enjoyable you may want to move in. It could take a lifetime to work your way through the menu and a wine list deep in Okanagan vintages.

> **ACCOMMODATION**

Deer Path Lookout B&B Inn (150 Saddlehorn Drive; 250-497-6833 or 1-877-497-8999; www.deerpathlookout.bc.ca): This high-end inn features three large suites plus a guest bungalow, heated outdoor pool, and adobe design in a suburban location between Penticton and Naramata.

Penticton Lakeside Resort, Convention Centre and Casino (21 Lakeshore Drive; 1-800-663-9400; www.rpbhotels.com). Kick back on this resort's private beach, or in the indoor pool.

Naramata Heritage Inn and Spa (3625–1st Street, Naramata; 250-496-6808 or 1-866-617-1188; www.naramatainn.com). This hotel has been completely renovated and restored to classic grandeur complete with antique decor, wine bar and restaurant and Aveda Concept Heirloom Spa. Take advantage of their complimentary mountain bikes.

> 28

OSOYOOS AND OLIVER

. . . . .

> ACCESS: Drive 395 km east of Vancouver on Highways 1 and 3 via Hope.

> WHY GO: Take in the Golden Mile of Vineyards.

> KEEP IN MIND: Osoyoos and Oliver triple in population in July and August.

OSOYOOS AND OLIVER are two equal-sized peas in a pod of vineyards, orchards, and truck gardens. What a cornucopia. And the ethnic make-up is just as varied: First Nation, European, East Indian, and the most recent arrivals, Albertans. As much as Vancouverites have embraced the Okanagan, even greater numbers of vacationing Wild Rose families arrive in droves, particularly during school breaks. Can you blame them? With the explosion of vineyards in the South Okanagan, this part of B.C. is designed with tourism in mind. And it's a vicious circle: the more tourists come, the more the valley is developed into golf courses, resorts and watering holes. With that development comes an increased threat to the most endangered ecosystem in the country. A proposed national park would provide a much-needed level of protection for what remains.

Destination Osoyoos (1-888-676-9667; www.destinationosoyoos. com) operates the British Columbia Visitor Centre at the junction of Highways 3 and 97 in Osoyoos. The Oliver Info Centre is located in a brightly painted former CPR station on Highway 97 in the heart of downtown Oliver.

> **INTERNATIONAL BIKING AND HIKING TRAIL**
ACTIVITIES: *Cycling, hiking, walking*
This partially paved 18.4-km multi-use trail links Osoyoos with Oliver from the north end of Osoyoos Lake and loops through both the Black Sage Road and the Golden Mile as the pathway parallels the Okanagan River channel. It's always difficult knowing which winery along the route to favour with your presence. I always believe that you'll know the right one when you see it. To find the trailhead, turn east off Highway 97 on Road 22, 9 km north of Osoyoos.

> **GOLDEN MILE**
ACTIVITIES: *Cycling, driving, walking*
The Osoyoos-Oliver region has 56 per cent of all B.C. vineyards and 86 per cent of all grapes growing in the province. With over twenty one wineries spread between Osoyoos and Oliver, including stalwarts such as Gehringer Brothers and Tinhorn Creek, it's obvious why this stretch along Highway 97 goes by the moniker "The Golden Mile." It's equally understandable that deciding which wineries to visit can be a daunting task. For starters, my advice is to visit the Wine Cave at the British Columbia Visitor Centre in Osoyoos, where you can arrange to join a half- or full-day escorted wine tour. Expert advice is also available at the VQA Wine Store and Gift Shoppe (34881–97th Street, Oliver; 250-498-4867 or 1-888-880-9463; www.winecountry canada.com).

> **NK'MIP DESERT CULTURAL CENTRE** *(1000 Rancher Creek Road; 250-495-7901; www.nkmipdesert.com)*
ACTIVITIES: *Nature observation, walking*
Opened in June 2006, the $9 million Nk'Mip Desert Cultural Centre is the latest in an impressive list of economic initiatives undertaken by the Osoyoos Indian Band over the past twenty five years. The centre's mission is to teach about the lands, the legends, and the peoples. Trails and interpretive displays surround the architectural marvel. Set into the antelope-brush– and sagebrush-covered hillside, the centre's rammed earth walls are striated with pastel shades that mimic its surroundings. One undulating exterior wall bears precise, colour-coded timelines that detail significant geological, historical,

and human events from the band's perspective. At the heart of this latest band-driven initiative—which also includes a winery, golf course, and resort complex—is a desire to preserve a way of life that's undergone considerable change over the past two centuries following European contact. Over time, the people's traditional relationship with the land has become as perilous as it is for creatures such as badgers, burrowing owls, and western rattlesnakes. A rich scent of sagebrush fills the sun-baked landscape as you head out from the cool confines of the centre's interior, which features a theatre, interpretive galleries such as a rattlesnake "hotel," and a revelatory display of Inkameep Day School children's drawings from the 1930s. (Unlike many Native bands, the Okanagan hired teachers to work on their reserve rather than send students away to residential school.) Life-sized metal figurine sculptures by Spokane artist Virgil "Smoker" Marchand installed beside pathways suggest what life was like in a traditional village environment. One balances hot rocks at the doorway of a sweat lodge while others spear and dry salmon. The most impressive of all depicts a stylized warrior on horseback offering a peace pipe to the sky.

Time spent under the desert sun quickly saps strength from even the most energetic souls. Benches in riparian groves of ponderosa pine and cottonwoods offer shade in which to relax. As you survey the brown hills that roll south into nearby Washington State and north towards Oliver through a stretch of vineyards known as the Golden Mile, take comfort in the thought of a cooling dip in Osoyoos Lake.

> **OSOYOOS DESERT CENTRE** *(146th Avenue just east of Highway 97; 1-877-899-0897; www.desert.org)* &
ACTIVITIES: *Nature observation, walking*
It's not exactly like walking on coals. More like stepping into a furnace. Welcome to the desert, southern Okanagan–style, where the air is as dry as dust and as hot as the bluebird that will pogo-dance above your head if you interrupt a flying lesson here at the Desert Centre in Osoyoos.

Four fledglings flit nearby among the gangly branches of blossoming antelope-brush. Their mother beckons encouragingly to join her

Nk'Mip Desert Cultural Centre, Osoyoos

atop a nearby fencepost. For inspiration, the bluebird chicks need look no farther than the sky above where ravens, practising their courtship aerobatics, are having soaring and flying-upside-down contests. Whichever raven soars longest gets the girl—no small feat, since soaring is tricky at the best of times for these open-country lovers.

You'll pick up on all this up from wildlife biologist Joanne Muirhead, the Desert Centre's education coordinator and site manager. She and her staff offer guided tours year round. As you survey the pancake-flat landscape, you may wonder what's to see. With the exception of the birds, just about every other living, breathing land creature—including the spadefoot toad—has taken cover under whatever shade is handy, such as that proffered by the portable trailers, which currently house the centre's reception room and administration offices. There are thirty different research stations spread out over the 27-ha site. The open countryside around Osoyoos still contains enough habitat to support a host of desert species, but such land is disappearing quickly. Less than 10 per cent of the original habitat remains. Thanks to irrigation, more and more property is cultivated each year as vineyards. This trend is why a visit to the Desert Centre, along with its counterpart across the valley, the Nk'Mip Desert Heritage and Cultural Centre, provides such a timely—and surprisingly entertaining—perspective on this unique Canadian microclimate, one characterized as the most endangered environment in Canada.

Unlike the Sahara, which formed 65 million years ago, the so-called pocket desert around Osoyoos (the northernmost section of the vast Great Basin Desert) is a mere ten thousand years old. Is this, in fact, a true desert? After all, if you wanted to be picky, a bona fide desert is defined as receiving 250 mm or less rainfall per year. The average annual precipitation around Osoyoos is 300 mm. But a desert is so much more than the amount of rainfall. Staff will point out the many desert indicators that surround the centre—ones that an uninformed eye would overlook, such as grey horsebrush and longleafed flox, plants so rare that no mention is made of them in regional plant guides. Boardwalks lead out above a thin layer of cryptogamic crust that covers the ground. If broken, sand seeps up through the cracks and creates dunes, hardly the scenario for sustaining plant life critical to the survival of a host of animal species, such as the monarch butterfly. At intervals around the 1.5 km of boardwalk that loop out over the desert, staff demonstrate that the cryptogamic crust is a living organism by sprinkling water on a small patch. It immediately begins to change from a dry, dead-looking crust to a vibrant green and brown mosslike mush. While you watch, look for tiny tunnels that lead underground where you can just distinguish the red hourglass design on a black widow spider's back as it rests near the surface. Despite its fearsome reputation, black widows only come out at night and bites are extremely uncommon. (However, scorpions have recently been reintroduced to the desert near here.)

If you're looking for a little shelter from the sun, the boardwalk is punctuated by a series of eye-catching, slope-roofed ramadas, where visitors can find some shade and rehydrate. Daytime summer temperatures often soar to 40°C or more. Such heat can trigger feelings akin to drunkenness, which is why water bottles are always kept at the ready. As a precaution, visitors to the centre are not allowed to explore on their own but must join one of the hourly guided tours. This requirement also ensures that no one will pick flowers or step off the boardwalk. A small pond nearby is the site of one of the Desert Centre's greatest success stories. Prior to the establishment of the centre (which hosts over twenty thousand visitors a year), this land was used for ranching. Great Basin spadefoot tadpoles were discovered when the former owner removed a water trough. As spadefoot toads always return to the same place to mate, the centre quickly constructed a pond to encourage them to stay. The tiny toads, which spend 90 per cent of their time underground, corkscrew themselves into the mud with the aid of their distinctively shaped feet, only emerging at night to feed on insects. The toads have tiger salamanders for company. Amphibians are extremely rare finds in the desert.

Each summer, the centre hosts a full-moon gala event called Romancing the Desert. In fact cool night tours are offered here on several evenings a week throughout the summer.

> ## OTHER ATTRACTIONS

Anarchist Mountain Viewpoint: The Boundary region is sandwiched between the Okanagan and the Kootenays along the B.C.–Washington State border. There's something about the rolling landscape here with its golden-hued hills that hold a tremendous appeal for me. As the population thins out between Osoyoos and Grand Forks, spacious tracts of open range roll off to both the north and south of Highway 3. Sporadic irrigation turns the fields a luminous green. Although hay is the principal crop newly planted vineyards hug the lower slopes of Anarchist Mountain that marks the western perimeter of the Boundary. Even if you venture no farther than to the viewpoint 11 km east of Osoyoos along the switchbacks to Anarchist Summit on Highway 3, make the effort for the geography lesson alone.

Festival of the Grape: Held from noon to sundown at Oliver Community Park by the Okanagan River on the last Sunday in September, the festival features wine tasting, exhibit booths, games, and the famous Grape Stomp Competition. The event includes more than thirty four wineries and seventeen food vendors. Adult tickets are $19 in advance or $22 at the gate. For tickets call 250-498-6321.

Golf: With a climate to rival Palm Springs, many visitors journey here as much to golf as to wine and dine. Of the five local courses, I suggest the thirty-six-hole Osoyoos Golf and Country Club (123000 Golf Course Drive; 250-495-3355 or 1-800-481-6665; www.golf osoyoos.com) on the west side of Osoyoos Lake south of downtown, the eighteen-hole Nk'Mip Canyon Desert Golf Course (37041–71st Street, Oliver; 250-498-2880 or 1-800-656-5755; www.inkameep canyon.com), and the eighteen-hole Fairview Mountain Golf Club (13105–334th Avenue, Oliver; 250-498-6050 or 1-866-534-7264; www.fairviewmountain.com) rated one of ScoreGolf's Top-100 courses.

Tickleberry's (Main Street, Okanagan Falls, 9 km north of Oliver; 1-800-667-8002; www.tickleberrys.com): Renowned throughout the Okanagan for its forty flavours of ice cream and *au naturel* chocolate-covered dried fruit, Tickleberry's is surrounded by extravagantly painted murals. If nothing else, stop for a photo op and test how long your rubber arm can resist being twisted into ordering a triple-scooper, especially when temperatures top 40°C.

> **DINING**

Dolci Deli (8710 Main Street; 250-495-6807; www.dolcideli.com): Noted for its Swiss-German inspired catering prowess, the Dolci is open every day for lunch. Pull up a stool, order a coffee, and choose from a selection of fresh local deli goodies at the counter showcase. *Dolci* (sweet) picnic fare.

Campo Marina Café and Restaurant (5907 Main Street; 250-495-7650; www.campomarina.com): If you dine out only once in Osoyoos, make Gemma and Mike Oran's Mediterranean-themed eatery the place.

Nk'Mip Cellars (1400 Rancher Creek Road; 250-495-2985; www.nkmipcellars.com): Go wild and splurge on the Nk'Mip Platter for Two at lunch. And of course enjoy a glass of wine from the barrel-roofed cellar.

Toasted Oak Wine Bar and Grill (34881–97th Street, Oliver; 250-498-4867 or 1-888-880-9463; www.winecountry-canada.com):

The Toasted Oak boasts the largest exclusively B.C. wine list in the world paired with local cuisine and is the perfect place for a refreshing pause while exploring the International Hiking and Biking Trail (see above).

> ## ACCOMMODATION

Nk'mip Campground and RV Park: Opened in 1982, and located directly downhill from the Nk'Mip Desert Cultural Centre, the campground was one of the band's first tourism-related ventures and remains the most perennially popular attraction. Recently many such privately run waterfront parks, the staple of family vacations for generations of visitors, have been sold for redevelopment as condominiums. In its own way, the Okanagan people are just as protective of this way of relating to the land as they are within the larger objectives of their Desert Cultural Centre. And that's good news for everyone who enjoys sleeping under the stars. Avoid July and August, when campers are squeezed together cheek by jowl.

Spirit Ridge Vineyard Resort and Spa (1200 Rancher Creek Road; 250-495-5445; www.spiritridge.ca): The Spirit Ridge is a great place to rub shoulders with Albertans, including in the resort's dining room, PassaTempo (www.passatempo.biz), run by transplanted Edmonton restaurateur Brad Lazarenko. This all-suite adobe-style resort sports full kitchens and enjoys an enviable location, although it is still a work in progress and will triple in size over the next several years. The resort sits adjacent to the Nk'Mip Desert Cultural Centre and Sonora Dunes golf course. Bicycles are available to ride the International Bike and Hike Trail or simply to cruise over to the beach and dining district.

Mount Kobau is the site for the annual Star Party in mid-August as part of a week-long gathering of astronomers and amateur star gazers.

Burrowing Owl Estate Winery (100 Burrowing Owl Place; 250-498-0620 or 1-877-498-0620; www.burrowingowlwine.com): When money is no object, stay here. Ten guest rooms surround an outdoor solar-heated pool and hot tub. Chef Bernard Cassavant of Whistler fame presides over the winery's Sonora Room restaurant.

Destination Index

. . . .

Active Pass, 98–99, 102–03,
 105–07, 109, 113
Agassiz, 7–8
Aldridge Point, 157
Alice Lake Park, 26–27
Alta Lake, 33
Anarchist Mountain, 245
Ancient Cedars Loop Trail, 36–37
Anderson Lake, 49
Apex Mountain Resort, 215, 223,
 232–34
Armours Beach, 65
Armstrong, 217
Atwell Peak, 30

Baker, Mount, 120, 125, 134
Bastion Square, 145–46
Battleship Lake, 188
Baynes Peak, 125
Beacon Hill Park, 142, 146
Bear Beach, 152
Beaumont/Mount Norman (GINPR
 South Pender), 117–118
Beaver Point, 129
Beaver Pond Trail, 6
Becher Bay, 157
Beaconsfield Mountain, 232
Beddis Beach, 123–24
Bedwell Harbour, 115, 119, 121
Bellhouse Park, 98–99
Bennett Bay, 108, 113
Bertram Creek Park, 226

Big White Mountain, 234
Big White Ski Resort, 188, 215, 223–24
Bike Ranch, the, 202
Birkenhead River Valley, 49
Blackcomb, 41–43
Blubber Bay, 90
Bluffs Park, 97–99
Blunden Island, 137
Boat Pass, 132, 135
Bonniebrook Beach, 63–64
Boot Cove, 132
Boston Bar, 11
Botanical Beach, 152–56, 159
Botany Bay, 154
Boundary, the, 245
Boundary Passage, 120, 134
Bowen Island, 18–24
Brackendale Eagles Park, 27
Brentwood Bay, 141, 161
Bridge River Valley, 54–55
Brooks Point Park, 120
Brown Lake, 81
Brown Ridge, 118, 133–35
Bruce Peak, 125
Burgoyne Bay, 125

Cabin Trail, 217
Cable Bay, 102–03
Callaghan Valley, 42
Campbell Bay, 109
Campbell Point, 108
Campbell River, 191

Cape Flattery, 153
Cape Roger Curtis, 22–23
Cariboo, the, 238
Carmanah Walbran Park, 162
Carpenter Lake, 55–56
Carr's Landing, 213
Cayley, Mount, 28
Cayoosh Pass, 49
Cedar Creek Park, 226
Chaster Park, 64
Chaster Creek, 68
Cheakamus Canyon, 30
Cheakamus Lake, 38
Cheakamus River, 28–29, 34, 38
Cheam Peak, 3
Cheekye River, 28, 34
Chemainus, 161, 166
Centennial Trail, 39
Channel Ridge, 127
Chehalis River, 2, 4, 9
Chilliwack, 2
Chimney Rock, 55
Chin Beach, 152
China Beach, 152–53, 159
Chittenden Meadow Trail, 14
Chute Lake, 235, 238
Clark Bay, 183
Coast Mountains, 2, 55, 173, 188
Coast Trail, 156
Comox, 186, 192
Comox Valley, 186–94
Coon Bay, 100
Coopers Green Park, 74
Copeland Island Marine Park, 91–92
Copeland Islands, 87, 93
Copper Butte, 234
Coquihalla Canyon Park, 11–12, 16–17
Coquihalla River, 16
Cordova Bay, 141
Cougar Mountain, 36–38, 42
Courtenay, 166, 186, 191–94
Courtenay River Walk, 194

Cowichan Bay, 125, 161–64, 169
Cowichan Gap, the. See Porlier Pass
Cowichan River Footpath, 164
Cowichan River Park, 164–65
Cowichan Valley, 161–69
Cox Park, 185
Craig's Crossing, 191
Creyke Point, 157
Crippen Park, 19–22
Crofton, 122, 128
Crown Lake, 55
Cumberland, 186

Dakota Ridge, 66
Dalton Dome, the, 30
D'Arcy, 48–49
Davis Bay, 75
DeBeck's Hill, 27
De Courcy Group, the, 185
Deer Lake, 6
Degnen Bay, 181
Denman Island, 191
Departure Bay, 170, 175–77, 183
Descanso Bay, 178, 182
Descanso Bay Park, 185
Desolation Sound, 87, 91–92
Dewdney Mule Trail, 10, 12
Dinner Bay, 110
Dionisio Point, 97
Dionisio Point Park, 100–01
Don App's Trail, 190
Drumbeg Park, 182–83
Duck Bay, 91
Duffey Lake Park, 49
Duncan, 161, 164–66, 168

Earls Cove, 78, 86
East Point, 132–34
East Sooke Park, 156–58
Egmont, 78–85
Elaho River, 28
Eldorado Trail, 215

Ellison Park, 213, 219
Enderby, 217
Entrance Island, 183
Esquimalt, 143, 146, 148

Fairway Channel, 183
False Narrows, 185
Fanny Bay, 191
Finn Bay, 93
Fintry Park, 214, 218–19
Fitzsimmons Creek, 41
5 Mile Trail, 210
Flat Top Islands, 179–80, 183–84
Forbidden Plateau, 188
Fort Rodd Hill, 141, 143
Forwood Channel, 183
Fountain (Kwotlenemo) Lake, 55
Fountain Valley, 55
Four Lakes Loop Trail, 27
Francis Lake, 11
Francis Point Park, 79–80
Fraser Canyon, 10–11, 16–17, 55, 202
Fraser River: at Harrison Hot Springs, 2–4; at Harrison Mills, 5; at Hope, 11, 16–17; at Lillooet, 58
Fraser Valley, 4–5, 7, 16, 167
French Beach, 152, 159
Fulford Harbour, 122, 125–26, 128

Gabriola Island, 176, 178–85
Gabriola Sands Park, 180–81
Galiano Island, 96–105, 107, 109, 127, 129–30
Galiano, Mount, 97–98, 102, 105
Gallagher's Canyon, 225
Galloping Goose Trail, 141, 144, 158–59
Ganges, 122–24, 128
Garden Bay, 78, 84
Gardiner, Mount, 18, 22, 65
Garibaldi Highlands, 27
Garibaldi Park, 30, 38

Garnet Point, 91
Gartley Point, 194
Gellatly Bay Park, 226, 228
Gellatly Nut Farm Park, 228
Georgeson Bay, 99
Georgina Point Park, 109–11
Gibsons, 62–69
Gold Bridge, 57
Golden Mile, the, 241–42
Gold Rush Trail, 48, 53
Goose Spit Park, 192
Gordon's Beach, 152
Gower Point, 64
Gowlland Point, 120
Grace Trail, 102
Grandfather's Trail, 233
Grand Forks, 245
Grandma's Beach, 127
Gray Peninsula, 102
Great Basin Desert, 238, 244
Green Lake, 36
Green River, 50
Gulf Islands, 96, 101, 105, 109–10, 112, 116–17, 125, 130–32, 134, 136, 143, 182–84. *See also individual Gulf Islands*
Gulf Islands Disc Park, 120
Gulf Islands National Park Reserve (GINPR), 108, 117–18, 121

Halfmoon Bay, 71, 74–75, 77, 82–83
Hannah Lake, 11
Harbourside Walkway, 171–72
Harrison Bay, 4–5
Harrison Hot Springs, 2–9
Harrison Lake, 3, 6, 10
Harrison Mills, 5
Harrison River, 3–5
Haywire Bay Park, 88–89
Heffley Creek, 206, 210
Hicks Lake, 6–8
Homesite Creek, 83

Hope, 10–17
Hope Bay, 116, 118–19
Hope, Mount, 12
Horseshoe Lake, 90
Horswell Channel, 175
Howe Sound, 18, 22–23, 25, 27,
    31, 64–65
Hurricane Ridge, 157

Inland Lake Forest Park, 88–89
International Biking and Hiking
    Trail, 241, 247
International Creek, 15
Iron Mine Bay, 157–58
Irvine's Landing, 78
Island View Park, 144

Jack's Trail, 27
Jervis Inlet, 79, 83, 85
Jewel Creek, 57
Joffre Lakes Park, 49
Jordan River, 152
Juan de Fuca Marine Trail, 152–53, 159
Juan de Fuca Park, 154, 156, 159
Juan de Fuca Strait, 142, 153, 156, 158

Kalamalka Lake, 212–14
Kaloya Park, 214
Kamloops, 131, 196–205
Katherine Lake Park, 83
Kawkawa Lake Park, 12, 16
Keats Island, 65
Kelowna, 213, 220–30, 234
Kettle Valley Railway Trail: at Hope,
    10, 12, 17; at Kelowna, 220, 224; at
    Penticton, 232, 234–35, 238
Kilby Park, 4, 6
Killarney Creek Trail, 21
Killarney Lake, 20–21
Kitty Coleman Park, 193
Klein Lake Park, 83–84
Kleindale, 78, 82–83

Klesilkwa River, 15
Knox Mountain Park, 228
Kootenays, the, 245
Kunchin Point, 73
Kuper Island, 133
Kwotlenemo (Fountain) Lake, 55

Ladysmith, 161
Lake Cowichan, 162, 164
Lake Helen Mackenzie, 188
Lakeshore Walk, 26
Langdale, 63
Lasqueti Island, 91
Layer Cake Mountain, 225
Leechtown, 158
Lighthouse Bay, 101
Lillooet, 49, 53–59
Lillooet River, 45, 47–48, 50
Lions, the, 18, 65, 103
Lock Bay, 182
Lois Lake, 89–90
Long Harbour, 122, 125
Lord Park Trail, 102
Lost Lake, 38–39
Lower Mainland, the, 108,
    176, 193–94
Lower Panorama Trail, 39
Lund, 87, 91–93
Lyall Creek, 136
Lyall Harbour, 131–32

Madeira Park, 78
Maffeo Sutton Park, 172
Malaspina Galleries, 180–83
Malaspina Peninsula, 65, 86–87,
    92, 112
Mallard Lake, 173
Manning Park, 14, 232
Maple Bay, 162, 164, 168
Marble Canyon Park, 55–57
Marie Canyon, 165
Marina Way Park, 237

Matheson Lake, 158
Matson Lands, the, 146
Maxwell, Mount, 125, 128
Mayne Island, 99, 102, 106–113, 130
McArthur Island Park, 197–99
McGillivray Lake, 208
Meadow Loop Trail, 30
Meadow Trail, 21
Medicine Beach, 119–20
Memorial Park, 15
Merritt, 203
Middle Bay, 80
Mill Bay, 161
Miller Creek, 47
Miners Bay, 102, 106–13
Mission, 4, 6–7
Mission Creek, 227
Mission Creek Greenway, 220, 224–26
Moha River, 55
Molly Hogan Trail, 40
Monarch Head, 120
Monashee Mountain, 223
Monashee Mountains, 220
Montague Harbour, 98, 103–04
Montague Harbour Park, 101–02, 104
Morrisey, Mount, 207–08
Mortimer Spit, 119–20
Mosquito Lake Park, 49–50
Motherlode Trail, 234
Mount Baldy, 234
Mount Currie, 48
Mount Douglas Park, 141
Mount Galiano Park, 102
Mount Knox, 228
Mount Maxwell Park, 123–25
Mount Parke Park, 110
Mount Washington Alpine Resort,
    186, 188–90, 193
Muir Beach, 152
Murder Point, 133
Myra Canyon, 224
Mystic Beach, 152–53

Nahatlatch Lake, 11
Nahatlatch Park, 10–11
Nahatlatch River, 17
Nairn Falls Park, 50, 52
Nanaimo, 75, 170–79
Nanaimo River, 176
Nanoose Bay, 175
Naramata, 234–36, 238–39
Narrows Inlet, 72
Narvaez Bay, 132, 136
Navy Channel, 121, 137
Neck Point Park, 175–77
Newcastle Island, 172–74
New Westminster, 6, 126
Nicola Lake, 202
Nk'Mip Desert Cultural Centre,
    241, 244, 247
Norman, Mount, 117–18
North Bend, 11
North Okanagan, the, 212, 214, 217–18
North Pender Island, 99, 114–21, 124,
    127, 130–31, 136
North Saanich, 141
North Side Trail, 165
North Thompson River, 196–97, 205
Nymph Falls Park, 191

Okanagan Beach, 237
Okanagan Falls, 246
Okanagan Highlands, 220, 224
Okanagan Lake, 212–14, 219, 222,
    225–28, 231, 235–36, 238
Okanagan Mountain, 229
Okanagan Mountain Park, 222, 228
Okanagan River, 241, 245
Okanagan Trail, 228
Okanagan Valley, 45, 126, 141, 167,
    209, 212, 227, 234, 237–38, 245
Okeover Arm, 87, 92–93
Old Mill Trail, 40
Oliver, 167, 240–47
Olympic Mountains, 102, 134, 157

One Mile Lake, 48, 50
Orlebar Point, 183
Osoyoos, 213, 238, 240–47
Osoyoos Desert Centre, 242–45
Osoyoos Lake, 241–42
Owl Creek, 49
Othello-Quintette Tunnels, 11–12, 17
Overlander Beach Park, 198
Oyama, 214
Oyster Bay Shoreline Park, 191

Paradise Meadows, 188–89
Paradise Valley, 28–29
Parksville, 191
Paul, Mount, 199
Pavilion Lake, 55
Payzant Creek, 159
Peachland, 226
Pebble Beach (Gibsons), 65
Pebble Beach (Sechelt), 75
Pebble Beach Reserve (Galiano),
  102–03
Pemberton, 45–52
Pemberton Meadows, 47
Pemberton Pass, 48
Pemberton Trail, 30
Pemberton Valley, 46–48
Pender Canal, 115, 119
Pender Harbour, 63, 78–80, 82–84
Penticton, 213, 226, 231–39
Petroglyph Park, 174
Pillchuck Creek, 28
Pilot Bay, 180
Pioneer Park, 64
Pipers Lagoon Park, 175–76
Plumper Sound, 118, 135
Point No Point, 159–60
Point Roberts, 108
Porlier Pass, 100, 103
Porpoise Bay, 70–71, 75
Porpoise Bay Park, 71–72, 76
Port Mellon, 63

Port Renfrew, 152, 156, 159
Powell River, 86–93, 188
Powell River Forest Canoe
  Route, 88–90
Prevost Island, 124
Princess Louisa Inlet, 79, 88
Prior Centennial (GINPR), 117
Protection Island, 172
Puntledge River, 191, 194

Quadra Island, 191
Qualicum Beach, 191

Race Point, 10
Race Rock, 157
Rainbow Mountain, 39
Rainier, Mount, 134
Raggeds, the. See Copeland Islands
Redroofs Park, 74
Reservoir Route Trail, 238
Riverside Park, 198–99
Riverside Trail, 38
Rivers Trail, 197, 204
Roberts Creek, 62, 64–67
Roberts Creek Park, 66
Roberts Creek Pier Park, 65–66, 69
Roche Cove Park, 158
Roe Islet, 118
Roe Lake, 118
Ross Lake, 14–15
Rotary Route Trail, 164
Rowland Point, 81
Ruby Lake, 78, 82, 84
Ruckle Park, 122–24, 129
Rusty Muffler Trail, 238
Ruth, 224
Ryan River, 47

Saanich, 141, 141
Saanich Inlet, 125
Sakinaw Creek, 82
Sakinaw Lake, 83

Salish Sea, the. *See* Strait of
    Georgia, the
Salmon Inlet, 72–73
Saltery Bay, 86
Salt Spring Island, 99, 109, 122–29,
    179, 184
Samuel Island, 135
Sandcut Beach, 151
Sandwell Park, 181–82
Sandy Beach, 7
Sandy Cove, 3
San Juan Islands, the, 120, 125, 134
Sargeant Bay, 74
Sargeant Bay Park, 72
Sasquatch Park, 6–8
Satellite Channel, 125
Saturna Beach, 133, 135
Saturna Island, 99, 111, 118, 120,
    130–37
Savary Island, 87, 91, 93
Scenic Canyon Park, 224–25
Schubert Park Lookout, 199
Seal Bay Forest and Nature Park,
    190–91
Sechelt, 70–77, 188
Sechelt Inlet, 70–72, 77, 81
Sechelt Inlets Marine Park, 72–73, 76
Sechelt Peninsula, 62, 65, 78, 86–87
Secwepemc Native Heritage Park,
    199–202
Seton Lake, 56
Seton River, 56–57
Shell Beach (Galiano), 101
Shell Beach (Saturna), 133
Showh Lakes, 36
Silva Bay, 182–84
Silverhope Creek, 15
Silvertip Mountain, 14
Shannon Falls, 30–32
Shawatum Mountain, 14
Shawnigan Lake, 164
Shelter Point Park, 90–91

Shoal Channel, 68
Shumway Lake, 203
Sidney, 141, 144
Silver Star Mountain, 234
Silver Star Mountain Resort, 190,
    210, 214–17, 223
Silver Star Park, 216
Similkameen Valley, 237
Sisters (Lions), the. *See* Lions, the
16 Mile Creek, 36
66 Mile Trestle, 164–65
Skagit River Trail, 14
Skagit Valley Park, 13–15
Skaha Bluffs, 237
Skaha Lake, 231, 235
Skaha Lake Park, 237
Skookumchuck Narrows, 79, 88
Skookumchuck Narrows Park, 80–82
Skutz Falls, 164–65
Smoke Bluffs, the, 32
Smuggler Cover Marine Park, 73–74
Snickett Park, 75
Snug Cove, 18–20, 23–24
Sombrio Beach, 152–54
Soo Valley Wildlife Reserve, 42
Sooke, 151–60
Sooke Potholes Park, 158
Sooke River, 158
South Chilcotin Mountains, 53, 57
South Okanagan, the, 237, 240
South Pender Island, 114–21, 137
South Thompson River, 196–97,
    199–200
Sovereign Lake Ski Area, 216
Spruce Lake Protected Area, 57
Squamish, 25–34, 193
Squamish Estuary, 30–31
Squamish River, 27–29
Squamish Valley, 28–29, 32
Stawamus Chief Mountain Park,
    30–32, 34
St. Mary Lake Watershed Lands, 127

Stoltz Pool, 164
Strait of Georgia (Salish Sea), the, 66, 70, 75, 91–92, 100, 105, 109, 111, 136, 176, 188, 191
Strathcona Park, 188
Stump Lake, 203
Summerland, 235, 238
Suncoaster Trail, 82–84
Sun Peaks Resort, 190, 205–11, 215
Sunshine Coast, 62–63, 65–67, 70, 75, 188
Sunshine Coast Trail, 88–89
Sturdies Bay, 96–98
Sutil, Mount, 103
Swan Lake, 212–13
Swan Lake/Christmas Hill Nature Sanctuary, 144
Swanson Channel, 127
Swartz Bay, 130

Tantalus, Mount, 28
Taylor Bay, 180
Taylor Point, 132, 135
Terminal Creek, 21
Texada Island, 87, 90–91, 176
Thacker Park, 16
Thieves Bay, 116
Thompson Plateau, the, 208
Three Blind Mice Trails, 238
Tin Pants Trail, 39–40
Tod, Mount, 206–07
Tod Mountain, 205
Trail Bay, 70, 75
Trans Canada Trail: at Cowichan Valley, 164–65; at Hope, 12; at Kelowna, 220, 224; at Penticton, 232, 234–35, 238
Trincomali Channel, 127, 129
Trout Lake, 72
Tuam, Mount, 125
Tumbo Island, 133
Tunstall Bay Beach, 22

Turquoise Lake, 55
Tuwanek, 72–73
28 Mile Creek, 14
Tyaughton Creek, 57

Union Bay, 191

Valdes Island, 100
Valley Trail, 39
Vancouver, 111
Vancouver Island, 99, 125, 141–42
Vernon, 212–19
Vesuvius, 122, 124, 128
Victoria, 108, 126, 140–50, 166
Village Bay, 102, 110
Virago Point, 101

Warburton Pike, Mount, 130, 132–35
Washington, Mount, 187
Welcome Passage, 73
Westbank, 220, 226–28, 230
West Coast Railway Heritage Park, 33
West Coast Trail, the, 159
Westside Centennial Park, 198
Whiffen Spit Park, 159
Whippletree Junction, 168
Whippoorwill Point, 4
Whistler, 33, 35–46, 188, 206
Whistler Interpretive Forest, 38
Whistler Mountain Bike Park, 42–43
White Tail Trail, 238
Wilkes Point. See Campbell Point
Willows Park, 146
Winegarden Waterfront Park, 65
Winter Cove (GINPR), 132–36

X̱á:ytem Longhouse Interpretive Centre, 7

Yale, 16–17

Zenith, Mount, 28

Activities Index

. . . . . .

Birding: information, 32; Lower
    Mainland region, 27, 30, 33–34;
    Vancouver Island region, 168,
    191–92

Camping: Gulf Islands region,
    100–02, 104–05, 117–18, 121, 125–27,
    129; information, 10, 32, 88, 187,
    197; Lower Mainland region,
    6–9, 17, 26–27, 31, 52, 55–57, 59;
    Sunshine Coast region, 71–74,
    76, 83–84, 88–92; Thompson
    Okanagan region, 213–14, 219,
    247; Vancouver Island region, 159,
    164–65, 172–73, 185, 193
Climbing: Gulf Islands region,
    124–25; information, 32, 79, 187;
    Lower Mainland region, 31, 55, 57;
    Thompson Okanagan region, 237
Cycling: Gulf Islands region, 99,
    108–10, 113, 127; information, 10,
    25–26, 35–36, 46, 54, 71, 87–88, 98,
    117, 142, 151, 171, 187, 197, 206, 213,
    222, 232; Lower Mainland region,
    6–7, 11–15, 20–22, 26–30, 46–48;
    Sunshine Coast region, 63–65,
    73–74, 82–83, 88–89; Thompson
    Okanagan region, 197–99, 202,
    204, 224–26, 234–36, 241–42;
    Vancouver Island region, 144–46,
    162–65, 171–76, 183, 190–91, 194

Driving: Gulf Islands region, 98,
    109–10, 128; information, 7, 98;
    Lower Mainland region, 28–30,
    46–48, 54–55, 57; Sunshine
    Coast region, 74–75; Thompson
    Okanagan region, 202–03, 241,
    245; Vancouver Island region,
    152–54

Fishing: information, 10, 32, 46, 54,
    71, 79, 88, 162; Lower Mainland
    region, 10–11, 26–30, 36–38,
    48–50, 56, 59; Sunshine Coast
    region, 84, 92; Thompson
    Okanagan region, 213;
    Vancouver Island region, 164–65

Gliding: information, 46;
    Lower Mainland region, 16, 46
Golfing: Gulf Islands region,
    103, 120; information, 32, 197;
    Lower Mainland region, 41–42;
    Thompson Okanagan region,
    217–18, 246
Guided tours: information, 35, 63,
    70–71, 88, 123, 223, 232

Hiking: Gulf Islands region, 102,
    110, 117–18, 124–27; information,
    32, 79, 180, 222; Lower Mainland
    region, 10–15, 26–27, 31, 36–38,

49–50, 57; Thompson Okanagan
region, 214–17, 228, 237, 241;
Vancouver Island region, 156, 159
Horseback riding: information, 46,
54, 206, 232; Lower Mainland
region, 36–38, 57; Thompson
Okanagan region, 224

Kayaking: Gulf Islands region,
100–01, 108, 113, 117, 119–20, 123,
125–27; information, 18, 32, 63,
79, 88, 108, 123, 133, 162, 197,
222; Lower Mainland region, 22;
Sunshine Coast region, 63–65, 68,
77, 85, 91–93; Vancouver Island
region, 185

Mountain biking: information, 25–26,
32, 36, 46, 79, 180, 187, 197, 207,
213, 232; Lower Mainland region,
26–27, 31–32, 36–40, 42–43,
49–50, 57; Sunshine Coast region,
182; Thompson Okanagan region,
202, 206, 214–17, 238; Vancouver
Island region, 188–90

Nature observation: Gulf Islands
region, 120, 134–36; information,
32; Lower Mainland region, 4–6,
16, 36–38, 40–41, 56–57; Sunshine
Coast region, 71–72, 79–83;
Thompson Okanagan region,
197–98, 224–26, 228, 237–38,
241–45; Vancouver Island region,
144, 154–58, 168, 190–92

Paddling: Gulf Islands region,
100–02, 108, 113, 117–18, 123–24,
133–35; information, 32, 35–36,
63, 71, 79, 88, 98, 117, 123, 151, 162,
171, 180, 187, 197, 213, 222; Lower
Mainland region, 3, 6–7, 10–11,

20–22, 26–27, 59; Sunshine Coast
region, 63–65, 71–73, 85, 91–93,
Vancouver Island region, 162–64,
183, 213–14
Picnicking: Gulf Islands region,
99, 108–10, 119–20, 124–27,
135–36; information, 32; Lower
Mainland region, 3–4, 6–7, 10–16,
20–22, 26–27, 32, 36–40, 48–49,
54–57; Sunshine Coast region,
63–66, 71–75, 79–80, 88–92;
Thompson Okanagan region,
197–99, 213–14; Vancouver
Island region, 143–44, 152–54,
156–59, 162–65, 175–76, 180,
183, 185, 190

Rafting: information, 32, 197;
Lower Mainland region, 10–11, 17,
28–30, 34
Running: Gulf Islands region,
125–27; information, 32; Lower
Mainland region, 20–22, 26,
38–40; Sunshine Coast region,
80–82, 88–89; Thompson
Okanagan region, 197–99,
224–26; Vancouver Island
region, 144, 188–90

Skylining: Lower Mainland region,
36–38, 40–41; Vancouver Island
region, 176–77
Snow sports (dog sledding, ice
skating, skiing, snowboarding,
snowshoeing, tubing):
information, 32, 36, 63, 187, 213,
222, 232; Lower Mainland region,
36–38, 42; Sunshine Coast region,
66, 69; Thompson Okanagan
region, 207–08, 210, 214–17,
223–24, 232–34; Vancouver Island
region, 188–90

Spas: Gulf Islands region, 104, 118;
    Lower Mainland region, 9, 17, 23,
    34, 43; Sunshine Coast region, 66,
    77; Thompson Okanagan region,
    209–10; Vancouver Island region,
    150, 169, 171, 193–94
Swimming: Gulf Islands region,
    100–03, 108–09, 117–18, 123–24,
    133–36, 164–65, 175–76, 180, 182,
    190–91; information, 32; Lower
    Mainland region, 3–4, 6–7, 16,
    20–22, 26–27, 48–50, 54–56;
    Sunshine Coast region, 63–66,
    71–74, 79–80, 83, 88–92, 100–02;
    Thompson Okanagan region,
    198–99, 213–14, 226, 236–37

Walking: Gulf Islands region, 98–102,
    108–09, 117–18, 124–27, 134–36;
    information, 32; Lower Mainland
    region, 3–4, 6–7, 11–15, 20–22,
    26–27, 30–31, 36–41, 49–50,
    58; Sunshine Coast region,
    63–66, 71–72, 75, 79–83, 88–80;
    Thompson Okanagan region,
    197–202, 213–17, 224–26, 228,
    234–37, 241–45; Vancouver Island
    region, 143–46, 154–59, 162–66,
    174–76, 180–83, 185, 190, 194
Wheelchair access: Gulf Islands
    region, 105, 125–27; information,
    32; Lower Mainland region, 3,
    11–12, 20, 27; Sunshine Coast
    region, 65, 71, 75, 79–83, 88–89;
    Thompson Okanagan region, 242;
    Vancouver Island region, 143–46,
    156–59, 164–66, 171–72, 174, 185,
    188–90